Research Reports on College Transitions | No. 7

What Makes the First-Year Seminar High Impact?

An Exploration of Effective Educational Practices

Tracy L. Skipper, Editor

Cite as:
Skipper, T. L. (2017). *What makes the first-year seminar high impact? An exploration of effective educational practices.* (Research Reports No. 7). Columbia, SC: University of South Carolina, National Resource Center for The First-Year Experience & Students in Transition.

Copyright © 2017 University of South Carolina. All rights reserved. No part of this work may be reproduced or copied in any form, by any means, without written permission of the University of South Carolina.

ISBN: 978-1-942072-01-0
Published by:
National Resource Center for The First-Year Experience® and Students in Transition
University of South Carolina
1728 College Street, Columbia, SC 29208
www.sc.edu/fye

The First-Year Experience® is a service mark of the University of South Carolina. A license may be granted upon written request to use the term "The First-Year Experience." This license is not transferable without written approval of the University of South Carolina.

Production Staff for the National Resource Center:
Project Manager: Tracy L. Skipper, Assistant Director for Publications
Cover Design: Allison Minsk, Graphic Artist
Design and Production: Joey Hilton, Graphic Artist

Library of Congress Cataloging-in-Publication Data

Names: Skipper, Tracy L. (Tracy Lynn)
Title: What makes the first-year seminar high impact? : an exploration of effective educational practices / Tracy L. Skipper, editor.
Description: Columbia, SC : University of South Carolina, National Resource Center for the first-year experience & students in transition, 2017. |
   Series: Research report on college transitions ; no. 7 | Includes index.
Identifiers: LCCN 2016045388 | ISBN 9781942072010 (print)
Subjects: LCSH: Seminars. | College teaching.
Classification: LCC LB2393.5 .W53 2017 | DDC 378.1/77--dc23
LC record available at https://lccn.loc.gov/2016045388

About the Publisher

The National Resource Center for The First-Year Experience and Students in Transition was born out of the success of University of South Carolina's much-honored University 101 course and a series of annual conferences on the freshman-year experience. The momentum created by the educators attending these early conferences paved the way for the development of the National Resource Center, which was established at the University of South Carolina in 1986. As the National Resource Center broadened its focus to include other significant student transitions in higher education, it underwent several name changes, adopting the National Resource Center for The First-Year Experience and Students in Transition in 1998.

Today, the Center collaborates with its institutional partner, University 101 Programs, in pursuit of its mission to advance and support efforts to improve student learning and transitions into and through higher education. We achieve this mission by providing opportunities for the exchange of practical and scholarly information as well as the discussion of trends and issues in our field through the convening of conferences and other professional development events, such as institutes, workshops, and online learning opportunities; publishing scholarly practice books, research reports, a peer-reviewed journal, electronic newsletters, and guides; generating, supporting, and disseminating research and scholarship; hosting visiting scholars; and maintaining several online channels for resource sharing and communication, including a dynamic website, listservs, and social media outlets.

The National Resource Center serves as the trusted expert, internationally recognized leader, and clearing house for scholarship, policy, and best practice for all postsecondary student transitions.

Institutional Home

The National Resource Center is located at the University of South Carolina's (UofSC) flagship campus in Columbia. Chartered in 1801, UofSC Columbia's mission is twofold: to establish and maintain excellence in its student population, faculty, academic programs, living and learning environment, technological infrastructure, library resources, research and scholarship, public and private support and endowment; and to enhance the industrial, economic, and cultural potential of the state. The Columbia campus offers 311 degree programs through its 14 degree-granting colleges and schools. In fiscal year 2015, faculty generated $243 million in funding for research, outreach and training programs. UofSC is one of only 32 public universities receiving both Research and Community Engagement designations from the Carnegie Foundation.

Contents

Structural Supports for Effective Educational Practices in the First-Year Seminar 7
Tracy L. Skipper

The American University of Rome 23
Jenny Petrucci

Cabrini University 27
Richard Gebauer, Michelle Filling-Brown, and Amy Perischetti

Clark University 31
Jessica Bane Robert

Coastal Carolina University 35
Michele C. Everett

Durham Technical Community College 41
Kerry F. Cantwell and Gabby McCutchen

Florida SouthWestern State College 45
Eileen DeLuca, Kathy Clark, Myra Walters, and Martin Tawil

Indiana University – Purdue University Indianapolis 51
Heather Bowman, Amy Powell, and Cathy Buyarski

Ithaca College 55
Elizabeth Bleicher

LaGuardia Community College, CUNY 59
Tameka Battle, Linda Chandler, Bret Eynon, Andrea Francis, Preethi Radhakrishnan, and Ellen Quish

Loyola University Maryland 65
Mary Ellen Wade

Malone University 71
Marcia K. Everett, Jay R. Case, and Jacci Welling

Montana State University 77
Margaret Konkel and Deborah Blanchard

Northern Arizona University 81
Rebecca Campbell and Kaitlin Hublitz

Southern Methodist University 87
Caitlin Anderson, Takeshi Fujii, and Donna Gober

Southwestern Michigan College 91
Christi Young, Jeffrey Dennis, and Donald Ludman

St. Cloud State University 95
Christine Metzo

Texas A&M University-Corpus Christi 101
Rita A. Sperry, Andrew M. Garcia, Chelsie Hawkinson, and Michelle Major

The University of Arizona 105
Marla Franco, Jessica Hill, and Tina Wesanen-Neil

University of Kansas 109
Alison Olcott Marshall and Sarah Crawford-Parker

University of Maryland Baltimore County 113
Lisa Carter Beall

University of New Hampshire 119
Neil Niman, Tamara Rury, and Sean Stewart

University of North Carolina Wilmington 123
Zachary W. Underwood

University of Northern Iowa 127
Deirdre Heistad, April Chatham-Carpenter, Kristin Moser, and Kristin Woods

University of Texas at Austin 131
Ashley N. Stone and Tracie Lowe

University of Texas at San Antonio 135
Kathleen Fugate Laborde and Tammy Jordan Wyatt

University of Wisconsin-Madison 139
Susan Brantly and Sorabh Singhal

Virginia Commonwealth University 143
Melissa C. Johnson and Bety Kreydatus

Conclusion: What Does It Mean to Be High Impact? 149
Tracy L. Skipper

Index 157
About the Editor 163

Structural Supports for Effective Educational Practices in the First-Year Seminar

Tracy L. Skipper

The responsibility for college success has historically rested with the student, but since the 1980s, educators have taken increasing ownership, designing structures to improve the likelihood of learning, success, and retention. These efforts have included a variety of initiatives—first-year seminars, learning communities, writing-intensive courses, common intellectual experiences, service-learning, undergraduate research, and senior capstones, among others—that have come to be known as high-impact practices. Evidence suggests these experiences may play a central role in helping students achieve important learning outcomes for the global marketplace, such as intellectual and practical skills, personal and social responsibility, and integrative learning (Kuh, 2008).

Kuh (2008) examined the characteristics of these educational experiences and suggested their effectiveness stems from a number of key factors. First, high-impact activities demand that students devote considerable time and effort to completing educationally purposeful tasks. They engage students with faculty and with their peers in formal and informal conversations "about substantive matters, typically over an extended period of time" (Kuh, 2008, p. 14). High-impact activities frequently engage students in authentic learning tasks, meaning that students have opportunities to apply knowledge gained in the classroom to problems and situations on the campus and in the community. Interactions with peers and faculty and opportunities for real-world learning experiences also increase the likelihood that students will encounter people who are different from themselves. Such experiences "challenge students to develop new ways of thinking about and responding immediately to novel circumstances" (p. 15). Finally, high-impact activities are effective in helping students achieve important learning outcomes because participation typically involves feedback about performance, which allows students to make the adjustments necessary to gain desired dispositions, knowledge, and skills.

The first-year seminar is perhaps the most common high-impact practice (HIP) on our campuses. National surveys of first-year curriculuar initiatives suggest that first-year seminars are in place at more than 90% of four-year institutions and over 80% of two-year institutions (Koch, Griffin, & Barefoot, 2014; Young & Hopp, 2014). Yet the way first-year seminars are defined in the HIPs literature may be at odds with the reality on many campuses. For example, the American Association of Colleges and Universities (AAC&U) defines first-year seminars as courses that

> bring small groups of students together with faculty or staff on a regular basis and place strong emphasis on critical inquiry, frequent writing, information literacy, collaborative learning, and other skills that develop students' intellectual and practical competencies. First-year seminars also involve students with cutting-edge scholarship and with faculty members' own research. (Kuh & O'Donnell, 2013, p. 49)

Such a definition clearly suggests an academic seminar focused on a disciplinary topic or question. Yet many institutions offer more than one type of first-year seminar, and the most frequently offered type—though it has trended downward in recent years—is the extended orientation course (Young & Hopp, 2014), which tends to focus on transition issues. Does this mean that other types of seminars are not high impact?

Recognizing that the quality of high-impact practices varied widely, Kuh and O'Donnell (2013), expanding Kuh's (2008) earlier work, identified eight "conditions that account for why students engage at high levels and benefit from a high-impact practice" (p. 7). These conditions or elements are a useful framework "for evaluating whether something that is 'called' a HIP has the necessary quality dimensions that foster student accomplishment in terms of persistence, graduation rates, and desired learning outcomes" (Kuh & O'Donnell, 2013, pp. 7-8) and include the following:

- performance expectations set at appropriately high levels;
- significant investment of time and effort by students over an extended period of time;
- interactions with faculty and peers about substantive matters;
- experiences with diversity, wherein students are exposed to and must contend with people and circumstances that differ from those with which students are familiar;
- frequent, timely, and constructive feedback;
- periodic, structured opportunities to reflect on and integrate learning;
- opportunities to discover relevance of learning through real-world applications; and/or
- public demonstration of competence. (p. 10)

Thus, it would stand to reason that first-year seminars incorporating some or all of these conditions could be classified as high impact, even if they do not mirror the AAC&U definition. One potential source of evidence about the presence of these conditions is the 2012-2013 National Survey of First-Year Seminars (NSFYS). In the section that follows, I explore what we have learned about different types of first-year seminars and how they may be organized to encompass these conditions.

Profiles of First-Year Seminars[1]

The National Survey of First-Year Seminars provides insight into the prevalence, structure, and administration of first-year seminars at colleges and universities in the United States. The NSFYS gathers data on the range of seminar types on a single campus while collecting in-depth information on the seminar serving the largest number of students at the institution (i.e., the primary type). For the primary seminar type, respondents report demographics about the students who are required to take the course or for whom special sections are offered; who teaches the course and how they are compensated, the number of credit hours, amount of classroom contact, and grading policies; the primary course objectives and course content; and how the course is assessed. In 2012-2013, a special section was added to the survey to collect additional data regarding the connection between the first-year seminar and other high-impact practices (e.g., service-learning, undergraduate research, learning communities, common intellectual experiences, writing-intensive courses); however, the researchers did not explicitly seek to identify the extent to which the conditions outlined by Kuh and O'Donnell (2013) were present in the seminar. That said, findings from the 2012-2013 NSFYS might suggest the existence of organizing structures or principles within seminars that make the presence of effective educational practices more likely. Here, I outline data points from the NSFYS that provide evidence for those organizing structures. In the sections that follow, I highlight the prevalence of those structures in the four most commonly reported seminar types: (a) extended orientation, (b) academic seminar with uniform content, (c) academic seminar with variable content, and (d) hybrid.

- ***Performance expectations set at appropriately high levels.*** At the institutional level, performance expectations are communicated through the number of credits offered for a course, whether it carries academic credit, and how it is graded (e.g., letter grade vs. pass–fail). Such basic expectations undoubtedly have an impact on how individual instructors design their own seminar sections and on the demands they place on students.
- ***Significant investment of time and effort by students over an extended period of time.*** The number of classroom contact hours associated with the first-year seminar provides some insight into what institutions expect from students in terms of their investment in the course.
- ***Interactions with faculty and peers about substantive matters.*** The NSFYS incorporates questions about who teaches the seminar, including the involvement of graduate and undergraduate student instructors. If engagement around substantive issues, especially opportunities for engagement outside the classroom,

---

[1] This discussion of first-year seminars draws on frequency data, seminar definitions, and the survey instrument as presented by Young and Hopp (2014).

is a hallmark of a high-impact practice, then it stands to reason that institutions that use full-time faculty, staff, and administrators to teach the first-year seminar are more likely to create the possibilities for such engagement than those who rely more heavily on contingent faculty. Similarly, whether the seminar is part of the instructor's regular workload might affect availability for interactions with students outside the course. The inclusion of undergraduate peer leaders in seminar design would create a structural possibility for interactions with other students that might move beyond simple social connections. The presence of specific course goals (e.g., *develop a support network or friendships, increase student-faculty interaction*) and the inclusion of *educational experiences that require collaboration and teamwork with other students* or undergraduate research suggest an intention to incorporate interactions about substantive matters at the department or institutional level. Seminars that report assessing *connections with peers* and *out-of-class student–faculty interaction* communicate the importance of this effective educational practice.

- **Experiences with diversity.** Seminars that include developing intercultural competence as a primary course goal, include diversity issues or global learning as important course topics, and intentionally incorporate educational experiences inside or outside the classroom that help students explore cultures, life experiences, and worldviews different from their own provide the structural support to make the presence of this effective educational practice more likely.

- **Frequent, timely, and constructive feedback.** The NSFYS provides little data on structural conditions or organizing principles that might support feedback within the seminar. Analysis of open-ended data related to the incorporation of writing in first-year seminars suggests that feedback is an important component of writing instruction (Skipper, 2014). The inclusion of writing or similar learning activities or assignments (e.g., undergraduate research) might suggest the presence of structural components that encourage feedback.

- **Periodic, structured opportunities to reflect on and integrate learning.** Departments or institutions that identify *self-exploration or personal development* as an important course goal may establish a greater expectation that reflection should be included in the seminar. Because reflection is a frequent component of service-learning, seminars that include service as part of the course may also create conditions more favorable to reflection. Additionally, critical thinking might be considered a proxy for integrative learning, although the two are not identical. As such, conditions may be more favorable for integrative learning to exist in seminars where developing critical thinking skills is listed as a priority goal, an important course topic, or an assessment outcome. Finally, because learning communities frequently include opportunities for students to synthesize content and integrate learning across courses, the intentional linking of the seminar to another course may also suggest the presence of this effective educational practice.

- **Opportunities to discover relevance of learning through real-world applications.** To the extent that seminars focus on career exploration and preparation as a course goal or topic, there may be some support for connecting learning in the seminar or other courses to real-world applications. However, the clearest evidence of structural support for this effective educational practice comes with the inclusion of service-learning experiences in the seminar. Respondents who indicate that civic engagement or involvement in service is an assessed seminar outcome underscore the value of real-world applications at the department or institutional level.

- **Public demonstration of competence.** An emphasis on the development of oral and written communication skills as an important course goal or topic may suggest structural support for this effective educational practice. The inclusion of *educational experiences that develop students' ability to produce and revise various forms of writing*—especially if that writing is for a public audience—is further evidence of that support. Finally, assessment of writing ability may provide some indication of the value of this practice.

The chapter appendix includes response frequencies for these survey items organized by seminar type for the 2012-2013 administration of the NSFYS.

Extended Orientation

The extended orientation first-year seminar is variously known as freshman orientation, college survival, college transition, or student success. These courses frequently include an introduction to campus resources, time management, academic and career planning, learning strategies, and personal development. They are the most common type of seminar, with 60.4% of respondents from the NSFYS reporting that they offer an extended orientation course. It is the primary type on 39.1% of campuses that reported offering a first-year seminar.

Expectations set at appropriately high levels. The vast majority of respondents reported that the first-year seminar is offered for academic credit (94.5%) and that students receive letter grades (85.2%), though the extended orientation course is more likely to be offered on a pass–fail basis than the other course types described here. The assignment of credit and emphasis on letter grades suggests that most first-year seminars communicate high expectations to enrolled students. As noted earlier, the number of credits earned may also suggest something about expectations of academic rigor associated with a course. Extended orientation courses were more likely to be offered for one credit (61.3%) and less likely to be offered for three credits (28.8%) than seminars in general (43.5% and 31.7% respectively). Fewer structural supports for high expectations (as evidenced by credits offered and grading policies) may be present for extended orientation courses than for other seminar types.

Classroom contact hours are closely related to credit hours earned, so it is not surprising that 43.6% of respondents reporting on extended orientation courses indicated that students meet for only one hour per week. Slightly more than a quarter (26.4%) reported students have three contact hours per week. The design of many extended orientation seminars suggests that students may have limited opportunities for significant investment of time and effort in learning activities.

Interactions with faculty and peers about substantive matters. Institutions employ a range of individuals to teach first-year seminars, including tenure-track faculty, full-time non-tenure-track faculty, student affairs professionals, other campus professionals, and adjunct faculty. Across all seminar types, the percentage of seminars employing full-time faculty and staff approaches 98%; for the seminar types examined here, the percentage of adjunct instructors ranges from 43.2% (hybrid seminars) to 58.8% (academic with uniform content). The survey data provide no way of knowing the percentage of instructional staff who are adjuncts, compared to full-time personnel; data show only the relative likelihood of institutions to include both types of instructors in their staffing patterns.

Given the relative stability of staffing patterns across seminar types, the way in which seminar instruction is treated with respect to the rest of instructor workload may be a better indicator of structural support for effective educational practices centered on student–faculty interactions than who teaches the course (i.e., full-time vs. part-time). Full-time faculty assigned to teach an extended orientation seminar appear to be equally likely to teach it as part of their regular course load (61.0%) as they are to teach it as an overload course (64.1%). However, when the course is taught by a student affairs or other campus professional, it is much more likely to be an extra responsibility than a regular component of the position (72.5% compared to 41.9%).[2] Although full-time faculty and staff are primary instructors of extended orientation courses, the finding that many of them are engaged in this work as an additional responsibility suggests an organizing principle for this type of course that may make interaction with faculty around substantive issues more challenging.

Among all seminar respondents, relatively few (4.1%) identified undergraduate students as course instructors. However, 46.3% suggested that undergraduates play a role in the course, such as teaching independently or as part of team, assisting the instructor, or performing some other function (Young & Hopp, 2014, p. 32), and 44.6% reported involvement of undergraduate students in extended orientation courses. Additionally, 19.7% indicated that developing a support network or friendships was an important course goal, and 69% indicated that opportunities for teamwork and collaboration were intentionally incorporated into the seminar. The value placed on peer-to-peer interaction is also evidenced by the percentage of institutions reporting *connections with peers* as an assessed outcome of the seminar (39.8%).

Periodic, structured opportunities to reflect on and integrate learning. Learning communities, by their nature, provide structural opportunities for integration. Slightly more than one third (36.9%) of extended orientation seminars were linked to another course or to a set of theme-based cocurricular experiences. Of those, 34.9% reported the seminar content was intentionally coordinated with linked courses by instructors, 23.6% indicated that content in the

---

[2] Two questions on the NSFYS ask about whether the course is taught in-load or as an extra responsibility—one about faculty instructors and one about staff instructors. For both questions, participants could select multiple responses. As such, percentages do not total 100. What the responses suggest is that on the same campus, some faculty may be teaching the course in-load while others teach as an extra responsibility. A similar situation exists with staff. These data suggest the relatively likelihood that seminar instruction is an assigned responsibility for a given type of instructor.

seminar and linked courses were connected to a common theme, and 27.4% noted that seminar students participated in a common set of theme-based cocurricular experiences. Intentional coordination of course content and connection to a common theme provide the structural support for integration of learning. Where the extended orientation course is linked to another course or a set of cocurricular experience, there may be a greater likelihood of opportunities for integrated learning.

Opportunities to discover relevance of learning through real-world applications. Among extended orientation courses, 20.3% indicated career exploration or preparation was one of the most important course topics. Slightly more than one quarter of extended orientation courses (28.6%) incorporate service-learning into the seminar, but outcomes involving civic engagement (11.4%) and involvement in service (14.2%) are rare, suggesting less value may be placed on real-world learning opportunities in this seminar type.

Public demonstration of competence. A focus on the development of written and oral communication may provide evidence of structural support for public demonstration of competence: 25.5% of extended orientation courses offered opportunities to produce and revise writing. The kinds of assignments described in open-ended responses suggest that few were intended for a public audience, however, with reflection papers and personal writing being the most common (Skipper, 2014).

Academic Seminar With Uniform Content

Academic seminars with generally uniform content are interdisciplinary or theme-oriented courses that focus on an academic theme and have a significant emphasis on academic skills such as critical thinking and expository writing. These courses may fulfill a general education requirement. For example, Hunter and Linder (2005) identified the Western Heritage in a Global Context course at Eckerd College as an academic seminar with uniform content, noting the course "introduces students to the arts and sciences of human civilization ... by discussing great works and ideas from Western civilization and comparing them or putting them into context with great works from non-Western civilization" (pp. 279-280). Academic seminars of this type are increasing in prevalence: 29.4% of respondents indicated that they offered such a course, and 19% reported that an academic seminar with uniform content is the primary seminar type on their campus.

Expectations set at appropriately high levels and significant investment of time and effort. The vast majority of academic seminars with uniform content are letter graded (89.9%), and nearly half of these courses are offered for three (41.5%) or four (4.9%) credit hours. Instructional time was consistent with credit hours—47.3% of the respondents reported that students spent three hours a week in class. Structurally, the uniform content seminar appears to meet the baseline for setting appropriately high expectations and supporting significant investment of student time and effort.

Interactions with faculty and peers about substantive matters. Nearly 80% of respondents reporting on uniform content seminars indicated that faculty teaching the course did so as part of their regular responsibilities, with 42.6% indicating that faculty taught the course as an overload. This pattern was reversed for staff instructors, with 42.5% of respondents reporting they taught the course as part of their assigned duties and 75.9% reporting it was as an extra responsibility. Uniform content seminars appear to emphasize out-of-class student–faculty interaction (22.2% of those formally evaluating the seminar had assessed this outcome in the previous three years), though they may be less likely (10.1%) to identify it as one of the primary goals of the course. For students enrolled in an academic seminar with uniform content, opportunities to engage with the seminar instructor around substantive issues may depend on whether the instructor is classified as faculty or staff.

For this type of seminar, 41.2% of the respondents reported that undergraduate peer leaders were involved in some way in the course, and 66.9% incorporated opportunities for teamwork and collaboration. Of the 57.6% of uniform content seminars that reported formally evaluate the seminar in the previous three years, 31.7% had assessed *connections with peers*. On the whole, structural support for peer engagement seems to be present.

Frequent, timely, and constructive feedback. Structural evidence related to opportunities for frequent, timely, and constructive feedback is limited within this dataset, yet we might find some clues in how writing and undergraduate research experiences are incorporated into the seminar. Among uniform content seminars, 54.7% reported providing experiences designed to help students develop their ability to produce various forms of writing while 9.7%

reported incorporating undergraduate research experiences into the course. Respondents who reported on writing offered modest evidence of using a process approach to writing instruction and incorporating peer review within the open-ended responses on writing activities (Skipper, 2014). The emphasis on writing activities suggests some support for feedback as an effective educational practice within uniform content seminars.

Periodic, structured opportunities to reflect on and integrate learning. Writing assignments in uniform content seminars may also support reflection. Skipper (2014) reported that journals, reflection papers, and personal writing were among the types of writing assigned in these courses. Of the uniform content seminars including service-learning, 29.2% reported using portfolios as a reflection technique—a tool that may also support integrative learning.

The development of critical thinking skills assumes greater importance in academic seminars with uniform content: 31.1% reported that this was among the top three course objectives, and 45.9% identified it as an important course topic. Of those reporting on uniform content seminars, 38.9% indicated the seminar was connected to another course or a set of themed cocurricular experiences. Opportunities for integrated learning within the seminar are evidenced by intentional coordination of course content across linked courses (33.9%), connection of courses to a common intellectual theme (32.1%), and connection of the seminar to theme-based cocurricular experiences (41.1%).

Opportunities to discover relevance of learning through real-world applications. Career exploration was identified by 20.3% of respondents as one of the most important course topics for uniform content seminars, but only 5.4% identified it as a primary course objective. Evidence of real-world application is more clearly communicated by the incorporation of service-learning, which was present in one third of uniform content seminars. Assessment of civic engagement (15.9%), while not one of the most commonly measured outcomes for this type of seminar, is more frequent in uniform content seminars than other seminar types discussed here. Involvement in service is measured at a slightly lower rate (11.5%) than it is for extended orientation or hybrid seminars. The higher prevalence of service-learning in this type of seminar, coupled with a greater emphasis on assessment for civic engagement, may suggest more structural support for real-world applications in uniform content than in extended orientation seminars, though a similar level of support is evident in academic seminars on various topics and hybrid seminars.

Public demonstration of competence. Greater structural support for public demonstration of competence, as evidenced by an emphasis on the development of writing ability, is apparent in the uniform content seminar. Writing skills are a primary course objective for 13.5% of these seminars and an important course topic for 23.6%. Further, more than half incorporate opportunities to produce and revise writing. The assignments described in open-ended responses mirror traditional college academic writing assignments (e.g., research papers, formal essays; Skipper, 2014), yet it is unclear to what extent these assignments are designed for an audience beyond the instructor.

Academic Seminar With Variable Content

Academic seminars on variable topics, similar to uniform content seminars, frequently emphasize academic skills in an interdisciplinary context. However, individual sections are driven by the instructor's disciplinary or research interest. As such, each section typically has a different topic. Examples of topical academic seminars offered at the University of Michigan, for example, include Looking at Traditional China Through Its Most Famous Novel: *The Story of the Stone*, The Poetry of Everyday Life, Colonialism and Its Aftermath, and Inventing Race (Hunter & Linder, 2005). The prevalence of academic seminars on various topics is roughly the same as those with uniform content. Of those responding to the 2012-2013 NSFYS, 28.7% indicated they offer this type of seminar; it was the primary type on 19.2% of campuses.

Expectations set at appropriately high levels and significant investment of time and effort. Variable content seminars are more likely than other seminar types to be letter graded (93.9%), with fewer than 4% being offered on a pass–fail basis. These courses are generally offered for three or four credit hours (36.1% each); the variable content seminar is the least likely to be offered for one credit hour. Students in variable content seminars also have more weekly contact hours than students enrolled other seminar types; nearly 60% of survey respondents report three contact hours and an additional 17.7% report four contact hours per week. Variable content seminars provide strong structural support for setting appropriately high expectations and significant investment of student time and effort.

Interactions with faculty and peers about substantive matters. Tenure-track faculty are more likely to be engaged in teaching the variable content seminars than the other types of seminars described here (91.2% vs. 63.2% -

77.5%). The vast majority of respondents reporting on variable content seminars indicated that faculty teaching the course did so as part of their regular responsibilities (91.7%), with 28.3% indicating faculty taught the course as an overload. Student affairs staff and other campus professionals are less likely to be involved in teaching variable content seminars (25.7% and 23.0%, respectively) than the other seminar types described here. When they do teach variable content seminars, only 21.8% of institutions report that they do so as part of their regular workload, with 83.6% indicating staff take it on as an extra assignment. The importance placed on student–faculty interaction is evidenced by its placement as the third most commonly cited course objective; nearly one quarter identified it as a primary objective. Similarly, of those formally evaluating variable content seminars, out-of-class student–faculty interaction is assessed by 34.5%. The high percentage of tenure-track faculty teaching a variable content seminar course in load, coupled with a priority placed on student–faculty interaction, suggests strong structural support for interactions with faculty around substantive issues.

Frequent, timely, and constructive feedback. Variable content seminars place a strong emphasis on writing instruction. Developing writing skills was the second most commonly reported objective (38.8%), and writing skills were the second most commonly reported course topic (49.0%). Not surprisingly, 71.4% of respondents reported that their variable content seminars provide experiences designed to help students develop their ability to produce and revise writing in various forms. Among these respondents, there is strong evidence of the use of a process approach to writing (Skipper, 2014), which may include multiple drafts of an assignment with written and/or verbal feedback from the faculty member. Peer review was more commonly mentioned in open-ended responses about variable content seminars than those about extended orientation or uniform content seminars. Undergraduate research was also more frequently incorporated into variable content seminars (27.4%) than the other seminars described here (6.2% - 15.9%). The clear emphasis on writing and increased opportunity for undergraduate research in variable content seminars suggest strong structural support for frequent, timely, and constructive feedback.

Periodic, structured opportunities to reflect on and integrate learning. Opportunities for integrative learning may find strong structural support within variable seminars. The development of critical thinking skills was the most frequently cited course objective (50.3%) and the most commonly cited topic (63.3%). Similar to uniform content seminars, 37.7% of variable content seminars are part of a learning community. Of those seminars embedded in learning communities, the larger structure seems to support integrative learning in many cases, including intentional coordination of course content across linked courses (30.9%), connection of courses to a common intellectual theme (25.5%), and connection of the seminar to theme-based cocurricular experiences (32.7%).

Opportunities to discover relevance of learning through real-world applications. When considering variable content seminars, respondents were more likely to report the inclusion of service-learning (37.7%) than they were for other seminar types, but they do not report assessing civic engagement and are less likely to report that they measure involvement in service (4.8%). Considering available data from the 2012-2013 NSFYS, the extent to which variable content seminars offer robust support for real-world applications of learning is unclear.

Public demonstration of competence. As noted earlier, the development of writing skills is a primary emphasis of variable content seminars, suggesting greater structural support for public demonstration of competence. As with uniform content seminars, it is difficult to determine the extent to which assignments are designed to address a public audience. Research papers and formal essays, which may include persuasive writing, are mentioned twice as often by respondents reporting on variable content courses compared to uniform content seminars (Skipper, 2014). Structural support for public demonstration of competence is also evidenced by an emphasis on oral communication skills. Of respondents reporting on variable content seminars, 16.3% indicated that the development of oral communication skills was among the primary objectives of the seminar. A similar percentage (14.3%) reported this was an important course topic.

Hybrid

Hybrid seminars bear the characteristics of one or more of the primary seminar types (i.e., extended orientation, academic with uniform content, academic with variable content, preprofessional or discipline-linked, basic study skills). Nearly one quarter of respondents (23.4%) said their institution offers a hybrid first-year seminar, with 14.1% indicating it is the primary seminar type on their campus.

Expectations set at appropriately high levels and significant investment of time and effort. Hybrid seminars offer a basic framework for setting appropriately high expectations and supporting significant investment of student time and effort. Nearly 90% reported that their hybrid seminars (86.1%) are letter graded, with about 45% offered for three or four credit hours. Consistent with credit hours earned, half report that students spend three to four hours a week in class.

Interactions with faculty and peers about substantive matters. Not quite three quarters of respondents reporting on hybrid seminars indicated that faculty teaching the course did so as part of their regular responsibilities, with 45.3% indicating faculty taught the course as an overload. The balance of assigned versus extra responsibility shifts in the other direction for staff, as it did for uniform content seminars, with 45.5% reporting that staff teach the seminar as part of their assigned duties and 62.1% teaching it as an extra responsibility. Of those reporting on hybrid seminar assessment, 29.4% assessed out-of-class student-faculty interaction. The emphasis on assessment suggests that hybrid seminars value student–faculty interaction and, thus, may offer structural support for this practice.

With respect to peer engagement, more than half (54.6%) reported involvement of undergraduate students in some way in hybrid seminars, and 71% noted that they incorporate opportunities for teamwork and collaboration. Although developing a support network or friendships was identified as a primary course objective by only 11.2%, 38.2% of those conducting formal evaluations of the seminar suggested that connections with peers *had been assessed in the previous three years*. Overall, the data suggest strong structural support for peer interactions around substantive issues in the hybrid seminars.

Frequent, timely, and constructive feedback. The emphasis on providing experiences designed to help students develop their ability to produce various forms of writing is present but not as pronounced in hybrid seminars (42.1%). Though undergraduate research opportunities are relatively rare in first-year seminars across the board, 15.9% of respondents reported intentionally incorporating such experiences into hybrid seminars. As suggested elsewhere in this analysis, writing and research activities frequently incorporate opportunities for feedback from instructors and/or peers, suggesting moderate structural support for this effective educational practice in hybrid seminars.

Periodic, structured opportunities to reflect on and integrate learning. Of the seminar types explored here, hybrid seminars were most likely to include personal development or self-exploration as an important goal for the course (indicated by 28% of respondents). Of the hybrid seminars including service-learning, all included some type of reflection. The most common reflection activities reported were class discussions (86.1%), writing assignments (83.3%), and student presentations (58.3%). These types of reflection experiences also seem to support discussions with peers around substantive issues and public demonstration of competence.

The development of critical thinking skills was the most frequently cited important course topic (by 37.4% of respondents), and 44.1% of those conducting formal seminar evaluations indicated that critical thinking had been assessed in the previous three years. Slightly less than one third indicated that hybrid seminars were connected to another course or a set of themed cocurricular experiences. Respondents reported intentional coordination of course content across linked courses (40%) and connection of the seminar to theme-based cocurricular experiences (40%); one quarter of respondents indicated the seminar was connected to the linked course(s) by a common intellectual theme.

Possible Gaps

The different seminars types described here provide varying levels of structural support for the eight effective educational practices identified by Kuh and O'Donnell, though some potential gaps are apparent. For example, 17% of respondents overall indicated that self-exploration or personal development—an outcome that is most likely driven by reflection—was one of the three most important course goals. Among the seminar types described here, hybrid seminars seemed to place the greatest emphasis on this, with 28.0% reporting it was an important course goal. Only 2.7% of variable content courses indicated this was an important course goal. Although it would be imprudent to assume that variable content seminars do not offer opportunities for reflection, these seminars may provide few opportunities for students to personalize their learning or to consider how content knowledge connects (or fails to connect) to their lived experiences. Such opportunities may be important drivers of engagement.

With respect to opportunities for public displays of competence, survey data suggest relatively little emphasis on this effective educational practice within first-year seminars. Only 4.3% of respondents overall indicated that the development of oral communication skills was an important course goal, with slightly more (5.1%) indicating it was an important course topic. Writing was more prominent, especially among academic seminars, but it is unclear how often writing assignments were designed to address audiences beyond the instructor. The lack of emphasis on oral communication and writing in first-year seminars may be due to an assumption that these topics are covered elsewhere in the first-year curriculum. Yet, such an omission may be a missed opportunity. Arguing specifically about the inclusion of writing instruction in first-year seminars, Runciman (1998) suggested it was an important chance to change institutional views about the value of writing—in particular, the recognition that content and context matter, that writing instruction is the responsibility of faculty from many departments, and that writing is an integral aspect of learning and articulating course content.

More striking is a potential lack of depth around experiences with diversity in first-year seminars. Less than 1% of survey respondents indicated that developing intercultural competence was an important course goal. Slightly higher percentages of respondents reported that diversity issues (4.7%) and global learning (3.3%) were important course topics. Yet 58.8% reported that diversity and global learning experiences were intentionally incorporated into the seminar. This pattern—fairly consistent across all seminar types—may suggest that a focus on intercultural competence is a one-off for many seminars. There is recognition of its value without the structural support to encourage a sustained emphasis on this effective educational practice.

Conclusion

For all seminar types, the organization and administration provide frameworks and structures that make specific effective educational practices more or less likely to occur. Some seminar types seem to have greater support for enacting certain practices and less for others. It seems logical that the presence of more educationally effective practices would lead to higher student engagement, yet there is nothing to suggest that all need to be present in order for an experience to be high impact. Moreover, simply having the conditions to support an educational practice does not mean that the practice will be enacted or that it will be high quality. Because the NSFYS provides a high-level view of only one type of seminar offered at each institution, we have limited insight into whether and how educational practices are deployed on the ground. For example, a majority of respondents for each of the seminar types reviewed here reported that diversity and global learning experiences were intentionally included in the seminar but did not emphasize these experiences as course goals or topics. Do such experiences happen in each section of that seminar taught at the institution? Are the experiences designed at the course level, where they would be common for all students, or at the section level, where they might not be? Is there a sustained focus on diversity and global learning throughout the course, or is it simply a one-off experience? In other words, how likely is it that all students enrolled in that type of seminar at a particular institution receive exposure to high-quality educational practices focused on diversity and global learning?

Understandably, these kinds of questions are difficult to answer using broad survey instruments. To fill this gap, the National Resource Center for The First-Year Experience and Students in Transition at the University of South Carolina invited contributions describing the presence of educationally effective practices within the first-year seminar. Our purpose in reviewing and selecting case studies for inclusion in this volume was two-fold. First, we hoped to suggest that first-year seminars as a whole rather than a single type could reasonably be called high-impact practices. As the foregoing analysis suggests, structural supports exist across seminar types for a range of effective educational practices. Second, we hoped to offer examples of how different types of seminars (i.e., extended orientation, academic seminars with common content, academic seminars with variable content, hybrid, and basic study skills courses) function as HIPs on their respective campuses.

This report includes case studies of 27 colleges and universities—both two-year and four-year, public and private, and representing a range of different types of first-year seminars. The cases have been arranged alphabetically; an index is included to help readers identify cases by institutional type or mission, seminar type, effective educational practices described, connections to other HIPs, and assessment methods or outcomes. We hope that these case studies provide readers with models of good practice for first-year seminars, a framework for evaluating whether and how the seminars function as HIPs on their own campuses, and strategies for improving the educational effectiveness of these courses in the future.

References

Barefoot, B. O., Griffin, B. Q., & Koch, A. K. (2012). *Enhancing student success and retention throughout undergraduate education: A national survey.* Brevard, NC: John N. Gardner Institute for Excellence in Undergraduate Education.

Hunter, M. S., & Linder, C. W. (2005). First-year seminars. In M. L. Upcraft, J. N. Gardner, & B. O. Barefoot (Eds.), *Challenging and supporting the first-year student: A handbook for improving the first year of college* (pp. 275-291). San Francisco, CA: Jossey-Bass.

Koch, S. S., Griffin, B. Q., & Barefoot, B. O. (2014). *National Survey of Student Success Initiatives at Two-Year Colleges.* Brevard, NC: John N. Gardner Institute for Excellence in Undergraduate Education.

Kuh, G. D. (2008). *High-impact educational practices: What they are, who has access to them, and why they matter.* Washington, DC: Association of American Colleges and Universities.

Kuh, G. D., & O'Donnell, K. (2013). *Ensuring quality and taking high-impact practices to scale.* Washington, DC: Association of American Colleges and Universities.

Runciman, L. (1998). Ending composition as we knew it. *Language and Learning Across the Disciplines, 2*(3), 44-53.

Skipper, T. L. (2014, February). *Writing in the first-year seminar: A national snapshot.* 33rd Annual Conference on The First-Year Experience, San Diego, CA.

Young, D. G., & Hopp, J. M. (2014). *2012-2013 National Survey of First-Year Seminars: Exploring high-impact practices in the first college year* (Research Reports on College Transitions, No. 4). Columbia, SC: University of South Carolina, National Resource Center for The First-Year Experience & Students in Transition.

Appendix

2012-2013 National Survey of First-Year Seminars, Selected Response Frequencies by Seminar Type

Survey question/responses	Extended orientation seminar Freq.	%	Academic seminar: Uniform content Freq.	%	Academic seminar: Various topics Freq.	%	Hybrid Freq.	%
Q28. Who teaches the first-year seminar?								
Adjunct faculty	152	50.0	87	58.8	78	52.7	48	43.2
Full-time non-tenure-track faculty	161	53.0	95	64.2	108	73.0	74	66.7
Tenure-track faculty	192	63.2	100	67.6	135	91.2	86	77.5
Student affairs professionals	215	70.7	71	48.0	38	25.7	55	49.5
Other campus professionals (please specify)	118	38.8	41	27.7	34	23.0	40	36.0
Graduate students	19	6.3	3	2.0	3	2.0	6	5.4
Undergraduate students	18	5.9	0	0.0	2	1.4	8	7.2
Total	304	100.0	148	100.0	148	100.0	111	100.0
Q29. Faculty who teach the first-year seminar teach the course as which of the following?								
Part of regular teaching load	153	61.0	112	79.4	133	91.7	70	73.7
An additional course beyond regular teaching load	161	64.1	60	42.6	41	28.3	43	45.3
Other (please specify)	13	5.2	8	5.7	5	3.4	7	7.4
Total	251	100.0	141	100.0	145	100.0	95	100.0
Q30. Staff (student affairs and other campus professionals) who teach the first-year seminar teach the course as which of the following?								
An assigned responsibility	93	41.9	37	42.5	12	21.8	30	45.5
An extra responsibility	161	72.5	66	75.9	46	83.6	41	62.1
Other (please specify)	24	10.8	12	13.8	8	14.5	16	24.2
Total	222	100.0	87	100.0	55	100.0	66	100.0
Q41. If undergraduate students assist in the first-year seminar, what is their primary role?								
They teach independently	6	2.0	1	0.7	4	2.7	3	2.8
They teach as a part of a team	55	18.6	8	5.4	9	6.1	17	15.7
They assist the instructor but do not teach	76	25.7	43	29.1	41	27.7	33	30.6
Other (please specify)	36	12.2	22	14.9	33	22.3	18	16.7
Undergraduate students do not assist in the seminar	164	55.4	87	58.8	69	46.6	49	45.4
Total	296	100.0	148	100.0	148	100.0	108	100.0
Q46. How many total classroom contact hours are there per week in the first-year seminar?								
1 hour	129	43.6	31	20.9	17	11.6	30	27.8
2 hours	81	27.4	33	22.3	14	9.5	20	18.5
3 hours	78	26.4	70	47.3	88	59.9	39	36.1

Table continues on page 18

Table continued from page 17

Survey question/responses	Extended orientation seminar Freq.	%	Academic seminar: Uniform content Freq.	%	Academic seminar: Various topics Freq.	%	Hybrid Freq.	%
Q46. How many total classroom contact hours are there per week in the first-year seminar? (cont.)								
4 hours	3	1.0	6	4.1	26	17.7	15	13.9
5 hours	1	0.3	2	1.4	1	0.7	0	0.0
6 or more hours	4	1.4	6	4.1	1	0.7	4	3.7
Total	296	100.0	148	100.0	147	100.0	108	100.0
Q47. Does the first-year seminar carry academic credit?								
Yes	275	92.9	142	95.9	144	98.0	104	96.3
No	21	7.1	6	4.1	3	2.0	4	3.7
Total	296	100.0	148	100.0	147	100.0	108	100.0
Q48. How many credits does the first-year seminar carry?								
1 credit	168	61.3	50	35.2	24	16.7	43	41.3
2 credits	35	12.8	16	11.3	9	6.3	13	12.5
3 credits	70	25.5	59	41.5	52	36.1	30	28.8
4 credits	0	0.0	7	4.9	52	36.1	17	16.3
5 credits	1	0.4	1	0.7	1	0.7	0	0.0
6 or more credits	0	0.0	9	6.3	6	4.2	1	1.0
Total	274	100.0	142	100.0	144	100.0	104	100.0
Q50. How is the first-year seminar graded?								
Letter grade	235	79.7	133	89.9	138	93.9	93	86.1
Pass/fail	50	16.9	15	10.1	5	3.4	12	11.1
No grade	7	2.4	0	0.0	0	0.0	0	0.0
Other (please specify)	3	1.0	2	1.4	4	2.7	3	2.8
Total	295	100.0	148	100.0	147	100.0	108	100.0
Q55. Select the three most important course objectives for the first-year seminar:								
Create common first-year experience	58	19.7	53	35.8	26	17.7	19	17.8
Develop a connection with the institution	166	56.3	54	36.5	46	31.3	53	49.5
Develop academic skills	102	34.6	56	37.8	47	32.0	49	45.8
Develop critical-thinking skills	23	7.8	46	31.1	74	50.3	22	20.6
Develop financial literacy	9	3.1	2	1.4	0	0.0	0	0.0
Develop information literacy	17	5.8	14	9.5	15	10.2	5	4.7
Develop oral communication skills	2	0.7	3	2.0	24	16.3	2	1.9
Develop study skills	81	27.5	30	20.3	7	4.8	13	12.1
Develop support network or friendships	58	19.7	21	14.2	12	8.2	12	11.2
Develop writing skills	2	0.7	20	13.5	57	38.8	7	6.5
Develop intercultural competence	1	0.3	3	2.0	0	0.0	2	1.9
Improve second-year return rates	59	20.0	15	10.1	11	7.5	18	16.8
Increase student–faculty interaction	21	7.1	14	9.5	36	24.5	15	14.0

Table continues on page 19

Table continued from page 18

	Extended orientation seminar		Academic seminar: Uniform content		Academic seminar: Various topics		Hybrid	
Survey question/responses	Freq.	%	Freq.	%	Freq.	%	Freq.	%
Q55. Select the three most important course objectives for the first-year seminar: (cont.)								
Introduce a discipline	4	1.4	2	1.4	14	9.5	4	3.7
Introduce the liberal arts	5	1.7	21	14.2	24	16.3	11	10.3
Provide orientation to campus resources and services	172	58.3	40	27.0	17	11.6	37	34.6
Provide career exploration	30	10.2	8	5.4	2	1.4	2	1.9
Provide preprofessional preparation	1	0.3	0	0.0	2	1.4	0	0.0
Self-exploration or personal development	56	19.0	24	16.2	4	2.7	30	28.0
Other (please specify)	13	4.4	15	10.1	17	11.6	15	14.0
Total	295	100.0	148	100.0	147	100.0	107	100.0
Q56. Select the three most important topics that compose the content of this first-year seminar:								
Academic planning or advising	139	47.1	52	35.1	18	12.2	34	31.8
Career exploration or preparation	60	20.3	30	20.3	7	4.8	13	12.1
Campus engagement	97	32.9	41	27.7	22	15.0	37	34.6
Campus resources	166	56.3	35	23.6	13	8.8	33	30.8
College policies and procedures	53	18.0	16	10.8	4	2.7	11	10.3
Critical thinking	32	10.8	68	45.9	93	63.3	40	37.4
Diversity issues	13	4.4	6	4.1	5	3.4	6	5.6
Financial literacy	14	4.7	2	1.4	1	0.7	1	0.9
Global learning	0	0.0	6	4.1	14	9.5	5	4.7
Health and wellness	5	1.7	3	2.0	1	0.7	1	0.9
Information literacy	22	7.5	19	12.8	21	14.3	5	4.7
Oral communication skills	2	0.7	8	5.4	21	14.3	6	5.6
Relationship issues (e.g., interpersonal skills, conflict resolution)	27	9.2	11	7.4	4	2.7	10	9.3
Specific disciplinary topic	1	0.3	15	10.1	49	33.3	22	20.6
Study skills	116	39.3	36	24.3	16	10.9	33	30.8
Time management	95	32.2	31	20.9	6	4.1	25	23.4
Writing skills	10	3.4	35	23.6	72	49.0	14	13.1
Other (please specify)	22	7.5	25	16.9	33	22.4	21	19.6
Total	295	100.0	148	100.0	147	100.0	107	100.0
Q57. Which of the following approaches associated with high-impact educational practices are intentionally incorporated into the first-year seminar? (Select all that apply):								
Writing-intensive experiences	75	25.5	81	54.7	105	71.4	45	42.1
Collaboration and teamwork	203	69.0	99	66.9	90	61.2	76	71.0
Diversity and global learning	162	55.1	99	66.9	84	57.1	72	67.3

Table continues on page 20

Table continued from page 19

Survey question/responses	Extended orientation seminar Freq.	%	Academic seminar: Uniform content Freq.	%	Academic seminar: Various topics Freq.	%	Hybrid Freq.	%
Q57. Which of the following approaches associated with high-impact educational practices are intentionally incorporated into the first-year seminar? (Select all that apply): (cont.)								
None of the above	53	18.0	8	5.4	12	8.2	12	11.2
Total	294	100.0	148	100.0	147	100.0	107	100.0
Q59. Which of the following high-impact educational practices are connected to the first-year seminar? (Select all that apply):								
Service-learning	83	28.6	48	33.3	55	37.7	36	33.6
Learning community	107	36.9	56	38.9	55	37.7	35	32.7
Common reading experience	92	31.7	67	46.5	54	37.0	54	50.5
Undergraduate research	18	6.2	14	9.7	40	27.4	17	15.9
None of the above	107	36.9	36	25.0	35	24.0	27	25.2
Total	290	100.0	144	100.0	146	100.0	107	100.0
Q60. How many total hours are students required to complete for the service-learning component?								
There is no requirement about the total number of hours.	27	32.9	18	37.5	33	60.0	17	47.2
5 or fewer	35	42.7	13	27.1	11	20.0	8	22.2
6 - 10	17	20.7	14	29.2	6	10.9	7	19.4
11 - 15	1	1.2	1	2.1	1	1.8	0	0.0
16 - 20	0	0.0	1	2.1	3	5.5	3	8.3
More than 20	2	2.4	1	2.1	1	1.8	1	2.8
Total	82	100.0	48	100.0	55	100.0	36	100.0
Q61. Which of the following are used as reflection techniques in the first-year seminar associated with the service-learning component? (Select all that apply):								
Class discussion	62	75.6	40	83.3	39	70.9	31	86.1
Portfolio	11	13.4	14	29.2	9	16.4	6	16.7
Student presentations	33	40.2	30	62.5	27	49.1	21	58.3
Writing exercise, such as writing a paper or journaling	63	76.8	38	79.2	40	72.7	30	83.3
Other (please specify)	5	6.1	6	12.5	9	16.4	3	8.3
There is no reflection associated with the service-learning component.	6	7.3	2	4.2	2	3.6	0	0.0
Total	82	100.0	48	100.0	55	100.0	36	100.0
Q63. Which of the following are characteristics of the learning community of which the first-year seminar is a part? (Select all that apply):								
Co-enrollment, not all courses	87	82.1	35	62.5	36	65.5	29	82.9
Co-enrollment, all other courses	9	8.5	5	8.9	6	10.9	2	5.7
Coordinated course content	37	34.9	19	33.9	17	30.9	14	40.0

Table continues on page 21

Table continued from page 20

Survey question/responses	Extended orientation seminar Freq.	%	Academic seminar: Uniform content Freq.	%	Academic seminar: Various topics Freq.	%	Hybrid Freq.	%
Q63. Which of the following are characteristics of the learning community of which the first-year seminar is a part? (Select all that apply): (cont.)								
Course content connected by common intellectual theme	25	23.6	18	32.1	14	25.5	9	25.7
Common set of theme-based experiences outside of the course	29	27.4	23	41.1	18	32.7	14	40.0
Living-learning community	30	28.3	12	21.4	25	45.5	11	31.4
Other (please specify)	8	7.5	4	7.1	6	10.9	4	11.4
Total	106	100.0	56	100.0	55	100.0	35	100.0
Q73. Has your first-year seminar been formally assessed or evaluated since Fall 2009?								
Yes	177	61.2	83	57.6	84	57.5	70	65.4
No	82	28.4	55	38.2	53	36.3	30	28.0
I don't know	30	10.4	6	4.2	9	6.2	7	6.5
Total	289	100.0	144	100.0	146	100.0	107	100.0
Q78. Please indicate each student outcome that was measured: (Select all that apply):								
Achievement of learning or course outcomes	114	64.8	55	67.1	60	71.4	54	79.4
Civic engagement	20	11.4	13	15.9	10	11.9	8	11.8
Connections with peers	70	39.8	26	31.7	29	34.5	26	38.2
Critical thinking	45	25.6	34	41.5	45	53.6	30	44.1
Grade point average	79	44.9	34	41.5	20	23.8	27	39.7
Information literacy	37	21.0	20	24.4	24	28.6	17	25.0
Involvement in service	25	14.2	9	11.0	4	4.8	10	14.7
Out-of-class student–faculty interaction	39	22.2	18	22.0	29	34.5	20	29.4
Participation in campus activities	74	42.0	25	30.5	22	26.2	26	38.2
Persistence to graduation	53	30.1	22	26.8	14	16.7	16	23.5
Persistence to second year	111	63.1	49	59.8	36	42.9	43	63.2
Satisfaction with advising	49	27.8	19	23.2	20	23.8	24	35.3
Satisfaction with faculty	76	43.2	47	57.3	49	58.3	47	69.1
Satisfaction with the seminar	135	76.7	60	73.2	62	73.8	56	82.4
Satisfaction with the institution	63	35.8	30	36.6	24	28.6	22	32.4
Student self-reports of course impact	78	44.3	44	53.7	39	46.4	42	61.8
Student self-reports of improvement	51	29.0	23	28.0	32	38.1	24	35.3
Understanding of institutional identity and culture	26	14.8	15	18.3	14	16.7	17	25.0
Use of campus services	69	39.2	24	29.3	16	19.0	26	38.2
Writing ability	17	9.7	26	31.7	40	47.6	15	22.1
Other (please specify)	10	5.7	4	4.9	8	9.5	5	7.4
Total	176	100.0	82	100.0	84	100.0	68	100.0

The American University of Rome
Jenny Petrucci

The Institution

The American University of Rome (AUR) is a four-year, private, independent, not-for-profit liberal arts college founded in 1969 and offering undergraduate and graduate degree programs to students from all over the world. Embodying a global breadth of vision in its work, AUR is firmly rooted in the local community, with strong links to Italian and European institutions. AUR hosts approximately 500 students from more than 40 countries every semester, including (a) resident students who complete their degrees at the University and (b) study-abroad students, coming mainly from the United States and Europe, who enroll for one semester or a year. The mission of AUR is to prepare students to live and work across cultures as skilled and knowledgeable citizens of an interconnected and rapidly changing world.

Description of the Seminar

AUR implemented a First Year Program (FYP) in 2007 in response to several student issues, such as integration, learning, and adjustment to college and to a different culture. The FYP is composed of several different yet complementary elements: an induction program, including preregistration; learning communities; a common reading; a first-year seminar (FYS); a peer mentor program; and a Passport program.

The FYS, the core of the program, is a three-credit (i.e., 42 hours of instruction), general education course required for all first-time-in-college students (FTIC). The seminar focuses on culture and diversity seen through different fields, such as Italian culture, film, sociology, and communication across cultures. AUR normally enrolls about 100 FTIC students every year. They represent 42 different countries, with 40% of students coming from the United States, 18% from Italy, and the rest from other countries all over the world. Moreover, 69% of the total population are female and 31% are male. Each student coming to AUR with fewer than 30 credits is considered FTIC, although because of the diversity in the international student population at AUR some students may be reclassified (e.g., students transferring with a low GPA or students who have been home schooled previously). The goal of the FYP is to level discrepancies arising from the different academic, social, ethnic, and cultural backgrounds of students. The seminar, in particular, provides students with the basic skills required to be successful in college and more specifically at an American college like AUR.

The FYS is designed to encourage all first-year students to become active participants in the AUR community and ensure a successful college experience. Courses are taught in English, and students develop the fundamental skills of writing, information literacy, information technology (IT), communication, and oral presentations and put them into practice through the examination of various cultural and multicultural themes. Special attention and dedicated support is given to ESL students, who can benefit from the peer-led workshops organized every semester to reinforce specific academic writing skills such as elaborating on a thesis statement, creating an outline, and developing an annotated bibliography. The course is project-based and includes many onsite lectures. *Laughing Without an Accent* by Firoozeh Dumas is assigned as a common summer or holiday reading and offers a reflection on the adjustment to a different culture.

The FYS is taught by the FYP director and includes a number of faculty and staff guest speakers. More precisely, full-time faculty members (mostly program directors) from the Italian Studies, Communication, International Relations, and Film and Digital Media departments teach one session each, at the beginning of the semester, focusing on culture as seen from the perspective of their own disciplines. Toward midsemester, a business professor comes to the FYS to teach two sessions on numeracy skills (primarily based on advanced Microsoft Excel skills). When addressing the oral presentation skills component of FYS, one professor from the International Relations department gives the students a workshop on persuasive public speaking. The librarian, the registrar, and the IT director are also involved in the FYS, providing students with workshops on how to use the library, register for classes, and build a PowerPoint or Prezi presentation, respectively. At the beginning of the semester, both Student Government and Writing Centre representatives introduce themselves during FYS to make the students aware of their services and activities. Moreover, professors from the Art History and Archeology programs give students two onsite classes around the city of Rome. This experience introduces students to the AUR mission that includes using Rome as the classroom.

The Peer Mentor program is an integral and fundamental part of FYP. Two peer mentors (PMs) are selected by the FYP director every semester from among the juniors and seniors. PMs assist with AUR orientation, mentoring and advising, finding campus resources, and facilitating FYS. They model successful student behaviors and leadership skills and help students get to know each other through introductions to classmates from the same country or with similar interests, informal and individual meetings, and organized events.

The FYS is structured as a discussion-based class where students are participating actively in the learning process. They receive materials to review before class and are expected to come prepared for in-class activities and group work. The course uses an engaged pedagogy comprising undergraduate research, cooperative learning, peer teaching, and an interdisciplinary approach, intended to take students out of their comfort zones to initiate a dialogue on cultural diversity. The students complete three major assignments in the course: a research paper, a group oral presentation, and a weekly journal.

The research paper is based on the topic of culture and diversity and developed in four phases (i.e., thesis statement, annotated bibliography, outline, and final draft), with students receiving feedback at each stage. The final draft of the research paper must be submitted to the Writing Centre for review. Learning objectives include fostering writing skills necessary for synthesizing information and communicating it clearly, developing critical- and creative-thinking skills, and gaining competence in gathering and presenting quantitative data.

During the semester, students are involved in individual oral presentations on assigned topics (e.g., time management and planning, studying preferences, the use of IT in the learning process) leading up to a final, graded, group presentation. To begin to hone students' skills, the first individual assignment is videotaped and reviewed by both peers and the instructor. Students then participate in a public speaking workshop led by a professional in the field, again receiving immediate feedback on their talks. The assessed assignment has students working in groups to produce a presentation on one of the topics covered in class. Learning objectives include a demonstration of oral presentation skills to carry on a brief line of reasoning to a target audience, development of critical- and creative-thinking skills, and competence in gathering and presenting quantitative data and using basic professional software programs.

Students are required to submit a weekly journal reflecting on issues discussed in class. This assignment fosters critical thinking and self-reflection, awareness of cultural differences, and a deeper understanding of the AUR mission. Students receive weekly feedback in a rubric format.

Educationally Effective Practices

The mission of AUR, the makeup of the student body, and the intentional focus of the FYP on multicultural themes ensure that students have relevant and real-world *experiences with diversity*. In addition, the Peer Mentor program, guest lecturers from cross-campus departments, and collaborative student group work encourage meaningful and multiple *interactions with faculty and peers*. Students receive *frequent and constructive feedback* from the instructor, other faculty members, and their peers at multiple stages during the three major assignments. *Periodic and structured opportunities for reflection and integration* are incorporated into all assignments, especially the weekly reflective journal.

Discussion

One of the most effective educational practices integrated in the FYS is the interaction with faculty and peers (i.e., through the Peer Mentors program). This program assists all first-year students in meeting the challenges of living, learning, and making connections throughout their university experience in Rome and beyond. The program is formally assessed on a three-year basis through student exit questionnaires and PM feedback (e.g., weekly meeting or focus groups with the FYP director, surveys). During 2015 assessment, first-year students almost universally found the PMs helpful. Only one out of 86 students found them unhelpful, and 84% described the PMs as a source of information and support that was on their level. About 10% of the students reported that the PMs contributed help for their research paper, and 15% found them inspiring, as indicated by the following comments:

> The Peer Mentors are good figures to have in class because they are always ready to help you.

> They were sort of friends and guides throughout the semester.

> They were helpful in the writing skills; they advised us well on how to start a research paper.

> They were helpful for the workshops, sharing their opinions in class and also being available outside class.

The benefits related to peer interactions are not limited to first-year students. The PMs themselves commented on the positive outcomes related to their involvement in FYS:

> As a Peer Mentor I feel that I have gained a naturally stronger psychological perspective, in the sense that I have grown much better at understanding subtle messages and feelings from students ... and I have gotten much better at dealing with different mixes of energy and emotion.

> I feel I have been very good at being able to connect with students ... to introducing students to other peers and upperclassmen that they would get along with, to ease the sometimes blunt assimilation freshmen might experience.

One of the learning objectives of the FYS is appreciation of cultural differences. Students have the chance to reflect on cultural differences and diversity through their journals and in the research paper on cultural diversity. Appreciation of cultural differences is assessed though journal and essay rubrics and an exit questionnaire administered to students at the end of their first semester in college. Students complete the questionnaire in the FYS; the PMs collect them and give them to the instructor afterwards. Student comments reflecting an increasing appreciation for cultural differences include the following:

> ... since I arrived to my multicultural college I discovered that it does not make sense to focus on the differences—they just put barriers between us—we should focus on what we have in common.

> I have discovered that the personal interactions I have within AUR depend, to an extent, on the cultural characteristics of the person I am interacting with ... I think this trait is what enables AUR to become a haven of diverse cultural interaction, where cultural differences are preserved and flourish rather than [being] lost among commonality. The FYS has greatly encouraged me to better understand that.

Out of 43 students responding to the survey, 33 agreed or strongly agreed that FYS contributed to fostering their appreciation of cultural differences, and 10 were undecided. Some of the comments included the following:

> By interacting with the peers from different cultures I gained firsthand experiences and point of views from them. It made me have an open mind about cultural differences on things that seemed strange to me. I know that I am not a freak!

> I opened my mind to want to meet everyone.

> It helps you to embrace it. (cultural difference)

> This course helped me to learn how to understand and get used to different cultures. It helped me welcome Rome and all that comes with it.

The nature of the FYS structure allows interaction with faculty members who teach specific sessions of the course. The students have responded in a very positive way to such interaction so far and have manifested their appreciation in the exit questionnaire. They have the chance to get to know more faculty members and are more informed about the educational offerings of the University. Moreover, the expertise and experience of the guest speakers have proven to have a great impact on students and to be an important source of inspiration for them.

Ultimately the weekly journal entries represent an important opportunity for reflection on the class material and the students' holistic college experience. The instructor meets with each student individually twice during the semester. During these private meetings the students frequently comment about their journal entries, asking for more personal feedback from the instructor. Both in their exit questionnaires and in those meetings, students highlight the value they place on the journals as a safe place to reflect on their own lives and be truly who they are. From the point of view of the instructor, rather than being a mere assignment, the journals are fundamental gateways into the private lives of students and ultimately their wellbeing.

Implications

The FYP at AUR was created with the aim of holistically supporting students in their transition to college. The educationally effective practices pertaining to the program (e.g., faculty and peer interaction, frequent and constructive feedback, periodic and structured opportunities for reflection, experiences with diversity) have been carefully selected, taking into consideration the skills the Association of American Colleges and Universities suggest are necessary for students to acquire in college and the unique make-up of our student population.

Given the urgency of addressing transfer students issues on campus, AUR is currently discussing creating a seminar that would keep most of the elements of the FYS, such as peer mentoring and experience with diversity, with transition content more suitable for this group of students. The transfer seminar may have elements of career planning as well as of more sophisticated research methods, such as autoethnography. The latter would provide students with a deep knowledge of a qualitative research method and the opportunity to reflect on their role within their new institutional home, and in doing so, find the place they most belong.

Contact Information

Jenny Petrucci
The American University of Rome
Via Pietro Roselli, 4
Rome Italy 00153
E-mail: j.petrucci@aur.edu
Phone: +44 06 58330919

Cabrini University
Richard Gebauer, Michelle Filling-Brown, and Amy Persichetti

The Institution

Cabrini University is a small, private, four-year, Catholic, liberal arts institution located in Radnor, Pennsylvania, dedicated to academic excellence, leadership development, and social justice. The student body comprises approximately 1,360 undergraduates with roughly 400 first-year students. Approximately 62% of undergraduates identify as White, 20% as Black or African American, 7.3% as Hispanic or Latino, 1.1% as Asian, .01% as American Indian or Alaskan Native, and 62% as female. The racial demographics of the institution have changed in the past year, with a 14.3% increase of Black or African American students and 5.9% increase in Hispanic or Latino students entering in fall 2015. Roughly 62% of the student body lives in on-campus housing, and 50% of the fall 2015 first-year cohort applied to participate in a living–learning community or learning community.

Description of the Seminar

During the first year at the university, students are encouraged to apply for living–learning communities (LLCs), each with a distinct thematic culture. Each LLC comprises 16-18 students who live on the same residence hall floor and participate in an integrated curriculum and cocurriculum that consists of four to five courses taught by a team of three faculty members. They take a four-credit, first-year writing seminar (FYS), Engagements With the Common Good: ECG100, as a part of their LLC course work. The seminar establishes an important foundation for learning about social justice, writing, and information literacy at the university. Connecting the LLC experience with the FYS builds collaboration, integrates real-world learning, and begins the important conversations about diversity and social justice that are the hallmark of the Cabrinian education, while also aligning well with the educationally effective practices identified by Kuh and O'Donnell (2013).

Educationally Effective Practices

Experiences with diversity. ECG100 is the first in a three-year sequence of courses focusing on social justice issues, such as domestic violence, watershed citizenship, foster care, refugees, and the criminal justice system. The series moves students from a place of individual reflection to community engagement and advocacy. Although the topic of each FYS is linked to the theme of the LLC it is attached to, learning outcomes are the same for all sections. Students examine real-world social justice issues through the unique lens of their FYS and LLC as they consider their own identities, their place in the campus community, and the broader context of the world.

Significant investment of time and effort. Each section of the FYS requires a signature assignment (i.e., a four- to five-page research paper using scholarly sources) tailored to the topic of the course. This effort is buoyed by an additional information literacy credit that has been added to the course (four credits total) and is taught by library staff. In addition to homework, students spend a classroom hour weekly learning how to use digital technologies to inform course content, evaluate research, and cite properly. The four-credit value of the FYS provides 25% more instructional time than the average first-year course, ensures academic rigor, and reinforces student understanding of expectations for college-level work.

Frequent and constructive feedback and periodic and structured opportunities for reflection and integration. The written component of ECG100 allows students multiple opportunities to reflect on material, process ideas, and receive feedback from instructors who guide not only the writing process but also the personalized development of critical-thinking skills. Although only the signature assignment is required for the purpose of artifact collection for assessment, faculty are establishing several shared writing assignments designed to ask students to reflect deeply on issues of diversity and inclusivity.

Reflection occurs in written assignments and is also an integral part of classroom discussions and activities. For example, in the IMPACT (Leadership) LLC, a year-long learning community that engages students in three courses in the fall and two courses in the spring, students take an FYS that challenges them to role-play in various modules using the Reacting to the Past (RTTP) curriculum developed by faculty at Barnard College. This innovative curriculum

> consists of elaborate games, set in the past, in which students are assigned roles informed by classic texts in the history of ideas ... [designed to] ... draw students into the past, promote engagement with big ideas, and improve intellectual and academic skills. (Reacting to the Past, 2015, para. 1)

In the seminar, students play a RTTP module entitled *The Threshold of Democracy: Athens in 403 B.C.* (Ober & Carnes, 2015). They assume roles and debate and write about the values and impact of taxation, slavery, democracy, and war from the perspective of these roles. At the conclusion of the module, they are challenged to reflect on their willingness (or refusal) to become Athenian leaders, consider the leadership qualities they exhibited individually and as a community of Athenians, and decide whether their approach to leadership was directed by ethical beliefs and values. Having tracked their own social, emotional, and cognitive development in their IMPACT LLC fall course, Metacognition for Leadership, students are more self-aware and can quickly connect the theories and models of leadership they are exposed to in their IMPACT LLC spring course, Foundations of Leadership, to their own approach to accepting or rejecting leadership opportunities that arose in the structure of the Athens RTTP module in ECG100. The Athens RTTP module and the debriefing that follows foster integration of learning across the LLC coursework.

Relevance through real-world application and public demonstration of competence. The FYS employs examples from daily life and current global issues to explore the theme of the linked LLC. For instance, in the Body Language LLC, students examine the formation of identity, beauty culture, icons, body image, and gender. In the fall semester of this year-long LLC, students take courses in social work and women's studies, studying the literary and cultural roots of gender and body image. In the spring, they take a psychology course focusing on the interface between media and psychological development. The linked FYS, taken in the spring and entitled Bodies in the News, has students examine how cultural beliefs about body and gender are communicated through media. One assignment has them develop a presentation they can submit for the campus's annual Undergraduate Arts and Research Symposium. At this event, in interactive sessions modeled on academic conferences, students present to their peers and faculty their analysis of how the media covered specific court cases and portrayed African Americans within the procedures leading to the court's decision.

Discussion

During a three-year cycle of assessment, the university's Assessment Committee collected student artifacts (the signature assignment) from all ECG instructors. A team of six interdisciplinary assessment readers attended a calibration session to understand how to apply a rubric, which was collaboratively developed by ECG instructors in alignment with national standards of writing assessment set forth by Association of American Colleges and Universities. Each student artifact was blind-read by two readers; a third reader contributed when initial scores differed by more than two points in any given domain on the rubric. Over three years, about 600 randomly sampled artifacts were scored. The data were disseminated through our shared governance structure, and all faculty were asked for feedback. Based on that feedback, the Assessment Committee made specific recommendations for change in areas such as curriculum or faculty development. The Committee then closed the feedback loop by documenting the progress toward or completion of those recommended action items.

Over the course of the assessment cycle, several tangible changes occurred, based on the student performance on the signature assignment. First, ECG100, which was initially a three-credit class, became enhanced with the fourth credit of information literacy instruction taught by an embedded course librarian. Second, the learning outcomes for the seminar were revised to capture the goals of the course more accurately. Based on those revisions, the rubric was updated to reflect the changes. Third, the university hosted multiple faculty development sessions on writing pedagogy, diversity, and cultural competence to address student weaknesses revealed through the data.

The Assessment Committee embedded the concept of the signature assignment across all areas of the core curriculum. All faculty were invited to contribute ideas to the formation of guidelines that would serve as a template for developing unique signature assignments, allowing for both standardization and academic freedom. The Committee hosted multiple faculty development opportunities and one-on-one sessions to assist faculty with developing assignments. Through this collegial experience, faculty were encouraged to use the writing process by building in multiple drafts, feedback on student writing, peer workshops, writing conferences, and opportunities for deep revision on the signature assignment. The assessment process itself helped encourage faculty to improve teaching methods and provide more meaningful feedback to students.

At the conclusion of the assessment cycle, Cabrini entered a Comprehensive Review Year. This period allowed the university the opportunity to reflect on what was learned and to plan for the next assessment cycle, which will focus on the newly approved learning outcomes and the effectiveness of the additional contact hours for information literacy instruction. A positive finding from the entire LLC program assessment over the past seven years is that LLC students have an average retention rate of 78.8%, compared to 68.9% for non-LLC participants.

Implications

With the hiring of a new president in 2014 came renewed energy and enthusiasm that permeated the campus community. Recognizing the value of academic and cocurricular experiences that are intentionally structured and threaded throughout the first-year experience, the president introduced the Cabrini Promise, centered on high-impact practices (HIPs; Kuh, 2008). By the fall of 2020, as part of this promise, the university will ensure that all entering students experience at least two HIPs by the conclusion of their first year and at least four by graduation. In an effort to make certain the university is successful in this endeavor, by 2020 all first-year students will be enrolled in either a living–learning community or learning community. The curriculum of each community will include an ECG100 to continue to strengthen the partnership and ensure the benefits of the connection between the FYS and the learning-community experience. The seminar serves as an introduction to diversity to all first-year students, providing students with the knowledge for future action involving diversity in ECG200: Service-Learning/Diversity in Action and ECG300: Diversity in Action/Community-Based Research in their sophomore and junior years.

Though students may go beyond the goal of participating in four HIPs, at the very least, they will experience diversity in action through community-based research, applying their service to research and advocacy in the ECG300 curriculum. Finally, as part of their majors—regardless of academic discipline—all students will complete an internship, complete a capstone experience, or participate in undergraduate research as defined by the academic department.

The scaffolding of these opportunities allows the institution to fulfill the promise we are making to our students. The relationship between the first-year seminar and the university's LLCs serves as the introduction to educationally effective practices, and these practices are threaded through the larger four-year experience. This case study articulates the importance of delivering a high-quality first-year seminar in an effort to promote college success.

References

Kuh, G. D. (2008). *High-impact educational practices: What they are, who has access to them, and why they matter.* Washington, DC: Association of American Colleges and Universities.

Kuh, G. D., & O'Donnell, K. (2013). *Ensuring quality and taking high-impact practices to scale.* Washington, DC: Association of American Colleges and Universities.

Ober, J., & Carnes, M. C. (2014). *The threshold of democracy: Athens in 403 B.C.* New York, NY: W. W. Norton.

Reacting to the Past. (2015). Retrieved from *https://reactingbarnard.edu*

Contact Information

Richard Gebauer
Director, First-Year Experience
Cabrini University
610 King of Prussia Road
Radnor, PA 19087
E-mail: gebauer@cabrini.edu
Phone: (610) 902-8592

Clark University
Jessica Bane Robert

The Institution

Founded in 1887, Clark University is a four-year, private, nonsectarian, teaching and research institution located in Worcester, Massachusetts, offering 32 undergraduate majors, 24 graduate programs, and 2 certificate programs. In Fall 2015, Clark had an enrollment of 3,395 students, of whom 2,301 were undergraduates, 671 were first-year, 147 were first-generation, 100 were international, and 571 were domestic. Among the domestic first-year students, 349 identified as White, 61 Hispanic, 55 Asian American, 33 African American, 3 Native American, 11 multirace or multiethnicity, and 59 unknown. In this cohort, 39% were male and 61% were female students. In 2009, Clark adopted a new model of undergraduate education, Liberal Education and Effective Practice (LEEP), which integrates classroom learning with real-world experiences to prepare students for life after college.

Description of the Seminar

In 2010, to increase first-year student engagement, persistence, and success, Clark began offering first-year intensive (FYI) seminars. By 2012 all first-year students were required to take an FYI, which became a graduation requirement and a foundational component in the LEEP academic journey. Students may select from one of three types of FYI experiences—topic-focused, introduction to a discipline, or research-intensive–which fulfill one of the eight required liberal studies core courses. This case focuses on a single seminar, Heart of a Poet–Heat of Poem, a small, writing-intensive seminar that fulfilled the liberal studies verbal expression requirement.

A part-time faculty member, who also serves as the assistant director of the Writing Center and Writing Program, taught the course. Students received one credit for the seminar, which met twice a week (2.5 hours total) for 15 weeks. Students were expected to commit a minimum of 180 hours of work in and out of class.

Course pedagogy centered on discussion and active- and applied-learning practices, with approximately 10% of the course delivered through faculty lecture. The mission of the FYI was to impart a variety of educationally effective practices though activities that created a collegial and fun environment where students felt safe and supported enough to impart diverse, personal experiences and perspectives on major life themes while they moved through shared intellectual and hands-on experiences.

Educationally Effective Practices

Interactions with faculty and peers and opportunities for frequent feedback. Frequent feedback from, and a close relationship with, the instructor was a primary goal of the course. As writing practice emerged central to the seminar, the instructor built in two one-on-one conferences to discuss each student's writing in addition to the one required academic advising meeting. This extra meeting time provided an opportunity for the instructor, doubling as the student's faculty advisor, to check in with individuals on personal matters of adjustment and making connections with others. The faculty member also had additional occasions to connect with class members in a less formal manner through various field trips and two group gatherings at the instructor's home: an informal, midsemester dinner and a formal end-of-semester reading event. These off-campus experiences had an auxiliary effect of creating a close-knit community of learners where individuals received both social and academic support from their professor and peers. They also provided additional contexts where students learned much about each other and their new community.

Not only did students have added contact with the instructor and peers outside class, but in class, participants also received frequent feedback from their peers through discussion, dialogue, and a staple of the course, the writer's workshop, during which students read and received constructive criticism of their work from a small cohort of classmates.

Throughout the course, collaborative approaches to poetry included study groups, team-based assignments, writing workshops, small-group interpretation and analysis of poems, and cooperative projects and research. One major collaborative project involved introducing students to research at the college level while enlisting help from Clark's research librarians, who familiarized students with the stacks, databases, and research methods. With a partner, students chose a type of poem (e.g., nature, rant, confessional, lyric, persona), researched, and co-authored a four-page paper on the selected form. They also developed and delivered a 15-minute oral presentation and created an original writing prompt. These activities asked partners to synthesize their research and apply their findings to a practical exercise. This informed-learning activity encouraged the pair to put their research into action and practice while offering them the opportunity to work more closely with a peer, contributing to the high-impact nature of the seminar.

Experiences with diversity and periodic and structured opportunities for reflection and integration. Collaborative learning activities occurred both inside and outside the classroom environment and combined two key goals: (a) learning to work and solve problems in the company of others and (b) sharpening one's own understanding by deeply listening to the insights of others, especially those with different backgrounds and life experiences. To the latter goal, poetry provided a rich field where students grappled with challenging material and major life questions while getting to know the views, stories, and strengths of their instructor, their peers, and authors from diverse backgrounds. Each class started with journal questions based on a poem that led to reflection and follow-up dialogue where students listened in turn to one another. The act of frequent reflection provided students with metacognitive experiences, the goal of which was personal insight and growth, with an additional benefit of bonding between participants in the FYI community. Frequent reflections and dialogue set a tone of trust and support and laid the foundation for productive collaboration and active-learning opportunities. Some of these moments came in the form of providing feedback on each other's writing in the writer's workshop and analyzing readings together in small groups and presenting their findings to the class as a whole. Students also interpreted and performed poems with their peers, intentionally emphasizing rhythm or theme. One memorable collaboration occurred when two male students faced the problem of teaching meter to the class. With the instructor's coaching, they decided to recite Theodore Rothke's, *My Papa's Waltz*, while they danced around the room emphasizing stressed beats with their bodies and delighting their classmates.

Relevance through real-world applications. The FYI applied practices to induce student engagement in the greater institutional and local community and provided context for relevant real-world application of poetry through community field trips and outings, visits from professional writers, and student publications and performances. During the semester, students were required to go to three literary events on campus or in the greater Worcester community. For example, students could participate in an open-mic event for local poets held at Barnes and Noble; attend an event hosted at one of the consortium schools, such as The College of the Holy Cross; or attend a graveside reading of Elisabeth Bishop poems hosted by the Worcester County Poetry Association and held at a cemetery near Clark's campus. Attendance at outside events maintained a two-fold goal: (a) students would witness practical application of our common intellectual and creative practice, and (b) they would become familiar with their new community.

Field trips provided relevant settings in which the instructor and students would experience poetry and write together, and again, students would become acquainted with their new place. One trip included an outing to Worcester native Stanley Kunitz's (10th Poet Laureate) boyhood home. Students read Kunitz's work within the very walls he wrote about; they stood beneath his mother's pear tree in the backyard listening to a reading of his poem, "My Mother's Pear Tree." On another field experience, students visited the world-renowned Worcester Art Museum to gain inspiration for writing ekphrastic poems (i.e., based on works of art). Later, these poems could be submitted for publication in an anthology of ekphrastic poems produced by the museum, or they could be shared at an end-of-semester reading—a celebration of their poetic efforts, open to the public and held at the instructor's home.

Public demonstration of competence. Students prepared for oral presentations of their work and for publication by frequent writing and oration practice in class and during visits from professional authors and editors working in the field who provided models for oral delivery and revision techniques. After revision and performance, some class members continued with submission practices and publication of their poems in campus or local journals.

Students entertained numerous in-class opportunities to present their reflections, research, and creative projects to their peers. They led discussions of poems, created dialogue and reflection questions, applied their knowledge of the elements of craft (e.g., word choice, line breaks, rhythm, meter) to critical and creative-thinking and problem-based activities. In addition, students taught lessons on types of poems and demonstrated their understanding of craft through mini presentations and group performances. Ultimately, the course culminated in students hosting a community reading of their polished creative work along with a brief talk on what they learned about poetry and about themselves as students and writers.

Discussion

No formal assessments of this course's practices or overall effectiveness as compared to other FYIs at Clark have been conducted. The following findings are based on qualitative methods: frequent student feedback during the semester; 16 end-of-course written evaluations from fall 2012; and recent, informal interviews with students almost four years after their FYI experience. The discipline of poetry as the foundation for an FYI not only helped develop research and written and verbal communication skills but also provided a rich field for discussing enduring questions, delving into various world views and diverse individual perspectives, and facilitating lasting practices of critical inquiry and reflection. Beyond disciplinary knowledge and skills, the educationally effective practices of the course provided purposeful opportunities for interaction and for synthesizing and implementing acquired knowledge.

The relationships that were fostered emerged as the major strength of the course and provided the most impact on first-year students. All students noted the connections made with the professor and classmates built through active-learning activities in the classroom and by experiences in the field. In all course evaluations, students expressed positive feedback and feelings toward the instructor (e.g., "approachable," "passionate," a "favorite" professor who "cared about helping students succeed") and appreciated the extra time spent on them (e.g., "[value the] openness and willingness to take [them] places and help outside of the classroom"). Evidencing this connection, all students who remained at the institution went on to seek the instructor's counsel and take other classes with her.

Additionally, social support and bonds had a lasting, positive effect on students. Most of the students' comments support research that suggest small class sizes are essential to "foster student-faculty interaction and peer relationships" (Padgett, Keup, & Pascarella, 2013, p. 135). As one student noted, "I got a lot of feedback not only from my professor but also my peers." Many of the students in the class have remained friends, and the majority have been retained at Clark all four years.

All students but one stated their writing improved through frequent assignments (some low-stakes and some public) and ample feedback from the instructor and peers. Students also noted the course's usefulness in acquiring self-awareness and adjustment to college expectations, as demonstrated in the following comments:

I have gotten to know myself and my strengths better.

[The course] helped me to adjust to college expectations.

[The course gave me] confidence that stuck with me ... and made me want to be an English major with a focus on poetry.

We had so much fun, we forgot we were learning.

Although the instructor aimed at relaying transparent outcomes to the class, one student mentioned the course lacked "structure" and "teacher presence." This came at the hands of giving students choice and input, allowing for flexibility, and perhaps trying to incorporate too many educationally effective practices and activities during one semester.

Many students only attended two of the three required outside events. In general, these first-year students experienced a less authoritarian model of teaching and were required to be self-directed for the first time in their academic careers. Although some stated they were not comfortable with this new pedagogy at first, ultimately, the class activities helped them become familiar with new expectations of collaboration and oral presentations at the college level.

Implications

This FYI focused on increased student–faculty and student–peer interaction and had implications for building long-lasting relationships while helping students acclimate to the campus and surrounding community. Involving students in enrichment activities outside of the classroom where they could apply their in-class learning and get to know their new community emerged as essential to student satisfaction and longevity at the University and introduced students to a culture of engagement in the community. All of these FYI students, who remained at Clark, adopted roles in community organizations and clubs, on and off campus.

Introducing students to student-centered, problem-based, and informed learning activities early on in a small, controlled, and supportive environment became important given that this institution values effective practices of collaboration. Clark has seen an increase in the activities and practices outlined in this case study throughout the college curriculum and has adopted a new philosophy and model of education institutionally that emphasizes effective practices across all disciplines and all years, not just in the first-year experience.

References

Pagett, R. D., Keup, J. R., & Pascarella, E. T. (2013). The impact of first-year seminars on college students' life-long learning orientations. *Journal of Student Affairs Research and Practice, 50*(2), 133-151.

Contact Information

Jessica Bane Robert
Assistant Director of the Writing Center and Writing Program & LEEP Advisor
Clark University
950 Main Street
Worcester, MA 01610
E-mail: JRobert@clarku.edu

Coastal Carolina University
Michele C. Everett

The Institution

Coastal Carolina University (Coastal) is a medium-size, four-year, public liberal arts institution located in Conway, South Carolina. Coastal offers bachelor's degrees in 70 fields, master's degrees in 17, and a doctoral degree in marine science. The University serves more than 10,000 students from diverse backgrounds. The Fall 2015 incoming first-year class consisted of 2,359 students; 70% of the students identified as White, 18% as Black/African American, and 12% as another race or ethnicity, including biracial and Hispanic. The geographic distribution of the 2015 first-year cohort was 40% from state, 59% from out of state, and 1% international. Roughly 88% of incoming students entered with a declared major. Nearly half (47%) enrolled as science majors; 21% as business majors, 13% as humanities and fine arts majors, 7% as education majors, and 12% were undeclared. Approximately 90% of newly entering students live in on-campus residence halls.

Description of the Seminar

The First-Year Experience (FYE) seminar is a mandatory three-credit, full-semester course for incoming first-year students. Although the overarching goal is to help students make a successful transition to college, each of the five colleges within the university (Science, Business, Humanities and Fine Arts, Education, and University College) shapes the content of the course to meet the needs of its students.

Undeclared students are enrolled in University College (UC) sections of FYE (UNIV*110U). In fall 2015, 277 students were enrolled across 14 sections of the course. The maximum class size for undeclared sections of FYE is 22 students. The course is taught by faculty from psychology and interdisciplinary studies and staff from a variety of areas, including housing, counseling services, information technology, and advising. Instructors for UNIV*110U are required to attend a one-day training session in June. Peer leaders, who are upper-division students and have completed a full-semester training course, also assist in teaching the seminar.

Undeclared students (also referred to as undecided or exploring) have been identified as "one of the largest clusters of potentially at-risk students on a university campus" (Reinheimer & McKenzie, 2011, p. 23). Because they are not associated with a specific college or department, they do not have the same kinds of opportunities that declared students have to engage with faculty and students who share academic and career interests and goals (Reinheimer & McKenzie, 2011). This may leave them "homeless" (Cuseo, 2005, p. 6) and feeling disconnected from the institution (Young & Redlinger, 2000). Research suggests that undeclared students not only have difficulties with academics and social integration but may also be at risk for engaging in higher levels of alcohol consumption and binge drinking (Smith, 2013; Wolaver, n.d.).

Awareness of the specific challenges faced by undeclared students has informed the content of UNIV*110U and the way UC approaches the course. UC's comprehensive, holistic approach to student development means providing support related to helping students identify a major and addressing personal, social, and academic skills required for student success. The 15-week course is divided into two main modules: (a) Module 1 - Developing personal, social, and academic skills and (b) Module 2 - Exploring interests and academic majors.

To ensure a level of consistency across all sections of UNIV*110U, instructors use the same student learning outcomes, course textbook, and curriculum. Learning outcomes include

- developing personal, social, and academic skills required for student success;
- identifying and developing personal, social, and academic goals and interests;
- demonstrating a greater understanding of campus resources and opportunities for engagement; and
- identifying and analyzing a major field of study that connects with academic and career goals.

Examples of common elements found in topics and assignments include practicing goal setting, identifying interests, getting involved on campus, developing academic skills, taking part in a common reading, exploring majors and careers, and participating in experiential learning. Although instructors are required to cover the same core elements, they are encouraged to add supplemental material and deliver the content in a way that plays to their individual strengths and meets their students' specific learning needs.

Educationally Effective Practices

Within UNIV*110U are examples of multiple effective educational practices as identified by Kuh and O'Donnell (2013). These include the following:

Expectations set at appropriately high levels. This practice is essential for achieving the course goals and objectives and is communicated early through in-class discussions about the purpose of the course. Through whole-class discussion, students and the instructor come to a shared understanding about the purpose of the seminar and what sets it apart from other required courses. The class also discusses what is required on the students' part to achieve the learning outcomes and why those outcomes are critically important to their future lives. In addition, students are provided with opportunities to engage in activities that encourage reflection and self-discovery. Through skills and interest self-assessment inventories and reflective writing assignments, students are develop the personal, social, and academic skills needed to succeed at Coastal and beyond.

Interactions with peers. Because undeclared students often feel like they do not have an academic home, establishing a sense of community and belonging in FYE is of paramount importance. To accomplish this sense of belonging, students spend a lot of time getting to know each other through ice-breakers and other activities, such as sharing cultural artifacts that represent their ethnic backgrounds and identities. Through these activities, students get to know each other's names, develop an appreciation of diversity, and form relationships with students who share their interests.

UC is very committed to building programs that foster a sense of connectedness and belonging among undeclared students. They are encouraged to consider UC their first-semester home and reminded that many other students, like them, are taking time to explore their options. In an effort to bring undeclared students together, during fall 2015 UC organized special events, such as an ice cream social and a movie night. Another tool to increase peer interaction and campus involvement is the event critique assignment. Each student is required to attend a variety of on-campus activities and programs (e.g., sporting, cultural, or arts events; a club or organization meeting) and write a critique including a description of the event and what they took away from the experience.

In addition to networking with classmates, UNIV*110U students also interact with peer leaders, who play an important role in helping them negotiate the challenges associated with the first semester of college by sharing their knowledge and experience. Students look to their peer leaders for guidance and support. In their role, peer leaders also serve as agents for engagement—getting students actively involved in and outside the classroom.

Interactions with faculty and periodic and structured opportunities for reflection and integration. Both of these educationally effective practices are achieved through the weekly reflective journal writing assignment. Students submit weekly journal entries via Moodle, the University's learning management system. The same prompt is used for 14 weeks: *Reflect on the events of the week (successes, challenges, etc.). Provide thoughts, questions, or feelings about anything you've experienced.* For the final journal entry, students are instructed to read all previous journal entries, reflect on their first semester at Coastal, and write about what they have accomplished; what they have learned about themselves; and what they still need to work on to achieve their academic, professional, and personal goals. Students derive significant benefits from engaging in this activity, such as self-discovery, stress relief, and personal well-being (Everett, 2013). Although this assignment is intended for personal reflection, instructors reply to journal entries, helping students understand that a faculty member cares about what is going on in their lives.

Significant investment of time and effort, public demonstration of competence, and relevance through real-world applications. The second half of the semester is devoted to exploring and identifying a possible academic major. The main assignment for this module is the capstone project. To complete the multiple-week project, students identify interests, make connections between their interests and majors, and engage in the research process to investigate a major field of study they are interested in pursuing. At the end of the semester, students submit individual research papers and present their findings to the class in small groups as a visual narrative entitled, "Where we have been and where we are heading." The instruction for the visual narrative is to use a series of images to tell the story of the first semester at Coastal (Everett, 2015). At the end of the presentation, students share the findings from their research and let the class know where they might be heading (major-wise).

Several features of this assignment make it educationally effective. Students are actively involved during the entire project, the topic relates directly to their lives, and they are provided with opportunities to engage with their classmates. At the same time, they are developing research, critical and creative thinking, oral and written communication, and collaborative learning skills.

Discussion

Assessment of UNIV*110U occurs at the individual student, instructor, course, and program levels (see Table 1). Individual student performance is assessed by instructors informally through classroom observation of levels of engagement and participation and formally through graded assignments. At the end of the semester, students complete two surveys: (a) an online survey administered at the University level and (b) a University College student course evaluation survey completed in class. Both surveys generate quantitative and qualitative data. The online and in-class surveys provide data concerning individual instructor performance and outcomes from specific sections of FYE. Classroom observations of first-time UNIV*110U instructors are also conducted. The University College survey provides the data for assessment at the program level.

Table 1
*UNIV*110U Assessment Strategies*

Level of assessment	Method	
	Informal	Formal
Student	Observation	Graded assignments
Instructor		Online course evaluations (University) Student survey (University College) Classroom observation
Course	Student feedback forms	Online course evaluations (University) Student survey (University College) Portfolio essay
Program		Student survey (University College)

In addition to the surveys, students keep portfolios of their assignments. At the end of the semester after reviewing all the work completed in the course, students write portfolio essays about what they gained from completing the assignments associated with each module. Students are asked to provide feedback throughout the semester by way of one-minute attendance response questions and other informal feedback request forms. Table 2 shows student comments about different educational practices employed in UNIV*110U.

Table 2

Student Comments About Educationally Effective Practices

Practice	Assignment	Data source	Student comments
High expectations		Feedback form	I knew this class was supposed to help us get used to college, but I don't think I realized exactly how helpful it would be in helping me figure out why I'm in college and what I want to do.
			I have learned how to manage my time and improve my critical thinking, problem-solving, communication, and research skills. I definitely needed this class as an undecided student.
			This class taught me how to find myself and become the person I strive to be.
			I hear from students in different FYE classes that their teacher doesn't take their class seriously and I am glad you do. You truly get out what you put into this course.
			[This class] helps us transition to college and helps us decide on a major and path, but it also helps us make our own decisions and to think for ourselves. It teaches us life skills that we can personally use forever.
Interactions with peers (peer leaders)		UC survey	Because of my peer leader, I am now going to be one. [She] helped give a perspective from an actual student who has been in my shoes.
			Our peer leader was a true inspiration and an amazing role model. She is awesome and gave great info!
			She did all she could to make herself available to us. She also genuinely cared about us.
Interactions with peers	Event critiques	UC survey	I have taken away a lot from participating in events. I have become more involved in activities and other events on campus.
			I went to my first football game. I got involved in international club and met great people as a result of the event critiques we were required to do.
			It helped me get out into the community to learn about new things and showed me what CCU had to offer.
			I was able to be around different types of people.
			I learned that life is what you make it and going to different events just expands your knowledge and creativity.
Interactions with faculty / reflection	Journal writing	Feedback form	I was able to express my feelings without anyone saying anything negative about it.
			I learned more about myself and who I want to become.
			It helped me relieve stress and get out my emotions.
			The journals helped tremendously with all the stress I have had throughout the semester and helped me to just breathe.

Table 2 continues on page 39

Table 2 continues from page 38

Practice	Assignment	Data source	Student comments
Interactions with faculty / reflection	Journal writing	Feedback form	I really enjoyed reflecting on the week and sorting out my feelings.
			I got to reflect on my successes and struggles and realize what I need to do to improve.
			I enjoyed talking out my issues for the week. It helped me keep everything straight in my head and get through it.
			A connection with my teacher and reflection on what I need to change in my life.

Note. Minor edits have been made to improve readability.

Implications

This case study offers important implications for future practice in first-year seminars. First, it highlights the specific needs of a large class of undergraduates—undeclared students. When working with the undeclared population, it is essential to build a sense of community by employing strategies that foster connectedness and belonging. Second, it documents the significant role that interactions with peers and faculty play in helping students negotiate the challenges they face during the first semester of college. Encouraging social interaction requires designing activities that provide students with opportunities to get to know their classmates, establish friendships, share experiences, and build relationships with peer leaders and instructors. These outcomes are reinforced by giving students assignments that help them expand their social networks through participation in campus activities and events. Third, this case illustrates how a curriculum can be shaped to meet the needs of a specific population. For FYE (undeclared) students at Coastal, this means adopting a comprehensive holistic approach to student development—one that helps students identify a possible major and addresses the wide range of personal, social, and academic factors that affect student success. Finally, this study provides support for employing pedagogical practices that encourage active engagement in and outside the classroom. This can be accomplished by developing activities and assignments that promote discussion, collaboration, reflection, and exposure to new experiences. Having students leave the course with a better understanding of who they are, where they are heading, and what is required on their part to achieve their goals is what makes teaching UNIV*110U meaningful and rewarding.

References

Cuseo, J. (2005). "Decided," "undecided," and "in transition": Implications for academic advisement, career counseling & student retention. In R.S. Feldman (Ed.), *Improving the first year of college: Research and practice* (pp. 27-48). Mahwah, NJ: Lawrence Erlbaum Associates.

Everett, M. C. (2013). Journal writing and the first-year year experience. *International Journal of Teaching and Learning in Higher Education, 25*(2), 213-222.

Everett, M. C. (2015). Fostering first-year students' engagement and well-being through visual narratives. *Studies in Higher Education.* doi: 10.1080/03075079.2015.1064387

Kuh, G. D., & O'Donnell, K. (2013). *Ensuring quality and taking high-impact practices to scale.* Washington, DC: Association of American Colleges and Universities.

Reinheimer, D., & McKenzie, K. (2011). The impact of tutoring on the academic success of undeclared students. *Journal of College Reading and Learning, 41*(2), 213-222.

Smith, A. L. (2013, April). *Proceedings of the National Conference on Undergraduate Research* (NCUR). University of Wisconsin, La Crosse.

Wolaver, A. M. (n.d.). *Bucknell University Economics 312 class survey on drinking habits, attitudes, and perceptions.* Retrieved from http://www.facstaff.bucknell.edu/awolaver/alcohol/acad.htm

Young, D. Y., & Redlinger, L. J. (2000). *Modeling student flows through the university pipelines.* Paper presented at the 41st Forum of the Association for Institutional Research, San Antonio, TX.

Contact Information

Michele C. Everett
Lecturer, Interdisciplinary Studies
Coastal Carolina University
Conway, South Carolina 29526
E-mail: meverett@coastal.edu
Phone: (843) 349-2239

Durham Technical Community College
Kerry F. Cantwell and Gabby McCutchen

The Institution

Durham Technical Community College (Durham Tech) is a regionally accredited community college serving Durham and Orange counties in North Carolina. The College offers a variety of transferable degrees, including Associate in Arts, Associate in Engineering, Associate in Fine Arts, and Associate in Science, as well as more than 100 Associate in Applied Science and career diploma programs. In 2015-2016, Durham Tech served 7,189 unduplicated students of whom 40% were Black, non-Hispanic; 35% were White, non-Hispanic; 13% were Hispanic, and 12% identified as other/unknown/multiple. The median age during fall 2015 was 25 ($n = 5,117$). In 2015-2016, Durham Tech served 1,100 (unduplicated) first-time in college (FTIC) students (defined as students with no prior postsecondary experience after high school as identified by the National Student Clearinghouse). Of these students, 35% were Black, non-Hispanic; 31% were White, non-Hispanic, 20% were Hispanic, and 14% identified as other/unknown/multiple. The median age for the fall 2015 FTIC cohort was 19 years.

Description of the Seminar

At Durham Tech, incoming students take a first-year seminar (FYS), ACA 122: College Transfer Success, during their first semester. Though the course name implies a focus on transfer success, the target population includes all students with fewer than 12 college-level credits who have the FYS on their program's plan of study. This one-credit, two-contact-hour course is transferable to North Carolina senior institutions and is required at Durham Tech for all degrees, most diplomas, and some certificates. Beginning fall 2014, students who registered for developmental math, developmental reading and English, and gateway English courses were required to co-enroll in the FYS. In spring 2016, 610 students enrolled in 40 sections of ACA 122 offered in 16-week seated, 8-week seated, 8-week hybrid (combination online and seated), and 16-week online formats, at both the main and the Orange County campuses.

A variety of personnel teach the FYS, including two full-time dedicated ACA instructors, faculty from other departments, academic advisors, and qualified staff members. To support instructors in the classroom, the chair for the First-Year Experience program maintains an ACA Instructor Resources site on the college's learning management system (Sakai) and provides sample homework assignments, explicit lesson plans, and accompanying materials (e.g., PowerPoint presentations, handouts, assessments, videos, web links). These materials are often used whole cloth by new ACA instructors for their first semester teaching the FYS, after which they often make their own amendments and additions to the course.

The FYS focuses on three major themes: (a) goal discernment, (b) learning strategies, and (c) college culture. Students complete one full cycle of goal discernment (i.e., self-assessment, goal exploration, goal setting) in the process of composing their final course portfolio. In the portfolio assignment, students present a synthesis of their reflections and research on their academic programs and chosen careers through the following required elements: a personal narrative, researched career summary with MLA citations, academic course plan, SMART academic and career goal statements, annotated list of relevant websites, informational interview transcripts, and reflections on the portfolio. The theme of learning strategies highlights traditional study skills (e.g., reading, studying, note taking, test taking) and time management. For college culture, students develop the skills and knowledge needed to navigate higher education, including resilience and grit; stress management; understanding transcripts and plans of study; citing research sources; and navigating financial aid, advising, and registration processes. ACA 122 brings together students of all abilities, with a wide range of college expectations, in one classroom community. For example, developmental reading and English students are mixed in with those in second-level English while dual-enrolled high school students mingle with individuals returning to college after 30 years. This *multilayered diversity experience* helps create a strong, supportive fabric of student experiences and rich learning opportunities, but it can also produce pedagogical challenges in meeting the needs of all students.

Educationally Effective Practices

Expectations set at appropriately high levels. Because the FYS is a credit-bearing course, many new students are challenged by the academic rigor of the college-level critical-thinking and writing expectations. By providing samples and purposeful scaffolding, instructors support students as they meet these high expectations. For example, the portfolio assignment, which requires students to research and reflect on their skills, goals, and plans, is assigned about two thirds of the way through the semester, but several weeks earlier students see the assignment along with a sample completed portfolio as part of a discussion about citing sources in MLA format. This strategy benefits global learners who need to see the whole in order to understand the parts. It also helps all students see that the assignment requires a substantial amount of effort and critical thinking.

Grading rubrics also help students understand each of the five major assignments: (a) the personal narrative and scavenger hunt, (b) career exploration and self-assessments, (c) academic course plan, (d) problem-solution paper, and (e) portfolio. Students see how points are allocated, giving them an opportunity to earn all possible points and better comprehend learning priorities and goals (e.g., only 5-10 points are attributed to grammar, punctuation, and mechanics compared to elements like organization, depth, and focus, which are each worth 10–15 points).

The academic course plan assignment is particularly challenging for FTIC students and may be complicated by academic placement, enrollment status (i.e., full-time vs. part-time), and degree options (e.g., Associate in Applied Science—Business Administration vs. Associate in Arts—Business). They must use their plan of study, transcripts, and the college website to list the classes they intend to complete each semester to meet their academic goals while considering the prerequisites and corequisites for their required classes and their individual circumstances. However, students have opportunities to check in with their instructor and classmates in the process and are provided step-by-step instructions for finding necessary information as well as completed samples, screenshots, and lists of on-campus resources for more assistance. These supports allow instructors to hold students to high expectations while validating their efforts and providing course correction along the way.

Periodic and structured opportunities for reflection and integration. In the personal narrative essay, students reflect on how they got where they are, what successes and failures they have already encountered, where they are headed, and how they chose their academic and professional goals. On the first day of class, instructors assess students' confidence in choice of major or career by asking them to make hash marks (labeled with their name, program, and desired career) along a horizontal line drawn on a whiteboard (one end marked *Very Sure* and the other *Not a Clue*). Then, students work together to write questions they might ask to become more sure of their academic and professional goals (e.g., What do you enjoy doing? What are you good at? How much time and money are you willing to invest into a college credential? Will this career have positions available when you graduate?) The activity sets the tone that the ACA class helps clarify goals, shows students they are not alone in their confusion, demonstrates that the others in the class can be sources of support and resources, and introduces them to their peers. Moreover, the questions students develop affirm the confidence of decided students while helping those who are undecided determine a certain direction in which to begin their career research later in the course.

Another opportunity for student self-assessment and reflection on the pathway to a suitable academic program is the 60-question Learning and Study Strategies Inventory (LASSI), which provides students a score on 10 different scales related to their skill, will, and self-regulation behaviors as applied to learning and study strategies. Reflecting on their highest and lowest scores through in-class facilitated discussion, students examine the reasons behind their scores and determine how the high and low scores have each affected their academic history. Students incorporate these reflections into a more thorough LASSI discussion in the learning strategies problem–solution essay in which they use a specific problem-solving process to address an academic problem they are currently experiencing, like minimizing distractions or difficulty taking notes in a particular class. They then examine long- and short-term consequences of the problem, research three possible solutions, determine pros and cons of each solution, select one solution to implement, and report results, altering the strategy as necessary to improve outcomes. Once this assignment is completed, students then reflect in a think–pair–share activity in class on how this method of problem solving (not the solution they chose) could be integrated into other areas of their lives. ACA instructors facilitate similar reflection discussions about problem solving in class each time students submit one of the five major assignments. In this way, reflection gets wrapped around each of the ACA 122 assignments.

Discussion

The end-of-term portfolio assignment is a summative assessment measuring students' ability to produce high-quality, college-level writing and engage in structured, meaningful opportunities for reflection. ACA instructors use rubrics to evaluate the quality of student writing and reflections on their academic and personal goals in their portfolios.

In addition to the traditional assignments described previously, ACA 122 instructors regularly use classroom assessment techniques (CATs), such as one-minute papers, to collect formative data on student learning and engagement. Students write their responses on index cards and turn them in at the end of class. As instructors review the questions, they consider how appropriate the challenge and supports were in that unit of instruction and plan to adjust accordingly.

Student feedback on the college-wide Student Evaluation of Course and Instructor also demonstrates the benefits derived from the FYS:

> This is my first year in college so I was lost in terms of managing class, time, studying, scheduling and more. I was overwhelmed until this class.

> This is the single most important class I could ever take at Durham Tech. I [am] very confident about my future in college just by the information received in this class. Many regrettable errors will [be] avoided due to taking this class.

> If I would have not taken this class I would have not been able to find out [where] I was struggling in order for me to better understand content in all my other classes.

> This course has helped me to think about my goals and has given me a clearer vision of what the college process is supposed to look like and how to navigate it successfully.

Finally, Durham Tech regularly tracks fall-to-spring persistence data on various cohorts of students. The First-Year Experience program collects longitudinal data on the persistence of students who take ACA 122 to compare with the persistence of students who do not take the seminar. Consistently, the data show that FYS students are likely to persist at an average rate of 25-30 points higher than first-year students who do not take the course.

Implications

Durham Tech's successful FYS is built on high-quality instruction and proven strategies of student engagement. Course instructors are trained and then supported as they set expectations at appropriately high levels and provide periodic and structured opportunities for reflection and integration. In fact, the purposeful inclusion of these educationally effective practices in ACA 122 has influenced teaching and learning in other courses. FYS professional development participants regularly report they have applied the pedagogical strategies in their other content courses. In addition, students leave ACA 122 expecting to be challenged in their college coursework and to integrate new learning with the foundation they have established during their first semester.

Lastly, by using educationally effective practices, community college FYS instructors not only help students from diverse backgrounds learn course content, but they also strengthen this high-impact practice and its emerging role in two-year institutions. Although the field of study surrounding FYSs at four-year schools continues to grow, there are still relatively few robust examples of successful and meaningful seminars at community colleges. At the same time, community colleges are regularly looking to these courses as a strategy to boost completion rates and support the diverse students who are welcomed to open-door institutions. Finally, FYSs at two-year institutions can be insufficiently supported and protected by the institution, which can result in the courses becoming the catch-all for the latest programming trend or informational content. Community colleges that offer seminars like Durham Tech's ACA 122 can protect the instructional integrity of their courses if they feature several educationally effective practices.

Contact Information

Kerry Cantwell
Chair, First-Year Experience
Durham Technical Community College
1637 Lawson Street
Durham, NC 27703
E-mail: cantwellk@durhamtech.edu
Phone: (919) 536-7200 ext. 8008

Gabby McCutchen
Dean, Student Engagement and Transitions
Durham Technical Community College
1637 Lawson Street
Durham, NC 27703
E-mail: mccutcheng@durhamtech.edu
Phone: 919-536-7200 ext. 8083

Florida SouthWestern State College
Eileen DeLuca, Kathy Clark, Myra Walters, and Martin Tawil

The Institution

Florida SouthWestern State College (FSW) is an open-access, baccalaureate-granting, state college. FSW is part of the Florida College System, offering bachelor's degrees in 10 fields, associate degrees in 20 fields, and 14 certificate programs. Located in Fort Myers, Florida, the college also has campuses in Collier and Charlotte counties and a regional center in Hendry/Glades. During the fall 2015 semester, FSW served more than 15,000 students. The unduplicated headcount for the 2014-2015 academic year was over 21,000. Within this cohort, 71.0% of students were 24 years old or younger, and the population was 60.9% female; 39.1% male. Among these students, 50.5% were reported as White, 28.5% as Hispanic/Latino, 11.1% as African American, and 2.5% as other minorities. Full-time students represented 34.3% of the student population, with the remainder (65.7%) being part-time. Of the full-time students, 1,874 were first-time, first-year students, and of the part-time students, 1,105 were first-time, first-year students.

Description of the Seminar

To promote the academic success of first-time-in-college (FTIC) degree-seeking students, FSW designed a three-credit course titled SLS 1515: Cornerstone Experience. The overall focus of the course is critical thinking as a tool to support student success in their studies at FSW and beyond. All incoming degree-seeking students who have earned less than 30 credits are required to take and successfully complete SLS 1515 in the first semester.

To achieve the goal of engendering self-reliant learners who apply critical thinking in the academic setting as well as their personal lives, the college has designed a series of professional development workshops for faculty, staff, and administrators. Training began in the summer of 2011 and has continued throughout each semester with external consultants and faculty experts. The majority of sections are consistently taught by full-time faculty. All faculty and staff who teach the course are required to hold (at least) a master's degree and complete 10 Cornerstone training modules for teaching certification. Training topics include critical thinking, universal design, understanding the first-year student, constructivist pedagogy, career planning, diversity on the college campus and beyond, learning styles, and workshops designed to familiarize faculty with the goals of the Cornerstone Course and program.

Educationally Effective Practices

Periodic and structured opportunities for reflection and integration. The SLS 1515: Cornerstone Experience curriculum emerged from best-practice literature review and is tailored to what is unique to the student experience at FSW. Although students are introduced to all of FSW's general education competencies, critical thinking is emphasized as a way to better achieve all the competencies. Students explore the nature and techniques of critical thought as a way to establish a reliable basis for claims, beliefs, and attitudes. Activities are based on Paul and Elder's (2005) elements of reasoning and the universal intellectual standards model adopted by faculty.

Faculty who teach the course use a standardized syllabus, which includes common assignments and assessments. A committee of faculty intentionally designed a series of critical reflection assignments to align with the course objectives, including a reflection journal and final essay.

For the reflection journal assignment, SLS 1515 students respond to six critical-thinking prompts throughout the course of the semester via an electronic journal entry submitted through the College's learning management system (see Figure 1). Their journal entries must be a minimum of 250 words and employ elements of Paul and Elder's (2005) Intellectual Standards, such as clarity, relevance, significance, and logic.

Reflection Journal Entries

1. Reflect and analyze why you are attending college. What motivated you to enroll? What goals do you hope to achieve?

2. Review the results of the critical-thinking assessment. What are your areas of strength? How do your strengths make you a better student? Which areas have room for improvement? Describe action steps you will take to improve.

3. Based upon your Personality Type report, identify three possible career choices that are suitable for you, and explain how one of those relates to your personality type, personal values, career interests, and success factors.

4. FSW has established the following general competencies: Communications (COM), Critical Thinking (CT), Technology/Information Management (TIM), Global-Sociocultural Responsibility (GSR), and Scientific and Quantitative Reasoning (QR) as listed in your syllabus. Please choose TWO and explain how developing each of these competencies will help you achieve academic and career success.

5. Discuss how time management and financial responsibility will help you successfully complete your college education.

6. Describe how your participation in the GPS (Go, Picture, Scribe) has helped you feel more connected to FSW. How has your participation helped you develop an understanding of diversity?

Figure 1. Reflection journal assignment.

Students also complete an essay assignment at the end of the course as a final critical reflection of the knowledge gained in the course (see Figure 2). The students must evaluate which course components resonate with them and use the reflection as a point of departure for building a plan for college success. As with the journal assignment, the final essay asks students to employ Paul and Elder's (2005) Intellectual Standards (i.e., clarity, relevance, significance, and logic). Both the reflection journal and the final essay assignments are assessed on a critical-thinking rubric that was designed by faculty and aligns with these standards.

Interactions with faculty and peers. Kuh and O'Donnell (2013) suggested that "high levels of discussion and collaborative problem-solving are present among students themselves and in concert with faculty" (p. 8). As a collegewide initiative, the majority of course sections are assigned to full-time faculty and staff, which facilitates early engagement with students. SLS 1515 is primarily offered as a ground course, and enrollment is limited to 25 students per section to ensure substantive class interaction (cf. Hunter & Linder, 2005).

Each professor who teaches the course is assigned a peer mentor, who is available during class to assist with group activities and inform students of other campus events. In keeping with the Cornerstone theme of Building the Foundation of Success, FSW's peer mentors are known as peer architects. They maintain weekly office hours to assist students and participate in offering extracurricular workshops and activities.

Two assignments common to all course sections are designed to promote campus engagement in general and with faculty, staff, and peers in particular: (a) the Go, Picture, Scribe (GPS) assignment and (b) a group project. To ensure students are engaged and connected to the college, they are required to document several activities ranging from scheduling and meeting with an academic advisor prior to registering for classes for the next term, attending a minimum of two academic or informational workshops, using the academic support and/or peer tutoring center, or attending six college events (see Figure 3). The name *GPS* relates the activity to a navigation tool, suggesting to students that there is a benefit to charting their course through college. Further, the intentional inclusion of the word *scribe* indicates that the students are not simply going on a treasure hunt; rather, they must engage in meaningful collegiate experiences and write brief critical reflections about how those experiences relate to college success.

> **Final Essay**
>
> The purpose of this assignment is to write an essay that reflects upon the main themes/topics of the course that were most influential or important to you. The essay will conclude with a description of a "new" plan for achieving success in college.
>
> The essay will be evaluated on the demonstration of Critical Thinking (see specific outcomes on the Critical Thinking Rubric). It is our expectation that all college written work must adhere to Standard English grammar and mechanics.
>
> Final essay guidelines:
> Write an essay that is a minimum of 500 words, including the following components:
>
> 1. Introduction. Start by describing your thoughts and feelings at the beginning of the term. Then introduce the topics/ideas that you found most influential across the semester. (1-2 paragraphs)
> 2. First idea/topic that was influential to you. Develop with specific examples and discussion. (1-2 paragraphs)
> 3. Second idea/topic that was influential to you. Develop with specific examples and discussion. (1-2 paragraphs)
> 4. Third idea/topic that was influential to you. Develop with specific examples and discussion. (1-2 paragraphs)
> 5. Conclusion. Describe your plan for achieving success and summarize the three topics/ideas that you found to be most influential. (1-2 paragraphs)

Figure 2. Final essay assignment.

Go, Picture, Scribe (GPS)

FSW offers many great activities and resources. The purpose of this activity is to engage and connect you to FSW. To be a successful college student requires that you utilize the resources to enhance your overall college experience. To successfully complete this assignment you will participate in 10 campus or community engagement activities that fall under the four categories in the chart below:

Category	Description	Required Interactions
Workshops	Attend a minimum of two academic or informational workshops at FSW, such as Critical Thinking in Careers Lecture Series, First-Year Experience (FYE), FSW Leads, Academic Success, Student Life, and Financial Aid Workshops.	2
Academic Advising	Schedule and meet with an academic advisor prior to registering for classes for the next term.	1
Academic Support Centers	Use an Academic Support Center (i.e., math, writing, peer tutor or the oral communication center).	1
Other Resources	Choose six from other resources: FYE social events, Service Saturday events, Student Life activities or events, use of the library services, use of the Tech Center, attendance at art events, plays, and any FSW-sponsored community event or activity. Note: Additional events from the "Workshops" category count toward "Other Resources."	6
Total		10

Figure 3. Go, Picture, Scribe (GPS) assignment.

Students learn how to work in a group during the semester through team-building and regular cooperative-learning activities. At a point in the semester when students have engaged in a sufficient amount of self-assessment and reflection and the class has reviewed diverse learning styles, personality traits, and multiple intelligences, the group project is introduced (see Figure 4). Faculty strategically group students with diverse learning styles and personalities, provide strategies for group communication, and encourage students to use creativity to design interactive presentations. Both the GPS assignment and the group project are scored on a faculty-designed rubric that aligns with Paul and Elder's (2005) Intellectual Standards.

Lastly, the First-Year Experience (FYE) Program offers a series of extracurricular programs aligned with SLS 1515 outcomes, including workshops regarding time management, academic technology, and study and test-taking strategies. In addition, FSW has implemented a Critical Thinking in Careers lecture series. Through this series, the College invites faculty, staff, and community leaders to give a 30-40 minute talk on how they use critical-thinking skills in their professions or academic disciplines or to discuss critical topics or concerns from their areas of academic interest. Through participation in this series, students are able to learn more about careers of interest and available programs of study, while analyzing a relevant application of critical thinking. They also have the opportunity to interact with faculty representing various disciplines and network with potential career connections.

Group Project

The purpose of this assignment is to reflect upon what it takes to be successful in academics and careers.

Groups must analyze, evaluate, and demonstrate what it takes to be successful in an academic degree program and ensuing career path. This includes applying effective success strategies, developing higher level communication, and using critical-thinking skills. The conclusions drawn by the group must be shared with the whole class in a final project.

Brainstorming is the first step demanded for a successful group project. Some of the best projects have been creative or outside the box and based on students' personal experiences.

Groups may choose to focus on a single major or career path, related majors or career paths, or general success and career acquisition strategies.

Think Critically!

Figure 4. Group project.

Discussion

The six critical-thinking reflection journal entries, GPS, final essay, and group presentation are scored on faculty-designed rubrics in the college's learning management system. The data from all course sections are extracted at the conclusion of each semester for reporting purposes. The faculty periodically engage in norming sessions to standardize the interpretation of the rubric dimensions and the associated levels of performance. Faculty have also engaged in an affinity process to identify anchor papers demonstrating various levels of performance. Overall mean scores on each dimension of the rubric and the percentage of students scoring a 3 or higher (on a 4-point rubric) are reported each term. Faculty and an assessment committee review the achievement data to note areas of strength and opportunities for improvement. Since 2013, the program has consistently met stated goals for overall mean scores and for the percentage of students scoring 3 or above on all aspects of a faculty-designed rubric. Other programmatic measures of critical thinking include pre- and post-assessments using the California Critical Thinking Inventory (CCTDI). The students consistently show significant gains in two or more dimensions measured by this tool, with Confidence in Reasoning and Analyticity showing consistent positive growth.

The students generally report benefits from completing the critical-thinking journal, GPS, and group project (the focus groups generally take place before students have completed the final essay assignment). Although the feedback is mostly positive, the focus groups also provide valuable information each term leading to course and program improvement. For example, many students report that the GPS assignment led them to engage in the campus in ways they would not have if the assignment had not been required. They report a positive change from engagement. However, many students over the traditional age and students who are working a significant number of hours have noted the difficulty in finding time to complete the activities, and the college has responded by offering more evening and weekend events and services. Also, the FYE program has begun to develop some content-rich, online activities as an option.

To determine the efficacy of the Peer Architect program, the college collects both qualitative and quantitative data midterm and end of term. These data include a 360-degree evaluation of peer architects by the FYE director, faculty, students, and peers themselves. The FYE director also reviews satisfaction and efficacy surveys from student consultations with peer architects. Finally, students respond to general questions about peer architects during focus groups held at the end of fall and spring semesters. These data are used to inform peer architect training sessions as well as topics for team meetings.

The students complete evaluation forms with Likert scale items and free response items following each Critical-Thinking Series session. The majority of the respondents consistently report learning gains and overall satisfaction with the sessions.

All Cornerstone assessment results are shared and discussed with the faculty in department and community-of-practices meetings. Assessment results are also shared collegewide by way of newsletters and an annual report and summary. The assessment of student learning, the interpretation of the results of assessment, and the use of those findings requires the participation of various stakeholders. Assessment is used to inform improvement, measure achievement, and make curricular and programmatic decisions in a continuous cycle of data-driven innovation.

Implications

The FSW model demonstrates the importance of periodic and structured opportunities for reflection and integration and interactions with faculty and peers in the first-year seminar. During focus groups, students consistently report that participation in the course made them feel as if they were part of a family. They also describe high levels of interaction with faculty and peers and the benefits of such interactions. Students have noted they would like to see this type of interaction in other college courses. Students are also connecting with advisors, librarians, and instructional assistants at increased rates based on participation in the course.

FSW's model is supported by a collegewide effort and several committees (e.g., advisory, implementation, assessment, orientation, advising and registration, FYE programming, early-alert, and marketing committees, as well as a faculty community of practice) that meet regularly to review progress towards Cornerstone goals and to find ways to enhance the course and the ancillary programming for first-year students. The committees include representation from both Academic and Student Affairs personnel across departments and campuses.

Students benefit from a coherent effort focused on student support, the development of critical thinking, and the acquisition of success strategies in the FYE seminar as well as the courses into which they will transition across the disciplines. The data from the first three years of implementation has demonstrated the efficacy of the seminar and its educationally effective practices in promoting achievement of critical thinking (as demonstrated by rubric scores), student satisfaction and engagement (as demonstrated by internally developed post-course surveys, increasing metrics on selected benchmarks from the Survey of Entering Student Engagement [SENSE], and focus groups responses), and positive (direct) correlations between course participation and retention (term-to-term and year-to-year to include subpopulations such as students testing in developmental coursework).

References

Hunter, M. S., & Linder, C. W. (2005). First-year seminars. In M. L. Upcraft, J. N. Gardner, B. O. Barefoot, and Associates (Eds.), *Challenging and supporting first-year students: A handbook for improving the first-year of college* (pp. 275-291). San Francisco, CA: Jossey-Bass.

Kuh, G. D., & O'Donnell, K. (2013). *Ensuring quality and taking high-impact practices to scale.* Washington, DC: Association of American Colleges and Universities.

Paul, R., & Elder, L. (2005). *Critical thinking competency standards.* Dillon Beach, CA: Foundation for Critical Thinking.

Contact Information

Eileen DeLuca
Associate Vice President, Academic Affairs
8099 College Parkway
Fort Myers, FL 33919
E-mail: ecdeluca@fsw.edu
Phone: (239) 218-9435

Indiana University–Purdue University Indianapolis
Heather Bowman, Amy Powell, and Cathy Buyarski

The Institution

Indiana University–Purdue University Indianapolis (IUPUI) is a large, urban, public university located in Indiana's state capital. In 2015, IUPUI had a student enrollment of approximately 30,000, including 22,000 undergraduates and 5,446 first-year students. Roughly 88% of IUPUI students are in-state, 56% are female, 17% are students of color, and 12% are international students. The majority of first-year students at IUPUI (60%) commute to campus, and about 40% are Federal Pell Grant recipients. For 13 consecutive years, IUPUI has been recognized by *U.S. News and World Report* (2015a, 2015b) for its efforts, including learning communities and first-year experience programs, which help ensure a positive collegiate experience for entering students and other undergraduates.

Description of the Seminar

First-year seminars (FYSs) at IUPUI are semester-based, credit-bearing classes aimed at providing new students with the tools they need to succeed in college. FYSs are offered in multiple formats, including themed learning communities (TLCs), linked learning communities, free-standing seminars, and classes connected to the Summer Bridge program. The number of credits attached to FYS varies from one to two depending on the format, and sections are offered by both degree-granting schools as well as University College, which holds classes for exploratory students and pre-health professions majors. The mission of the FYS is to support entering students in making a successful transition into the life and community of IUPUI and enhance rates of retention and persistence by providing early academic and social support. All sections of the FYS are taught by a team consisting of a faculty or staff instructor, academic advisor, and student peer mentor.

This case examines the FYS offered by University College. The FYS is a required component of IUPUI degree programs, which all incoming students with 17 or fewer credit hours must take during their first semester of college. All sections share common goals and learning outcomes; however, individual instructional teams may develop, emphasize, and assess these differently:

- *Goal 1: Belonging*—Students will connect with peers and instructional team members; identify individuals who can provide a personal support network; become familiar with campus programs and resources related to academic, professional, and social development.
- *Goal 2: Transitioning*—Students will identify strategies to increase self-awareness and personal responsibility; explore and develop academic success skills, such as information literacy and critical thinking; and recognize differences in the human experience and the ways those differences enrich the academic learning environment.
- *Goal 3: Planning*—Students will practice academic and personal time management techniques; explore and plan for majors, minors, and careers; and identify areas of cocurricular involvement and engaged learning that enrich academic pursuits and goals.

University College uses an electronic personal development plan (ePDP) to enhance the implementation of educationally effective practices in the seminar. ePDP is a tool for helping students engage in a process that facilitates greater understanding of who they are and enables them to set meaningful goals. Students create curricular and cocurricular plans while developing the sense of agency that will lead them toward achievement of their goals. The outcome of the ePDP is a personalized eportfolio that is open to revision and re-evaluation throughout the college experience. Students can build on the work they do in the FYS to continuously develop an eportfolio that integrates and makes visible their in- and out-of-class learning. This pedagogical tool, which supports seminar Goal 3—Planning, helps students make meaning of their college experience.

The ePDP includes five modules with proposed prompts, all of which can be adopted or adapted as faculty see fit:

- Landing Page: Snapshot of Who I Am
- About Me: Developing Identity
- My Academics: Shaping Learning and Experiences
- My Career: Planning for the Future
- My Involvement and Impact: Documenting and Showcasing Involvement

On the Landing Page, students may provide an introduction to who they are in a creative and engaging way, such as a quote, photo, short video, word cloud, or piece of art. The About Me section is the students' opportunity to introduce themselves and describe key aspects of their identity, including their strengths, values, beliefs, and personal mission. This section may contain multiple sub-pages with supporting artifacts from class activities that are synthesized into their introduction at the end of the semester. The My Academics section is used for academic planning and may include the students' two- or four-year plans as well as some research and reflection on their chosen major. The My Career section includes artifacts from class activities where students explore their strengths and interests and make connections between those and possible majors and careers. Finally, the My Involvement and Impact section captures students' experiences on and off campus, including their connections to IUPUI and the Indianapolis community. Each section is designed to be completed in a manner that, when read together, provides an integrated and cohesive narrative about students' goals and accomplishments.

Educationally Effective Practices

Periodic and structured opportunities for reflection and integration. Within ePDP, students are encouraged to integrate and document in- and out-of-class learning, engage in academic and career planning, and develop a sense of meaning within themselves, their college experiences, and their lives beyond college. Through reflective assignments, such as a classroom activity or discussion followed by structured reflection prompts, students are guided toward a deeper understanding of who they are and where they are going.

Relevance through real-world application. By creating a portfolio that can be built upon beyond the FYS, students begin to connect their in-class experiences to longer term academic and career goals. Prompts in the My Career module lead students through exercises, such as résumé and cover letter writing, researching career alternatives, and creating concrete action steps for career planning—all of which are designed to help students better understand the progression from academics to careers and to begin to make progress toward career goals. The My Involvement and Impact module allows students to plan for and begin to engage in recognized high-impact educational experiences, such as service-learning, international learning opportunities, and undergraduate research, while reflecting on the role of those experiences in their overall college experience.

Frequent and constructive feedback. Students typically tackle modules of the ePDP as point-bearing assignments, allowing them multiple opportunities to receive feedback on specific elements of their portfolio during its creation. Some sections incorporate feedback not only from the instructor but also from the academic advisor and/or student peer mentor. Students often benefit from feedback from classmates in the form of class discussion, as some instructors use ePDP prompts as starting points for reflective thinking. For example, one instructor begins a class discussion by asking, "Who remembers the exact moment when you decided you were going to attend college?" and uses that discussion starter to explore educational aspirations. Another instructor structures the FYS course using the ePDP, with each class activity, artifact, and reflection becoming part of the eportfolio. Students build sections of the ePDP as the semester progresses, using peer review to step back and consider the ePDP as a whole, and finish the semester with final reflections and presentations that synthesize their learning.

Public demonstration of competence. This educationally effective practice is sometimes difficult to capture in the FYS. When implemented holistically, the ePDP provides a framework to situate much of the content of the seminar, culminating in a product that allows students to showcase artifacts of their learning, goals and plans, and academic and cocurricular accomplishments. Most faculty help students create a web-based portfolio that can be shared electronically, though some ask students to display their portfolios in binders or another physical format. One FYS instructional team requires students to present elements of their ePDPs during a public event focused on multicultural awareness and diversity; another asks students to share aspects of their ePDPs through in-class presentations. Finally, all students are invited to submit their ePDP work to an annual campuswide ePortfolio Showcase, which is open to undergraduates in all stages of their academic program as well as to graduate and professional students. The event accepts up to 20 eportfolios and awards a top prize for student sumbissions in the first-year experience category. Students accepted into the showcase present their eportfolios and engage in discussion with attendees. In all these cases, the ePDP creates a framework in which student learning can be made visible and meaningful.

Discussion

A comprehensive evaluation of the ePDP in FYSs took place in fall 2010 and included sections offered by both University College and the degree-granting schools. Results indicated that students participating in sections that incorporated the ePDP had significantly higher fall GPAs (2.95 in ePDP vs. 2.79 in non-ePDP sections) and one-year retention rates (80% in ePDP vs. 74% in non-ePDP sections), even after adjusting for high school GPA, SAT score, gender, income level, and admit date.

In subsequent years, the positive effects of the ePDP on students' levels of academic success and persistence were not sustained. Possible reasons for this shift include the adoption of the ePDP platform across FYS sections campuswide; a shift away from mandatory multiday training on ePDP technology and pedagogy for all participating faculty; and increased flexibility in options for implementation, resulting in less uniformity in the ways and the extent to which the ePDP was used across sections.

In fall 2012, students participating in University College FYS sections who completed all five modules of the ePDP had significantly higher mean scores on student success and self-reported learning outcomes than students who did not complete ePDPs. Means were calculated using a 5-point Likert scale (1 = *no gain/strongly disagree* and 5 = *great gain/ strongly agree*). Students who completed ePDPs were more likely than those who did not to note gains in the following areas (ePDP vs. non-ePDP, respectively):

- using reflective writing to understand their experiences (3.93 vs. 3.46),
- adjusting to college (4.31 vs. 3.82),
- successfully transitioning to IUPUI (4.22 vs. 3.69),
- deciding on a major or future career (4.15 vs. 3.54),
- understanding self (4.38 vs. 3.79), and
- understanding motivations for attending college (4.34 vs. 3.81).

Implications

Data suggest that although the ePDP has the potential to impact retention and GPA positively when fully and consistently implemented in the FYS, the effects may be diluted when faculty are not fully versed in the pedagogy or are not fully invested in using the portfolio. Currently, faculty are encouraged (but not required) to attend a short training session prior to implementation of the ePDP in their sections. Although they are required to use the ePDP in some respect in their classroom, they are free to incorporate as many or as few of the modules as they want, customizing the prompts as they see fit. Some faculty reduce the ePDP to an independent assignment or two, whereas others use it to create a fully integrated framework to which students can connect much (or all) of their work in the FYS.

To take full advantage of the ePDP's potential to engage students in educationally effective practices in the FYS classroom, it seems evident that more in-depth and consistent faculty development and training is necessary. Incorporating an integrative portfolio into the typical FYS pedagogy is a new concept to many instructors, and without proper guidance, training opportunities, and ongoing resources and support, the initiative runs the risk of being reduced to yet another curricular requirement that faculty are forced to incorporate into an already-packed semester. Instructors must be provided with the tools and knowledge to fully implement the ePDP as it was conceived—as an integrative framework that brings together the various components of the FYS in a meaningful and relevant way.

Likewise, without clear guidelines related to the extent to which the ePDP is implemented from section to section, we are likely to continue to see uneven results. To reach the full potential of the ePDP in FYSs, more guidelines regarding the number of modules covered from section to section and the ways in which those modules are incorporated into the curriculum are necessary, while preserving some degree of flexibility and creativity among the instructional teams.

The ePDP is clearly a useful tool for ensuring high-impact delivery of FYS content, incorporating frequent and constructive feedback; multiple, structured opportunities for reflection and integration; relevance through real-world applications; and public demonstration of competence. Some fine-tuning of its implementation moving ahead, both in the area of faculty development and support and curricular guidelines, will serve to enhance the impact of the FYS program on the IUPUI campus.

References

U. S. News & World Report. (2015a). *Best colleges ranking and listing: First-year experiences.* Retrieved from http://colleges.usnews.rankingsandreviews.com/best-colleges/rankings/first-year-experience-programs.

U. S. News & World Report. (2015b). *Best colleges ranking and listing: Learning communities.* Retrieved from http://colleges.usnews.rankingsandreviews.com/best-colleges/rankings/learning-community-programs.

Contact Information

Heather Bowman
Director of First-Year Programs, University College
IUPUI
815 W. Michigan St
Indianapolis, IN 46220
E-mail: hebowman@iupui.edu

Ithaca College
Elizabeth Bleicher

The Institution

Ithaca College (IC), is a private, residential, midsized, comprehensive college located in Ithaca, New York, offering 100 undergraduate majors, 70 minors, and 30 graduate majors across five schools: Business, Communications, Health Sciences and Human Performance, Humanities and Sciences, and Music. IC enrolls approximately 6,300 undergraduates and 400 graduate students of whom 22% self-identified as persons of color, ethnicity, or nationality: American Indian or Alaska Native 0.1%; Asian 4%; Black or African American 6%; Hispanic/Latino 7%; two or more races 3%; Native Hawaiian or Other Pacific Islander 0%; international (nonresident aliens) 2%. The majority of the student body are degree-seeking, full-time, first-time college students, and approximately 8% of the first-year cohort are enrolled in the Honors program.

Description of the Seminar

Ithaca Seminars (ICSM) is a four-credit, hybrid first-year seminar (FYS) combining three credits of interdisciplinary academic content with one credit of transition-to-college content. ICSM is requirement for all first-year students and constitutes the foundation of the Integrative Core Curriculum. The goals of the FYS are to offer first-year students an intellectual liberal arts experience in a small class; provide a classroom experience for learning to analyze and critically evaluate ideas, arguments, and points of view; connect learning with other aspects of academic and college life; and help make a successful transition to college. With an incoming class of 1,600 to 1,700 and classes capped at 18 to 22 students, the IC offers approximately 100 seminars each fall, of which six are restricted to Honors students. The Why Are We Here: Student Culture and Problems of College (WAWH) Honors section is the focus of this case study.

All FYSs meet three or four times a week (200 minutes weekly), with one 50-minute Common Hour session devoted to transition to college. Faculty and peer leaders can choose from a robust menu of workshops and presentations on common transition issues (e.g., locating campus and community resources, self-care and mental health concerns, registration preparation, balancing academic and personal demands) and are encouraged to develop and submit their own trainings. Students in WAWH are required to participate in four events outside regular class hours: (a) a one-day weekend retreat with all first-year Honors students, (b) the performance of a play previously studied in class, (c) attendance at seminar-specific discussion of the first-year diversity speaker's presentation, and (d) participation in a cultural simulation (BaFa BaFa).

WAWH is taught by a tenured faculty member, in collaboration with a peer leader, an alumnus/a of the seminar who facilitates Common Hours, the diversity discussion, and the cultural simulation. The peer leader also conducts four activities to help students make the transition to collegiate academic standards and complete a final research assignment successfully, including modeling their own final projects, running networking and troubleshooting workshops, and moderating a panel of course alumni who discuss how they managed their major research projects and the stresses of the first semester. Faculty members and peer leaders hold weekly office hours or meet with students individually to discuss academics and transition-to-college issues.

WAWH was designed to address a growing sense that first-year students do not make a conscious decision to attend college but blindly enroll based on social and/or family customs, pressures, or assumptions. A first-day poll of class members reveals that the vast majority have never been asked why they are attending college, the exceptions being first-generation students. As such, WAWH challenges first-year students to (a) become intentional learners who take responsibility for their own education, can articulate their personal academic goals, and are increasingly motivated by intrinsic rewards and satisfaction; (b) identify issues that are important enough to make them want take action; and (c) cultivate the academic skills necessary to address the issues they care about and to use their powers as educated persons for greater good.

Educationally Effective Practices

Expectations set at high levels and interactions with faculty and peers. The seminar engages students in a metacognitive inquiry into multiple issues in the American education system of which the majority of these students are products. By analyzing and arguing about academic articles, journalistic exposés, college admissions materials and ads, essays, fiction, plays, song lyrics, film, TED talks, YouTube videos, political cartoons, and social criticism, students explore the tangled relationships among language, power, art, economics, and education as well as the ways American youth are seen as pressure points where these competing discourses intersect. They trace the evolution of the assumption that a college education is a universal good and an experience to which every American youth should aspire and is entitled. Finally, students seize their intellectual, writing, and rhetorical powers to construct interventions into the problems they have identified as most urgently in need of attention.

Further evidence of high expectations and meaningful interactions with faculty and peers can be found in the three-segment course design. The instructor begins the course by modeling and analyzing pedagogical methods (e.g., readings, discussions, experiential activities) as a form of scaffolding to prepare students to assume leadership of the seminar later in the semester. This shifts the understanding of the seminar from a behaviorist, top-down model to a constructivist experience (i.e., collaboration to generate new knowledge). Students study the concepts of high-impact educational practices (Kuh, 2008) to clarify the relevance of the course, as well as Bloom's taxonomy, which introduces them to the higher order thinking needed to become effective discussion leaders.

Students assume class leadership in the second segment. To prepare, they complete a preference survey after reviewing the syllabus and scanning a collection of potential readings for each unit that are posted on the course management system. Based on survey results, students are divided into 2-3 person teams and receive a compilation of 25 active-engagement discussion methods to spark their planning. Student teams curate readings and media; assign roles for balanced leadership; determine discussion format(s), pedagogical methods, and activities; and create all instructional materials for their units. As students become the class leaders, they begin to hold each other accountable for completing the readings before class, and they learn to do so diplomatically. After each unit, class members write one-page reflections on the unit and the extent to which their positions changed or were solidified by it. The student leaders comment on and assess the written reflections using a rubric. The instructor then reviews and records the reflections, assessing each team member and the team as whole on preparation, collaboration, and execution, including the extent to which questions led to higher order thinking.

In the final week of the semester (the last segment), the instructor resumes leadership of the class. Students complete final reflections and a systematic assessment of the course, giving them voice for improving it for next year's entering class.

Periodic and structured opportunities for reflection and integration. In addition to the individual unit reflections, students compose pre- and post-seminar reflections on why they are attending college. This activity enables them to chart the evolution of their beliefs about education and the purpose of college and to articulate their personal philosophies and academic goals. They store the post-seminar reflections in electronic portfolios that include artifacts from their Integrative Core Curriculum courses. In the capstone semester, this portfolio provides a springboard for reflection on progress since the first semester in college and the ways in which core requirement courses related to each other and shaped their college experiences.

Significant investment of time and effort and relevance through real-world application. Along with the multiple reflection papers, the seminar includes three academic writing assignments that are graduated in difficulty and sequenced developmentally to build skills: an analytical, thesis-driven essay examining a cultural artifact's impact on youth (4-5 pages); an argumentative essay identifying, explaining, and advocating for change of a social problem affecting young people (5-7 pages); and a 25-page research report (Synthesis Project). This final project requires students to conduct primary (IRB-approved) and secondary research to create interventions into issues affecting youth. It encourages students to connect what they are learning in their first-semester courses with prior knowledge and their experiences of being young adults in a U.S. college at this point in history. The report can take a variety of forms, from traditional research or white papers to documentary films to fully developed curricula for student workshops and courses.

Experiences with diversity. The content of the seminar deals explicitly with social justice, access to education, and inequality in the U.S. education system and higher education. Diversity is also directly addressed in two evening sessions: (a) when students attend the First-Year Diversity Speaker presentation and process it with the peer mentors and (b) during the cross-cultural simulation where students experience what it is like to be an outsider and are guided to connect their encounters with difference to that of students who are not like them.

Frequent and constructive feedback. Written feedback is provided on all assignments, and students receive midterm advisory grades and midterm assessments based on the final grade criteria. After this, they complete anonymous, online, midterm course assessments to indicate what is and is not working in the course and to offer suggestions for improvement. The instructor responds to the critiques and suggestions in class to reinforce students' ownership of the course and model how to use criticism and collaboration to solve problems.

Discussion

Seminar and assignment effectiveness are assessed via two anonymous, online course evaluations administered by the ICSM administration and the Honors Program administration and by a systematic written and oral group evaluation in the last class (Bleicher, 2011). In these evaluations, students repeatedly rate the course as challenging or highly challenging (78% in 2015) and regularly attribute to the course structure their realizations about collegiate study: specifically, the intentionality of pedagogy and design; the purpose of assessment, shifting it from performance to evidence of learning and implications for instruction; and a new awareness of how long grading takes. Further, although they sometimes complain about the required activities outside of class time, when students deconstruct and rebuild the course, they consistently retain these events and frequently volunteer to return as facilitating alumni. In reflections, many note a sense of achievement after meeting the rigorous demands of the Synthesis Project.

Real-world application of these students' newly acquired and honed skills can be found in the numerous occasions where they have presented their findings to school boards, at IC's undergraduate research symposium, and at annual conventions of the National Council on Undergraduate Research (NCUR) and the National Collegiate Honors Council (NCHC); led workshops at their former high schools; and developed and taught mini-courses on campus. Students have taken action at IC, some of which has led to a nationally covered change in the college's administration, and have made their voices heard though the student paper, hometown newspapers, and undergraduate research journals. One seminar graduate's Synthesis Project led to her appointment as a consultant to her hometown school board.

Anecdotal evidence suggests the effectiveness of a small class size in creating community and fostering participant interactions. Some classes have elected to eat together one night a week, and many have created and maintained a class page on social media; a significant number of students return as peer leaders or facilitators for the cross-cultural simulation or as guest speakers at the Synthesis Project panel. The students often call on the instructors for letters of recommendation, saying they know them better than their other first-year faculty.

Based on WAWH's success in helping college students discover academic purpose, become intentional learners, and engage actively with the campus, the founding instructor was charged with developing a one-credit, mini-course derived from the WAWH content as an optional, personal- and academic-enrichment opportunity for all undeclared students. The mini-course spawned by WAWH now serves as the foundational academic experience for IC's Exploratory Program.

Finally, alumni of both the seminar and the mini-course are disproportionately represented in the ranks of President's Hosts, Dean's Hosts, Student Government (including president and vice president of different years), ICSM Peer Leaders, Student Career Consultants, Orientation Leaders, and Resident Assistants. These numbers correlate more strongly to the seminar than does general membership in Honors.

Implications

WAWH has demonstrated that student ownership, responsibility, and engagement inside the classroom are reflected outside the class. The practices that have generated student success are student control of course content and discussion leadership; significant academic and time demands; explicit, metacognitive study of the relationships among youth and the institutions of secondary and higher education; writing assignments that are graduated in difficulty and sequenced developmentally to build skills; and opportunities to access their own power to affect change in themselves and their world. The seminar's impact is directly attributable to its structure, which requires students to take responsibility for their own learning and that of their peers and involves class alumni. The model described is easily replicable if faculty are committed to empowering students and working alongside instead of above them. It can have a positive impact in four-year and two-year institutions enrolling primarily young adults as its focus on cultivating and clarifying a sense of purpose could benefit youth populations.

References

Bleicher, E. (2011). The last class: Critical thinking, reflection, course effectiveness, and student engagement. *Honors in Practice.* Retrieved from http://digitalcommons.unl.edu/cgi/viewcontent.cgi?article=1129&context=nchchip

Kuh, G. D. (2008). *High- impact educational practices: What they are, who has access to them, and why they matter.* (2008). Washington, DC: Association of American Colleges and Universities.

Contact Information

Elizabeth Bleicher
Associate Professor of English
Director, Ithaca College Exploratory Program
Honors Program Faculty Member
313 Muller Faculty Center
Ithaca College
953 Danby Rd.
Ithaca, New York 14850
Phone: 607-274-1531
Email: ebleicher@ithaca.edu

LaGuardia Community College, CUNY

Tameka Battle, Linda Chandler, Bret Eynon, Andrea Francis, Preethi Radhakrishnan, and Ellen Quish

The Institution

Based in Queens, New York, LaGuardia Community College (CUNY) serves 20,000 degree students, all nonresidential. LaGuardia offers 54 majors, from accounting to liberal arts to nursing. Each year, 7,000 to 8,000 students enter the College; two thirds are first-time college students. CUNY tests place 90% of entering students in basic skills reading, writing, or mathematics courses. Approximately 50% of LaGuardia students are foreign born; 41% are Hispanic, 21% Black, 22% Asian, and 16% White. Roughly 60% are first-generation students; 69% report a family income of $25,000 or less (LaGuardia Community College, 2015).

Description of the Seminar

To support students' transition to college, LaGuardia has created eight required, discipline-based first-year seminars (FYS) that integrate an introduction to the major with college success content and advisement. These courses engage thousands of high-risk students with an integrated set of educationally effective practices, deployed to achieve course goals and advance student development as college learners. Piloted with 300 students in 2013-2014, LaGuardia brought its FYS program to scale with nearly 7,000 students in 2015-2016.

All CUNY students must choose a major before matriculation. LaGuardia students take the FYS designed for their meta-major. For example, students entering any business major take BTF 101. Credits and faculty contact hours vary, due to limits imposed by professional accreditation, but all eight courses integrate aspects of extended orientation, basic study skills, and discipline-linked seminars.

Discipline faculty teach FYS courses, assisted by peer mentors who support faculty assignments and introduce students to digital learning tools in the Studio Hour, a weekly tutorial held in a computer lab. Student Life staff offer in-class workshops on time management, wellness, and financial aid. All courses incorporate reflective ePortfolio practice (Arcario, Eynon, Klages, & Polnariev, 2013; Eynon & Gambino, 2017) and ask students to complete an ePortfolio-based "Graduation Plan," which scaffolds educational planning to support advisement, growth mindsets (Dweck, 2006), and purposeful self-authorship (Baxter Magolda, 2009).[3]

A year-long faculty seminar, required for all FYS faculty, has oriented more than 150 faculty to peer mentoring partnerships, advisement, ePortfolio pedagogy, and the needs of first-semester students. All courses address at least one of the College's three Core Competencies: Inquiry and Problem Solving, Global Learning, and Integrative Learning.

Educationally Effective Practices

LaGuardia's FYS courses incorporate many educationally effective practices, including interaction with faculty and peers, application to real-world problems, significant investment of time and effort, and regular opportunities for reflection and integration (Kuh & O'Donnell, 2013). These practices are deployed to enhance Integrative Learning

---

[3]The LaGuardia Graduation Plan is modeled on the ePersonal Development Plan (ePDP) created at Indiana University – Purdue University, Indianapolis (Buyarski & Landis, 2014; Eynon, Gambino, & Torok, 2014). See also the IUPUI case elsewhere in this volume.

(defined as strengthening students' understanding of the connection between their studies and their lives) and support course goals, including successful transition to college, engagement with the discipline, preparation for signature work, strengthened advisement, and improved retention.

In this case study, evidence related to these practices takes two forms. First, four vignettes of specific FYS courses describe the ways educationally effective practices are embedded in a particular course. These vignettes illuminate the broad parameters of the course as well as faculty creativity. In each, faculty describe their evaluations of the impact of such practices.

Second, we share highlights from external evaluation of the FYS for a U.S. Department of Education grant (Finley, 2016), which confirms the widespread use of educationally effective practice, such as those described in the vignettes. Finley's analysis of institutional evidence reveals a statistically significant impact on student outcomes, including retention, credit accumulation, and progress towards degree completion.

BTF 101 for Business Majors. In this two-credit course, the Me, Inc. term project integrates several educationally effective practices, including ***significant investment of time and effort***, ***relevance through real-world applications***, and ***periodic opportunities for reflection and integration***. Structured as a real-world business plan, the project requires students to apply business principles to themselves and create a value proposition for staying in college.

This staged project addresses student background; personal mission statement and brand management; career plan; degree plan; and financial information relating to tuition, future earnings, and retirement. These topics parallel those included in a traditional business plan, such as business background, mission, product and markets, management, and financial statements. The project requires weekly reflections and sustained effort, unfolding over the course of the semester. It is grounded in Integrative Learning, a LaGuardia core competency. Through focused reflection activities, the project weaves together the topics covered in the 12-week syllabus, helping students synthesize learning across the semester.

Integration is fostered as students connect the business discipline and their evolving sense of self and articulate that connection within the framework of the business plan. The project culminates in oral presentations where students engage in further real-world application by pitching their business/life plans to their peers and faculty, modeling the presentation an entrepreneur would make to potential investors.

Accounting professor Andrea Francis evaluated the role of educationally effective practices in her fall 2015 section of BTF101:

> My evaluation of the Me, Inc. term project in fall 2015 revealed that nearly all my students made a significant investment of time and effort, submitting three drafts of the project for my review and completing weekly written reflections in ePortfolio. Of my 21 students, 20 completed all aspects of the integrative term project, with an average grade of A, manifesting deepened understanding of fundamental real-world business concepts and new insight into themselves as learners. As one student put it, "I have discovered a lot about myself these past few months while writing and researching parts of my business plan. I have discovered that my story is not an ideal one, but it is a unique one and I will overcome any adversity that is put in my way on [the] path to my degree."

HSF090 for Health Science majors. Students in this zero-credit FYS ***explore diversity*** and ***reflect on their learning*** to develop the cultural competency they need as professionals. Cultural competency is introduced as part of a scaffolded reflection activity to help students understand the rich cultural traditions they bring to LaGuardia. Students write about the cultures reflected in their diverse communities and the health practices found there. Through shared reflection, students identify commonalities across different cultures, understand complex social systems, and deepen their understanding of Global Learning—a LaGuardia core competency.

Students then ***apply their learning to real world contexts***, exploring the role of culture in patient care. Engaging in purposeful service-learning activities, such as visiting farmers' markets to educate the community on healthy eating or volunteering at hospitals, HSF students apply classroom learning about culture to real-life situations and reflect on their experiences.

Recreational Therapy professor Tameka Battle reviewed the impact of these practices on the development of her HSF090 students:

As a zero-credit course, HSF090 is ungraded, but I conduct surveys and analyze reflections where students process their learning. Surveys show that more than 85% of students felt the course deepened their understanding of cultural issues in nursing. Student reflections demonstrated significant engagement with cultural competency. While students initially hesitated to share insights into culture, they became more enthusiastic about open dialogue as the semester progressed. In their final reflections, where students list skills acquired during the semester, a majority of students listed improved cultural competency among the most important areas for their learning.

LIF101 for Liberal Arts Majors. Advisement, flanked by research papers and other assignments, plays a crucial role in the three-credit LIF101. Many Liberal Arts students are uncertain about their educational directions, in part because Liberal Arts is where LaGuardia students are placed when they have difficulty choosing a major.

For faculty collegewide, the term *advising* conjures images of course selection. However, FYS advising is more complex, focusing on both developmental and prescriptive advising and involving staged student ***reflection*** and ***frequent and constructive feedback from faculty and peers,*** and building Inquiry and Problem Solving (a LaGuardia core competency). LIF101 ***students invest a significant amount of time and effort*** not only to understand the requirements for their majors but also to increase awareness of their strengths and weaknesses.

Students begin a semester-long engagement with advisement by completing the extensive Understanding Myself section of the Graduation Plan. Week by week, through integrative reflection, they examine their goals, strengths, values, and career interests. They map courses they plan to take in upcoming semesters; however, they must first understand the requirements for their degree, as taking courses that "do not count" has implications for financial aid, retention, and graduation. To build this insight, students gather needed information and use it in games and quizzes.

In the Educational Planning Advisement Worksheet, students list their upcoming courses and the requirements they satisfy. Using a peer-review worksheet, students evaluate each other's education plans, which they then post to their ePortfolios for faculty to review before clearing the students for registration. The process ends with students reflecting on what they learned from the FYS about their majors, the college, themselves, and being a successful student. English professor Linda Chandler reviewed the development of her LIF101 students:

> I reviewed the ePortfolios of the 21 students who finished LIF101 and found that all 21 had completed their entire Graduation Plan, including the reflective sections on Understanding Myself and course selection. In their final reflections, students discussed their growth, with one student writing, "This semester has been amazing…I feel like I have grown a lot this semester because [now] I know who I am as a student." Of my 21 students, 17 registered for classes the following semester (an 80% retention rate). These data, together with my assessment of students' ePortfolio content, suggest that students' investment of time and effort focused on integrative course content helped them learn not only the courses needed to graduate but also the importance of planning and taking ownership of their education.

NSF101 for Science Majors. In this two-credit FYS, students explore fundamental questions about nature, ***reflect on and integrate their learning***, and prepare to ***apply knowledge and skills to important real-world problems***. The scientific method (i.e., observing, questioning, predicting, experimenting, and collaborating to share results) is used to develop students' competency in Inquiry and Problem Solving—a LaGuardia core competency.

Components of the scientific method are introduced through TED-MED talks, which curate ideas in medicine and health. Librarians and student affairs staff helped faculty create research and scientific writing modules to help students practice the inquiry-based scientific method in both academic (e.g., understanding the effects of mood elevators on brain function) and nonacademic settings (e.g., constructing an effective time-management schedule). Student comprehension is deepened through three prompted reflective writing assignments in students' ePortfolios.

During the semester's final weeks, students complete research papers, incorporating scientific hypothesis testing. In accompanying reflective videos, students chronicle their development as science students and connect their academic skills to their Graduation Plans.

Biologist Preethi Radhakrishnan evaluated student work from NSF101, identifying the impact of educationally effective practices:

> I developed a rubric to evaluate the reflective writing and the culminating research paper, which together required sustained engagement with discipline-based real world topics. Of the 24 students in class, 100% submitted all staged reflections as well as the research paper. Of the research papers submitted, 15 students received a score between 89-100%. This high level of success was mirrored in other assignments including the Graduation Plan. Of the 25 students enrolled, 22 registered for the subsequent semester (88 %), and 76 % registered for science classes in their second semester. This advanced level of student success suggests that the inquiry into real world topics and recursive reflective writing in NSF101 effectively built students' engagement with the discipline as well as their ownership of their learning.

Discussion

These vignettes suggest that LaGuardia's first-year seminars use many educationally effective practices. Assignments incorporate interactions with faculty and peers as well as frequent feedback, often enacted through comments on students' ePortfolios. They embed experiences with diversity, application to real world problems, and significant investment of time and effort, as well as regular opportunities for reflection and integration, using prompts embedded in the ePortfolio. Faculty evaluation suggests that student engagement with these practices meaningfully contributed to the achievement of the FYS integrative course goals, including engagement with the discipline, strengthened advisement, and students' development as successful college learners.

More formal evaluation has been conducted. Student survey evidence confirms that similar practices are common in the LaGuardia FYS, contributing to improved student outcomes (Eynon, 2016). Institutional data were also analyzed to compare success outcomes for LaGuardia FYS students exposed to such practices with a matched set of LaGuardia students who did not take the FYS (Finley, 2016).

Student survey data revealed the widespread use of educationally effective practices in the FYS. For example, data from a survey conducted with 2,520 FYS students in fall 2015 (Eynon, 2016) confirmed that reflective ePortfolio practice was a crucial element of the FYS collegewide, that regular feedback from faculty and peers was widespread in the FYS, and that students perceived the course as having a positive impact (see Table 1).

Table 1

Selected Responses to FYS End-of-Course Evaluation, Fall 2015 (N = 2,520)

Survey Item	Percentage responding *Agreed* or *Strongly Agreed*
1. The ePortfolio was an important part of this course.	88
2. In this course, I examined my own strengths and weaknesses.	86
3. Using ePortfolio has allowed me to be more aware of my growth and development as a learner.	82
4. In this course, I got useful feedback on my ePortfolio from my professor.	87
5. In this course I got useful feedback on my ePortfolio from other students.	63
6. This course helped me study what successful college students do.	81
7. This course helped me feel more confident as a student.	77

The FYS survey also included several questions adapted with permission from the Community College Survey of Student Engagement (CCSSE). Responses to these questions were compared to those of LaGuardia FYS students college-wide and to the national CCSSE dataset (see Table 2). That FYS students were more likely than the college-wide or national sample to attribute increases in personal understanding and integrative learning to the course suggests the potential positive impact of the reflective element of FYS. FYS participants were also more likely to indicate applying classroom learning to real-world problems than the collegewide or national samples.

Table 2
Impact of FYS on Student Learning, Fall 2015

Survey item	Percent responding Very much or A lot		
	FYS Fall 2015 ($n = 2{,}520$)	LaGCC CCSSE ($n = 1{,}091$)	National CCSSE
8. How much did this course contribute to your knowledge, skills, and personal development in understanding yourself?	87	65	58
9. How much has your work in this course emphasized synthesizing and organizing ideas, information, or experience in new ways?	88	73	63
10. How much did this course emphasize applying theories or concepts to practical problems in new situations?	84	71	64
11. How much did this course contribute to your ability to explore and solve complex, real world problems, such as those you might face in your life, including your career?	87	NA	NA

Note. The FYS survey asks these questions about "your experience in this [the FYS] course." Administered collegewide, the CCSSE asks these questions about "your experience at this college." Question 11 is drawn from the National Survey of Student Engagement (NSSE) and does not have a comparable question on the CCSSE.

These data indicate that educationally effective practices, including feedback, engagement with real-world problems, and integrative examination of the self were widespread in the FYS. It also suggests ways these practices shaped students' learning, contributing to their development related to course goals.

The impact of the FYS on retention, progression, and academic success was also examined. Compared to a matched set of students from the same department who did not take the course, FYS students had a one-semester retention rate that was 11 percentage points higher ($p < .001$). Similarly, FYS students had a two-semester retention rate that was 9 percentage points higher ($p < .001$) than non-FYS students. Even three semesters after the intervention, FYS participation still showed a statistically significant impact on retention.

Other outcomes for FYS students were equally striking, particularly the increased rate of progress toward the degree, as measured by credit accumulation. By the end of their second semesters, FYS students earned, on average, 2.38 credits more than non-FYS students ($p < .001$). Again, the significant, positive impact persisted, actually increasing to 4.22 credits ($p < .001$) by students' fourth semester, suggesting an enduring effect on students' capacity for success. The seminar had a similarly significant, positive impact on cumulative GPA. The most current evaluation concluded:

> High-impact practices, such as FYS, often demonstrate only short-term effectiveness; as students move forward and distance from that exposure increases, effects tend to dramatically wane or disappear. That does not appear to be the case for the LaGuardia FYS program. Up to three semesters past exposure, highly significant differences continued to be found across every indicator of student success, whether related to progress toward the degree or academic achievement. This suggests that the connections students are making in the FYS course through development of ePortfolios, introduction to their chosen major, team-based and peer advising, development of an education plan, and cocurricular experiences are creating lasting impacts on students' development. (Finley, 2016)

Implications

Together, the faculty vignettes and the formal evaluation data suggest that educationally effective practices are widely used in LaGuardia's FYS courses. The vignettes and course-specific evaluations illustrate ways that LaGuardia FYS faculty deploy educationally effective practices, particularly investment of time, connection to authentic problems, and regular opportunities for feedback and reflection. Faculty adapt these practices to suit their courses, and course-specific evaluations suggest they help advance integrative course goals.

Formal evaluation confirms that such practices are common across FYS courses and that students perceive them as contributing to their growth related to key FYS course goals, including a deepened sense of self and educational purpose. These gains are key factors to contributing to dramatic and statistically significantly improvement in retention for literally thousands of high-risk students.

The significance of LaGuardia's FYS initiative is magnified by success in bringing it to scale. Structured professional development has been crucial to this effort. Our findings underscore the need to examine scaling and the ways that educationally effective practices are shared and adapted, shaping student learning and success college-wide.

References

Arcario, P., Eynon, B., Klages, M., & Polnariev, B. A. (2013). Closing the loop: How we better serve our students through a comprehensive assessment process. *Metropolitan Universities, 24*(2), 21–37.

Baxter Magolda, M. B. (2009). The activity of meaning making: A holistic perspective on college student development. *Journal of College Student Development, 50*(6), 621-639.

Buyarski, C., & Landis, C. (2014). Using an eportfolio to assess the outcomes of a first year seminar: Student narrative and authentic assessment. *International Journal of ePortfolio, 4*(1), 49-60.

Dweck, C. S. (2006). *Mindset: The new psychology of success.* New York, NY: Random House.

Eynon, B. (2016, September). *Project Completa: Comprehensive support for student success* (Project Director's Report Year 2). New York, NY: LaGuardia Community College.

Eynon, B., & Gambino, L. (2017). *High-impact eportfolio practice: Catalyst for student, faculty and institutional learning.* Sterling, VA: Stylus.

Eynon, B., & Gambino, L. M., & Torok, J. (2014).What difference can ePortfolio make? A field report from the Connect to Learning project. *International Journal of ePortfolio, 4*(1), 95-114.

Finley, A. (2016, October). *Project Completa: Comprehensive support for student success* (Evaluator's Report Year 2). New York, NY: LaGuardia Community College.

Kuh, G., & O'Donnell, K. (2013). *Ensuring quality and taking high-impact practices to scale.* Washington, DC: Association of American Colleges and Universities.

LaGuardia Community College, Office of Institutional Research.(2015). 2015 institutional profile. New York, NY: Author.

Contact Information

Dr. Bret Eynon
Associate Provost
31-10 Thomson Avenue
Long Island City, NY 11101
Phone: (718) 482-5405
E-mail: beynon@lagcc.cuny.edu

Loyola University Maryland
Mary Ellen Wade

The Institution

Founded in 1852, Loyola University Maryland is a four-year, private, Jesuit, Catholic university located in Baltimore, Maryland, offering 35 undergraduate majors in its three schools. The university is committed to the educational and spiritual traditions of the Society of Jesus and to the ideals of liberal education as well as the development of the whole person. In fall 2016, the institution had an enrollment of 6,050 students, of whom 4,068 were undergraduates and 1,033 were first-year students. Among undergraduate students, 77% are White; 6% are African American; 9% are Hispanic; 4% are Asian; less than 1% are American Indian, Alaska Native, Native Hawaiian or other Pacific Islander; 2% are two or more races (non-Hispanic); 42% are male; 18% are residents of Maryland. Loyola is a residential campus with 98% of first-year students and 81% of undergraduates living in campus housing.

Description of the Seminar

Loyola's first-year living-learning program, Messina, was developed as a key initiative from Loyola's Strategic Plan. As part of Messina, more than 200 faculty members, administrators, and student leaders partner each year to provide all first-year students an experience embracing the assertion that engaged learning, community engagement, and psychosocial well-being are interrelated. Launched in 2013 with the help of a Challenge Grant from the National Endowment for the Humanities, Messina was completely phased-in for all first-year students in 2015.

Students in Messina participate in an interdisciplinary seminar course in both the fall and spring semesters connected to one of four themes: Self and Other, Stories We Tell, The Good Life, and The Visionary. The themes function as bridges between fall and spring seminar courses and the academic and student development aspects of the first-year experience, which students often perceive as being separate and distinct. Building the learning community around broad, interdisciplinary themes provides a stimulus and locus for cross- and interdisciplinary conversations.

Within their seminar pairings, students experience how faculty from diverse disciplines approach similar topics but in the process pose different questions, assert differing viewpoints, and attack problems in a variety of ways. Over the course of their first year, students develop these same approaches in their own work both within and outside the classroom. Faculty in these pairings foster an integrated learning experience in a variety of ways, including using the same textbook or readings in both the fall and spring seminars, incorporating common topics across both semesters, or designing common projects with different components completed in each seminar. Sample pairings might include writing and philosophy, computer science and two-dimensional design, engineering and theology, communication and mathematics, or chemistry and philosophy. These small (14-16 students), three-credit, academic seminars meet for three hours a week in residence hall classrooms and usually satisfy general education requirements. Seminar faculty also serve as academic advisor for students in the pairing, thereby strengthening that important relationship in the first year.

Along with their academic seminar course, students participate in weekly enrichment sessions team taught by a working group composed of the seminar faculty, a student development administrator (the Messina Mentor), and a student peer leader (Evergreen). Enrichment sessions provide a chance to expand on the Messina theme and its connection to the seminar course, facilitate conversations and activities related to the transition to college life, and serve as a tool for students to connect to the Loyola and greater Baltimore community. Students are expected to treat enrichment sessions as a continuation of their seminar course; attendance is not optional. Some faculty members opt to include the enrichment session in their grading of the seminar, to emphasize its importance.

Students in Messina live in proximity to other students in their seminars (but not necessarily in the same room or on the same floor) and are housed according to their Messina themes. Commuter students have access to the common spaces of the residence halls where their seminar themes are situated so they can participate in the cocurricular programs. The intent is that Messina takes seminar-based conversation out of the classroom and into students' lives, providing students with an impetus to engage in informal intellectual conversation outside class and develop relationships with their peers that has a basis in intellectual community. Figure 1 depicts the basic structure of Messina.

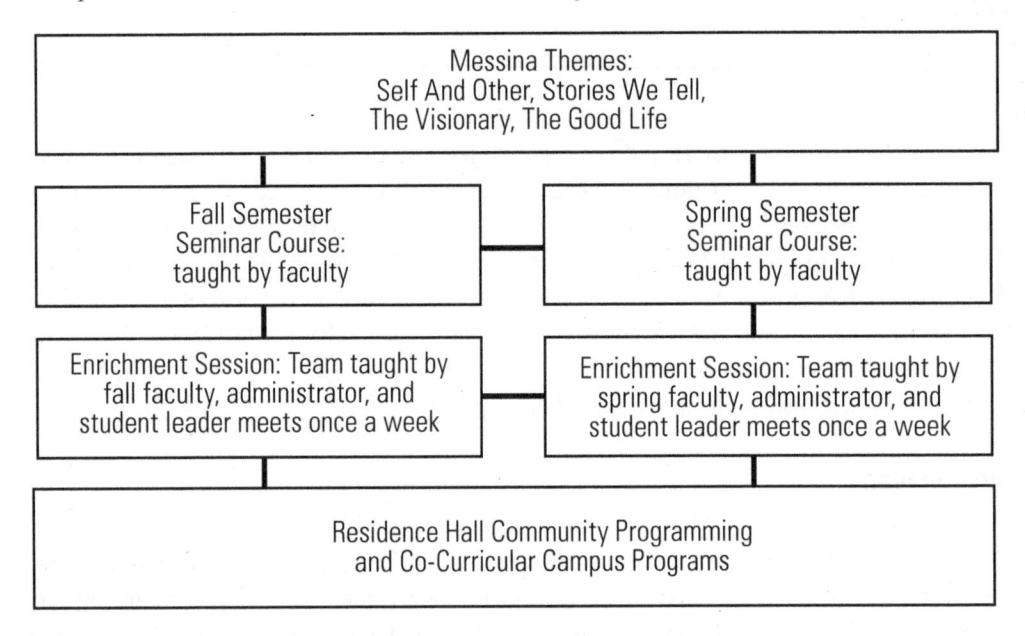

Figure 1. Structure of Messina Living-Learning Program at Loyola University Maryland.

Messina is grounded in the learning outcomes articulated in the Association of American Colleges and Universities (AAC&U) VALUE rubrics (Rhodes, 2010), especially in the areas of personal and social responsibility, integrated learning, ethical reasoning, foundations and skills for lifelong learning, and integrative and applied learning, along with the school's unique mission. First-year students are expected to show progress in the following areas as a result of participating in Messina.

Jesuit Mission and Values
- Develop habits of discernment and reflection in the Ignatian (Jesuit) tradition
- Explore and articulate the values and principles involved in their personal decision making

Critical Understanding
- Develop habits of reading, writing, and intellectual conversation that support academic excellence and engagement
- Demonstrate increased knowledge and use of campus resources that aid critical thinking

Connections to Loyola Community
- Establish healthy, mutually beneficial, and respectful relationships with others, including faculty, administrators, staff, and peers
- Demonstrate a sense of belonging to the community at Loyola both in and out of the classroom

Integrated Learning
- Integrate multiple sources of knowledge gained through various disciplinary lenses, texts, instruction, out-of-class experiences, and personal reflection to offer a perspective on the interdisciplinary theme of their community

Educationally Effective Practices

All Messina course pairings display aspects of educationally effective practices—the structure of Messina naturally fosters meaningful interactions with faculty and peers, experiences with diversity, and opportunities for reflection. However, each pairing demonstrates these practices in different ways because what works in a writing seminar may not work in an engineering seminar and vice versa. This case study highlights one Messina course pairing, a writing and philosophy seminar, under the Self and Other theme. Across both courses and within their cocurricular experiences, students explore how they imagine the other and how those imaginings shape their willingness to learn from, sympathize with, and open themselves to the other. Students in this pairing take Effective Writing: WR100 in the fall and Philosophy: PL201 in the spring semester. Both courses fulfill core requirements at Loyola.

Interactions with faculty and peers and experiences with diversity. From the moment first-year students arrive on campus, they spend Fall Welcome Weekend in their Messina groups led by their Messina Evergreens. Their first seminar-style moment with their fall faculty members begins with a discussion of the common text they were assigned to read over the summer. Throughout this weekend, students develop rapport with each other and the members of the working group so that when they attend their first official week of classes, they already have formed strong connections with each other.

Working group members coordinate 10 to 12 enrichment sessions per semester (i.e., 15 to 25 contact hours), which are included on the course syllabus. Enrichment sessions may include field trips, speakers, performances, and experiences specifically tied to the course and the theme (e.g., excursions to Baltimore's unique restaurants, museums, cultural institutions, and neighborhoods). The working group collaborates throughout the academic year to plan these enrichment activities—all at no additional cost to the student.

Enrichment sessions are also an extension of the seminar course. For example, many groups use a session during the first two weeks of the fall semester to facilitate a demonstration and conversation about expectations for critically examining and discussing texts at the college level. In other cases, faculty use an enrichment session to pass back the first writing assignment and facilitate a discussion about expectations related to college-level writing. The small, seminar-style design of these sessions fosters a setting where students have an opportunity to ask questions and assert perspectives in a supportive environment among peers.

Relevance through real-world application, expectations set at appropriately high levels, and periodic and structured opportunities for reflection and integration. In one Messina seminar course, WR100, students use a rhetorical framework to study the contemporary essay critically and creatively. They develop their writing process by learning how to conceive an original idea, use language effectively, conduct basic library research, construct an outline, plan a draft, and make revisions based on feedback. "The goal is to teach students to approach writing as a rhetorical activity, not as a set of rules or conventions. In achieving this goal, the course attends to writing as both process and product within a community of writers" (Leary, 2015).

In this seminar, students also have the option to participate in a service-learning experience, partnering with the after-school program serving prekindergarten through grade eight students at a local charter school. They have the opportunity to continue this service experience in PL201. Along with traditional texts and discussions, students read material related to service in the community. Writing assignments are tailored to the service experience, including an essay on Baltimore and the local community; a paper covering an issue with local and global impact on literacy and illiteracy, and a class project creating a newsletter for the charter school around literacy, with book recommendations and activities for their students. In addition to these projects, students keep a weekly reflection journal. Because some students may have scheduling conflicts with the time allotted for the service experience or may not be personally ready to make the commitment, alternative assignments have been designed for those who choose to opt out of service. Regardless of which option students decide to pursue in WR100, they are expected to reflect thoughtfully and engage with the topic of literacy within a personal, local, and global context.

Significant investment of time and effort. Students enrolled in the spring version of the WR100 course[4] have a similar service-learning option at the charter school; however, their newsletter project (*New Hounds*) involves developing a resource for the next incoming first-year class at Loyola. This newsletter is distributed during Fall Welcome Weekend and provides the stories of how students acclimated to the University during their first year. In addition to creating articles of relevance and importance to incoming first-year students, the class is responsible for design and layout decisions. A highlight of this Messina seminar is the emphasis on using the technical skills developed through course assignments and applying these skills in a way to give back to Loyola and surrounding community members.

Frequent and constructive feedback. Over the course of the semester, students move from learning, understanding, and demonstrating fundamental areas of writing related to purpose, audience, and idea development to assignments concerning the movement from local to global thinking. Throughout this process, students receive feedback not only from their instructor but also from their peers. This is achieved through peer critique and group writing assignments related to each of the essay readings.

Discussion

Messina is a relatively new program, and Loyola is still exploring ways to best assess individual student works. Part of the challenge is that while Messina is a universal program for all first-year students, experiences vary greatly among all programs offerings (e.g., not every student is in a Messina-specific WR100 seminar). Therefore, assessment tools must be broad enough to apply to student work in multiple classes and across a variety of disciplines. Another goal of Messina is to collect data and information that can best be used by other offices and departments at Loyola beyond just the first year.

During the upcoming year, Messina is developing a project that will examine student experience in Messina seminars through the collection of examples of direct evidence of student learning. Many Messina seminar faculty have students write or present end-of-semester or end-of-year reflections. These artifacts will provide a better sense of how students are making meaning from their seminar experiences and suggest potential areas of growth for our program.

Presently there is an interest at Loyola to see how students develop critical thinking and writing skills over the course of their four years, beginning with their experiences in Messina. In 2014-2015, Loyola piloted a Critical Thinking and Writing Assessment rubric to evaluate a select group of first-year writing samples (collected after course completion) with the intent that this rubric would also be used to evaluate a writing sample from the senior year. Faculty participating in the pilot attended several norming sessions where they practiced using the rubric. Following these sessions, faculty scored papers from students enrolled at the time and provided additional feedback and recommendations about the process. Because pilot faculty did not evaluate work from students in their own courses, all were provided with a copy of the original assignment instructions to help with scoring. At times, this project proved to be challenging in that expectations about writing styles sometimes differed across disciplines. A key takeaway of this group was that assignments that provided a more detailed emphasis on expectations around critical thinking resulted in student works that demonstrated higher levels of competence in this area.

Messina faculty involved in the pilot also engaged in discussions on how the findings could benefit both students and instructors (e.g., shaping future faculty development workshops or contributing to follow-up assessment projects). An additional consideration suggested by the group is that sharing this information with other faculty may help them better structure experiences that foster student development of critical thinking and writing.

Implications

First-year living-learning programs have the potential to provide a strong foundation to undergraduate students embarking on a collegiate experience. Through its interdisciplinary teaching, learning, and cocurricular programming, Messina strives to inspire lifelong intellectual curiosity among first-year students. For any institution looking to create a similar experience, it is important to examine the existing strengths of the programs or experiences offered. At Loyola, our emphasis focuses on our liberal arts core curriculum and a values-based educational mission.

---

[4] The two faculty teaching these seminar options also teach a second pairing within the program, where students complete PL201 in the fall and WR100 in the spring. This assignment description comes from the WR100 spring seminar.

During the training of Messina faculty and administrators, it has been helpful to provide time for them to highlight assignments and strategies they have incorporated in their Messina seminars that demonstrate creative ways of fostering effective educational experiences. Every year, more ideas are presented that inspire new approaches in other courses. A strength of Messina is that the trainings provide opportunities to create and strengthen cross-divisional partnerships and encourage the modeling of effective educational practices so students are able to see the purpose of these activities for themselves. Messina's unique model of having tenured and tenure-track faculty from different departments and disciplines collaborate in the course pairing allows for a high level of creativity in making cross-disciplinary connections in sometimes very different fields. In the WR100 sequence, a service-learning component and a writing project related to that experience support integrated learning. Incorporating educationally effective practices into a first-year program has the ability to foster transformative experiences among students early on in their collegiate careers, further strengthening the contributions these students will make toward the campus and community both during college and beyond.

References

Leary, A. (2015). *WR100.01S Effective Writing Service-Learning Optional* [Syllabus]. Baltimore, MD: Loyola University Maryland, Writing Department.

Rhodes, T. L. (Ed.). (2010). *Assessing outcomes and improving achievement: Tips and tools for using rubrics.* Washington, DC: Association of American Colleges and Universities.

Contact Information

Mary Ellen Wade
Associate Director of Messina, First-Year Living-Learning Program
Loyola University Maryland
4501 North Charles St.
Maryland Hall 145
Baltimore, MD 21210
Phone: 410-617-2225
E-mail: mewade@loyola.edu

Malone University
Marcia K. Everett, Jay R. Case, and Jacci Welling

The Institution

Malone University is a four-year, private, Christian university of the arts, sciences, and professions, located in Canton, Ohio, offering 48 majors, seven pre-professional programs, and four master's degree programs. Faculty and staff represent a wide range of religious affiliations (e.g., Orthodox, Catholic, Mennonite, Quaker, Pentecostal, Reformed) and affirm a common statement of faith; however, student enrollment is open and approximately one third of the student body do not identify with a particular faith commitment. Enrollment has varied in the past several years, reflecting a number of national and regional economic and demographic shifts. In fall 2015, enrollment was 1,750, of whom 245 were traditional-age, first-year students. Within this cohort, 82% were White, 10% were African American, 57% were women, and 86% lived on campus. A high percentage of first-year students are Pell Grant eligible (40%), and close to a third (30%) are first in their families to attend college.

Description of the Seminar

Malone's first-year seminar (FYS), GEN 100: The College Experience, is considered the beginning course in the general education curriculum and is required of all traditional-age, first-year students. The content of the seminar is oriented around four key questions about the purposes of a college education at Malone: (a) Who am I? (b) Why college? (c) What do I believe? and (d) With whom will I surround myself? A one-credit academic seminar with uniform content (i.e., common course requirements and readings), the course meets one day a week for 75 minutes throughout the fall semester. The FYS is taught by full-time faculty (60%) from multiple disciplines, as well as staff and administrators from Student Development, Admissions, and Campus Ministries. Full-time faculty receive two credits of teaching load for the course, and staff and administrators are paid at the adjunct rate for two credits. All of the GEN 100 faculty participate in course-specific professional development with each other and the peer leaders. The team of GEN 100 faculty has a significant level of ownership in course design and evaluation.

Each FYS section has a peer leader (course assistant or CA) who works closely with the instructor in teaching and facilitating the seminar. The CAs are expected to establish relationships with new students, helping them engage with faculty members and the larger campus community. CAs have a number of out-of-class responsibilities: They meet weekly with the other CAs in small groups or together with the director of the program; are responsible for major segments of orientation; have weekly contact (i.e., through e-mail or social media) with FYS students as well as several scheduled individual meetings over the course of the semester; and plan academic and social events, such as study groups and activities to engage FYS students with each other and the local community.

Because the seminar is discussion-oriented, enrollment in each section is limited to 15-20 students. FYS students are introduced to the academic mission, culture, and goals of Malone as well as the nature of a Christian liberal arts education, and they reflect on the role of a college education in their own lives. They are encouraged to think critically about choices and issues they encounter in their college experience and are invited to examine the relationship of faith to personal, community, and learning contexts. Additionally, students read and listen to the ideas of others to foster understanding and discernment, and they engage in self-reflection about learning.

The pedagogy for the course is highly interactive. While sitting in a circle, students engage in structured discussions and experiential activities to achieve course objectives. Other class assignments and components include reading assessments, writing, learning about campus resources, and participation in social events (e.g., games at a professor's house, First Friday in downtown Canton, 9-square-in-the-air with another section) and academic activities outside the classroom (e.g., study groups, attend campus lectures as a section, syllabus party.)

Educationally Effective Practices

Interactions with faculty and peers. The structure and design of the course incorporates effective educational practices that begin during a five-day orientation immediately preceding the fall semester. When new students arrive on campus, their first official meeting is with their FYS instructor, CA, and fellow classmates from their section. During that two-hour session, they are introduced to each other and the schedule, and they are guided to think about what it means to be a college student. On the second and third day of orientation, first-year students spend the day as a class at a camp engaging in initiative games, ropes courses, and problem-solving activities together.

The discussion-based nature of the seminar also fosters community building. Using small- and whole-class group formats, students engage in collaborative assignments, such as mini case studies examining integrity, diversity, relationships, general education, and the role of the liberal arts, among other issues. The textbooks for the course are a course reader unique to Malone and a common read book connected to the topics of the course.

In addition to required personal meetings with the CA and attendance at CA-organized social and educational events, students meet individually with the course instructor and are often invited to his or her home as a section. Interaction with other Malone faculty is facilitated through several course assignments, such as speaking to faculty members and reflecting on fields of study at a Major Fair. Students must also arrange a meeting with a professor (other than the FYS instructor) to talk about their performance in the course they are taking with that professor. The faculty–student and CA–student relationships often continue beyond the fall semester and reinforce a sense of belonging within the larger Malone community.

Experiences with diversity. Although the institution is working on increasing the racial and ethnic diversity of its student body, the majority of students come from small or rural communities in Ohio and Pennsylvania that are often homogeneous in nature. Many students arrive with little experience with people who are different from themselves. Because a significant number are first-generation students, many view college as a job training process. They have not been introduced to the idea that higher education should also present them with people, perspectives, and ideas that are quite different from what they have experienced previously. Therefore, one of the explicit goals of the FYS includes exposing students to differing viewpoints, introducing them to new experiences, and teaching them to listen well to others.

This exposure begins during orientation, when each first-year student participates in the Into the Streets event where small groups spend an afternoon doing service projects for various nonprofit organizations in Canton, a small rustbelt city struggling economically and experiencing population loss and demographic change. Into the Streets, then, not only orients and connects students to their new community but also exposes them to social situations that are often quite different from their prior experiences. The FYS later follows up these experiences with readings, writing responses, and discussions about investing in the local community.

The seminar also embeds practices designed to introduce students to new ideas and perspectives from various writers and fellow students. These practices model respectful civil discourse and careful listening to the views of others. Class sections commonly employ a Take a Stand action sociometric where students respond to a statement (related to course content) by standing in sections labeled *Strongly Agree, Agree, Disagree,* or *Strongly Disagree.* They then explain to others why they chose to stand where they did. Students are free to switch to a new section during the discussion if they find new ideas to be compelling, but the goal is understanding, not persuasion.

A variety of similar exercises are used throughout the semester to elicit responses from students and to prompt them to consider new perspectives. One of these is the use of partner assignments. During the week, students meet with a classmate to discuss several specific questions related to the following week's topic. In class, students report on what their partners said in their discussions, an exercise that encourages good listening and consideration of different perspectives. The next week, the partners change, so that by the end of the semester each student will have been a partner with just about everyone in the class.

The content of the course is also designed to encourage consideration of diverse perspectives. One of the criteria for the selection of the common read book is that it addresses some sort of theme related to differences in race, ethnicity, gender, religion, class, or culture. As students contemplate the four key questions, they write reflection papers on their own cultural upbringing and share these stories with one another. Finally, outside programming is tied to the course theme and common read. For example, a Holocaust survivor and individuals with experiences as refugees talked to students, a debate about Native American mascots was hosted, in conjunction with Communications classes, and various speakers were invited to share their experiences about being homeless or rescuing children from slavery in Nepal.

Diverse perspectives are also addressed in the custom-published textbook, which is divided by the topics of the course and includes readings that reflect and invite discussion about difference and how people engage diversity. Some of the readings are themselves stories about differences, whether in experiences with faith or a delineation of arguments for and against promoting abstinence from alcohol (written by the same author.) Others tend to evoke agreement or disagreement in the reader, such as an essay about why millennials are postponing relationships.

Periodic and structured opportunities for reflection and integration. The FYS director and director of composition work together formulating assignments for student writing (and reading) that are consistent with first-year writing courses. Students are assessed on their reading completion and comprehension each week. Whatever form the assessment takes, they must articulate the central ideas and supporting details of what they read, making a response to those ideas with connections to their own experiences and learning.

Writing (both formal and informal) is incorporated in the course in multiple ways. Students' formal essays are exploratory writing requiring them to reflect on their experiences in light of what they have been reading and discussing. Midway through the semester, they engage in meta-reflection and integration exercises based on a reading that articulates some of the habits, struggles, and intentions of college students when writing (Davis, 2006). This essay is returned without a grade but with considerable comments and feedback. Students then write a letter to their instructors responding to a number of posed questions, helping them reflect on the process of their writing and integrating what they have read (see Appendix – Malone University).

Discussion

Because the FYE seminar at Malone is required for all entering students and sections share the same objectives, readings, and assignments, there is no comparison group against which to measure the outcomes. Learning outcomes have been evaluated using pre- and post-, Likert-scale surveys related to course objectives, and students also complete open-ended responses. These narrative data are then collated and analyzed for common themes. When asked how interaction with faculty and the CA contributed to their experiences, first-year students consistently identify themes of feeling supported, encouraged, challenged, welcomed, and given important assistance (e.g., finding a major, navigating the transition to college, making decisions). Specific activities, such as Take a Stand and partner assignments, in addition to the faculty and student interactions, are among factors frequently identified as *most meaningful.*

When students were asked to identify topics covered in the FYS that they thought the most about after the class was over, topics involving reflection and integration assignments were in the top quarter of responses. Further, 87% agreed or strongly agreed that they read and listened to the ideas of others with discernment and understanding, and 91% indicated they engaged in thinking thoughtfully and critically about issues concerning the college experience. Although not a direct measure, institutional National Survey of Student Engagement (NSSE, 2014) data in the areas of collaborative learning, integrative and reflective learning, and student–faculty interaction corroborate these findings.

The assignments, pedagogy, and content of the course are regularly evaluated by the team of faculty who teach the seminar. Instructors meet several times during the semester and at its conclusion to discuss how things are working, review assessment and feedback results, and consider what changes could be made. Malone continues to explore ways to measure the outcomes of these educational practices more directly.

Implications

Small schools have some unique opportunities to employ best educational practices in integrated ways. Malone has been able to weave student–faculty interaction; respectful civil dialogue; a common reading; and multiple practices of careful listening, diverse viewpoints, and reflection and integration into a required seminar. The FYS lays the groundwork for similar but more advanced practices in the general education program. Malone has successfully adapted practices and ideas from institutions that are very different from ours. At the same time, we believe some of our practices could be readily appropriated for different educational contexts. Specific assignments related to writing and reading can be used in any seminar that has those components. The use of discussion strategies to engage diversity and encourage thoughtful and careful attention to other perspectives can similarly be adapted to a wide variety of contexts.

References

Davis, J. C. (2006, Fall). Making the most of college: Writing with purpose. *Comment*. Retrieved from https://www.cardus.ca/comment/article/336/making-the-most-of-college-writing-with-purpose/

National Survey of Student Engagement (NSSE). (2014). *NSSE 2014 engagement indicators: Malone University*. Retrieved from http://www.malone.edu/academics/assessment/background-resources/nsse-2014-engagement-indicators.pdf

Contact Information

Marcia K. Everett
Professor, Communication Arts
Director: The College Experience
Malone University
2600 Cleveland Ave NW
Canton, OH 44709
E-mail: meverett@malone.edu
Phone: 330-471-8335

Appendix
Reflection and Integration Assignment

Writing Reflection Assignment: Read through your paper and reflect on the process of writing it. Then, look over my comments on your paper, the comment sheet, and the paper assignment sheet. Write me (a letter? Just answer the questions? Either way ... write TO me) and respond to the following:

- Tell me how it feels to you to not get a grade on this paper. What difference does not getting a grade, but getting lots of comments, make? What difference do you think not assigning a grade made for me as a reader of your writing?
- Tell me about the process of your writing: How did you go about writing it? What did you do? What kind of time did you spend? How was that distributed between the drafting and revising? Look again at Davis's essay "Writing with Purpose." Which of the struggles and habits he identifies did you experience in writing this paper? Discuss how you saw this evidenced in your writing.

Choose ONE of the self-analysis blocks below that you think would be most helpful to reflect on more. Answer the self-reflection questions on the right side of the block.

Self-Analysis Block	Self-Analysis Questions
Choose three of the four questions (one of which must be, Why am I going to college?) and further develop a response to these three larger questions. Paper has a beginning that draws the reader in and a conclusion that pulls together what was said (but does not just restate it.)	Which of these questions did I answer? How did I weave them together? How did my beginning draw the reader in? How does my conclusion pull together what I have said without restating it? What, in retrospect, would have been helpful for me to consider? What could I have done differently in these areas to strengthen or improve my paper?
Responses are thoroughly articulated and organized in a coherent manner with good transitions between ideas.	In what ways can I see the flow of my paper? How might I have made it more coherent?
Paper incorporates, in meaningful and fluid ways, at least two examples from your own experience for each question or area you write about. Support (e.g., examples, experiences, explanation) has quality, depth, and variety.	What kinds of support did I use? Do I explain, give examples, and show what I mean when I use terms that represent broad concepts?
Paper provides evidence of a commitment to excellence in preparation, including professional appearance and use of standard English (e.g., voice, style, word choice, sentence structure, completeness, variety.)	What kinds of themes did I see in my writing related to this area? Were there particular strengths that I repeated or weaknesses or problem areas that recurred?

Reflect on what you think to be the strengths of this piece. Is it well-written? If so, what makes it well-written?

Choose TWO of my comments (that deal with your content) and restate them—demonstrating to me that you understand what I was saying. Overall, in what ways have my comments helped you to see what you did well and what you could have done better? Discuss.

Do you choose to rewrite and resubmit your paper? Why or why not?

Montana State University
Margaret Konkel and Deborah Blanchard

The Institution
Established in 1893 as a land-grant institution, Montana State University (MSU) is a four-year, public, research university located in Bozeman, Montana. In fall 2015, MSU enrolled 15,688 students, of whom 84% were White, 4.6% were international, 3.5% were Hispanic/Latino, 3.1% identified as two or more ethnicities, 1.6% were American Indian/Alaskan Native, and less than 1% were Native Hawaiian/Pacific Islander/Asian/Black/African American. First-time, first-year student enrollment was 3,024.

Description of the Seminar
US 101US First-Year Seminar (FYS) is an academic, place–identity themed, three-credit course open to students of all majors. The course contributes to MSU's general education core, serves approximately 20% of the first-year cohort, and is front-loaded with 40 to 41 sections in the fall semester and 4 to 5 sections in the spring. The seminar is a student-directed classroom experience that explores questions of place, region, and identity through a range of texts in a discussion format, meeting for three hours a week. Each section is capped at 17 students and facilitated by an adjunct or administrative faculty member. It is a shared curriculum—all sections engage with the same information at the same time. Common content (i.e., syllabus, course questions, assignments, rubrics, and resources) is compiled into a course packet, which students purchase as the text.

Approximately half of the fall sections are assigned peer leaders, who serve as problem solvers and connectors to the University community and as a campus resource for incoming first-year students. Peer leaders attend all FYS classes during the week and work directly with the instructors to co-facilitate the seminars, encouraging student engagement with the texts and classmates. They also assist in organizing provost-funded out-of-class community-building activities, such as picnics, day hikes, bowling, or pizza nights.

The seminar texts allow students to engage in issues that foster the development of critical-thinking skills based on Elder and Paul's (2009) model of raising questions, gathering information, coming to well-reasoned conclusions, engaging with multiple points of view, and communicating those conclusions in an effective manner orally and in writing. Place and identity theories (Altman & Low, 1992; Chow & Healy, 2008) form the foundation of the seminar as students consider how their views have been shaped by their home place and how their changed surroundings affect those views. Social constructivism provides a vocabulary by which students can appreciate that place is relative and that understanding diverse perspectives happens in part by understanding the relationship between place and mindset (Berger & Luckmann, 1967). The course is designed with four units (i.e., Education and Identity, Place and Identity, Morality and Social Justice, and Reflection), each of which presents a series of questions students consider as they engage with texts and complete assignments.

The Education and Identity unit begins during the first three weeks of class with the goal of building community. Students examine questions such as, Why are we here? What does it mean to be sitting in this classroom? Is this the right place to be? What role does education play in our lives, and how does that translate to where we are sitting today? They start the process of critical thinking by drawing connections from their personal experiences to the texts in discussion and collectively establish the foundation for dialogue-based learning. The unit assignment is a five-minute oral presentation in which students respond to a text by developing a field guide to help themselves and their peers understand who they are, why they are at MSU, and why they may engage in discussion from the perspectives they do. The low-stakes assignment helps students get to know one another and builds community through their shared uneasiness of oral presentations so soon after the start of term. Students provide peer feedback, focusing on one meaningful strength of the presentation and one constructive critique in a commendation and recommendation format.

The second unit, Place and Identity, tackles the core question, What responsibilities do we have to this place (Montana) and time (now) as an informed and engaged citizen? Students are challenged to move beyond personal responses to texts to draw connections between articles that offer a range of viewpoints and perspectives around the relationship between place and identity. They develop new interpretations as readings progress and strengthen expository writing skills through two assignments: (a) a portfolio of quick writes providing a low-stakes opportunity for students to explore deeper thinking and (b) a five- to seven-page paper asking them to respond to a prompt with a clearly articulated claim and to support that claim through multiple texts in an analytical, critical, and creative manner.

The Morality and Social Justice unit poses the questions, What is my place in the world? and How do we develop a moral framework for engaging with issues of justice in this society? Students examine complex issues of right and wrong in an objective, scholarly way; translate place and identity concepts to an empathetic approach to social justice; and examine both sides of an issue through the use of argument and counter-argument. Learning is demonstrated through a four-part research assignment that also incorporates a library skills workshop. Students are led through the research process from choosing a topic, to developing research questions, documenting preliminary research in an annotated bibliography assignment, and finally developing a storyboard outline with works cited for a Pecha Kucha (i.e., a 6-minute-and-40-second presentation comprising 20 slides shown for 20 seconds each) delivered during the last two weeks of class.

The final Reflection unit is intended to synthesize course experiences (e.g., discussion, oral presentations, readings) with personal experience through careful, reflective writing. The goal is for students to design a moral framework with which to navigate the college experience and demonstrate analytical, creative, and critical thinking in written communication. Students write a four- to six-page reflection paper on how their ideas and self-understanding have evolved throughout the course. Students are asked to consider how their understanding of place and identity has evolved, organizing their reflections in the theoretical framework of the course.

In addition to the unit assignments, the FYS includes two semester-long assignments that contribute to the overall course design and delivery of educationally effective practices: leading class discussions and the portfolio. In this student-centered course, the FYS participants are required to lead class discussion in teams throughout the semester. The team is responsible for creating a series of discussion questions, including an outside source that will help their peers understand something about the reading in a new or different manner, and developing an activity to get everyone involved. The student team runs the discussion and is evaluated on quality of questions, engagement of the whole class, and teamwork. Pedagogical goals include experiencing classroom leadership, building teamwork, and taking responsibility for their own active learning.

Students develop their critical-thinking skills throughout the semester by maintaining a portfolio of short writing assignments, which offers opportunities for consistent cultivation of deeper thinking with respect to the texts and the course work. Short writes vary by instructor: some are in-class writings, others are weekly reflective pieces, but most are prompts that scaffold new ideas and assess student engagement.

Educationally Effective Practices

Expectations set at appropriately high levels. Embedded in the objectives of US 101US is the goal of introducing first-year students to the demands and expectations of college work. The reading list and assignment criteria reflect this. In fall 2015, the reading list includes 16 texts discussed in a 10-week time period (MSU, n.d.). With the exception of full-length books, which may span two or three class sessions, students read and discuss a new text each class meeting. Texts vary in length and difficulty but consistently provide a challenge to first-year students.

Experiences with diversity. As the seminar is grounded in dialogue as a means of collective learning, texts are selected purposefully to provide a variety of genres and perspectives. Students are introduced to academic journal articles, fictional short stories, book-length creative nonfiction, persuasive articles, poetry, and video as examples of the range of texts they are likely to be exposed to throughout their college careers. These reading assignments also present a variety of viewpoints, challenging students to engage with a diverse set of ideas, perspectives, and opinions. In-class discussion supports this practice: Instructors guide students through the experience of cognitive dissonance that comes when assumptions are challenged and curiosity is piqued.

Relevance through real-world applications. Students apply critical thinking skills to a research project on issues of social injustice. They each select an issue they feel strongly about and are challenged to frame that real-world concern in the lessons of the course. This engagement with application allows students to experience the empowerment of expertise on a meaningful topic, the struggle of engaging in objective critical thinking about a topic that stirs their emotions, and the satisfaction of observing how that knowledge and thinking informs and persuades their peers through the oral presentation.

Discussion

The seminar is currently assessed in three different modes: (a) at the program level, to determine success of shared objectives and to establish standards of achievement across other general education core courses; (b) at the institution level, to ensure instructor outcomes on a section-by-section basis; and (c) at the section level, at the midsemester, to determine how students are engaging with the work, ideas, and individuals involved with their seminar experiences. Each of these modes of assessment offers formal and informal opportunities to evaluate the success with the educationally effective practices highlighted.

The assessment of high levels of expectation is informal at this stage. Midsemester evaluations from the past two years allow students to identify which of the texts was most interesting and which was most challenging. An analysis of the open-ended responses to the latter question shows an even distribution of course texts identified as most challenging. This suggests that the rigor of the seminar is recognized by a majority of the students, and the expectations for challenge do not rest on one single text or effort.

Experiences with diversity are assessed both informally, via a specific question on the midsemester evaluation, and formally, in the programmatic evaluation of the demonstration of analytical, critical, and creative thinking in written communication. At midterm, students are asked whether *In-class discussions challenge me to think differently about ideas*. Two years of data suggest that a majority of students (73% in fall 2014, 75% in fall 2015) agree with that statement. A content analysis of the open-ended comments following that question revealed that terms such as *different, interesting, think, ideas, and opinions* form the basis of what students find important to share. Formal, program-wide assessment of learning objectives is conducted on a three-year cycle, and the learning objective related to experiences with diversity and the critical, creative, and analytical thinking that stems from such exposure was assessed for fall 2015. One measure of that assessment, *Exploration and Synthesis of Multiple Perspectives*, specifically targeted this thinking; students in the FYS met or exceeded the expectations of the core program at a rate of 75%.

Relevance through real-word applications is directly connected to the third unit research project and associated Pecha Kucha presentation. Effective oral communication is formally assessed at a programmatic level, most recently following the fall 2014 semester. FYS students excelled in this assessment, meeting or exceeding program expectations by at least 79% in criteria of central message, content development and organization, and support of their arguments. Although this assessment shows strong outcomes, its emphasis is more in the delivery of effective oral communication, so MSU is developing a plan to assess this project more specifically in how it demonstrates the effective educational practice it supports.

Implications

The case study presented on US 101US provides a compelling example of intentional integration of educationally effective practices in an academic FYS. Integrated theories of place and identity allow the course to frame stimulating academic issues in a larger conceptual context that fits the transitional stage of first-year students. Balancing rigorous academic expectations with a classroom environment that encourages shared perspectives and engagement with the real world delivers a transformational experience.

The lessons of this case study, critical thinking grounded in personal growth and identity formation, can inform a range of seminar types and campus profiles. An FYS focused on concepts of place and identity provides an appropriate design for courses that emphasize orientation and integration to the campus community, based on the assumption that every place (i.e., campus, community, or region) has compelling issues and questions around which to organize student growth. The pedagogy outlined in this case study provides a translatable model to consider.

References

Altman, I., & Low, S. (1992). Place attachment: A conceptual inquiry. In I. Altman & S. Low (Eds.), *Place attachment* (pp. 1-12). New York, NY: Plenum.

Berger, P. L., & Luckmann, T. (1967). *The social construction of reality: A treatise in the sociology of knowledge.* New York, NY: Anchor.

Chow, K., & Healey, M. (2008). Place attachment and place identity: First-year undergraduates making the transition from home to university. *Journal of Environmental Psychology, 28,* 362-372. Retrieved from http://www.sciencedirect.com/science/article/pii/S0272494408000236

Elder, L., & Paul, R. (2009). Close reading, substantive writing and critical thinking: Foundational skills essential to the educated mind. *Gifted Education International, 25*(3), 286-295.

Montana State University (MSU). (n.d.). *US 101US: First year seminar: Tentative reading list.* Retrieved April 21, 2016, from http://www.montana.edu/universitystudies/firstyearseminar/F15%20Reading%20List.pdf

Contact Information

Margaret Konkel
Director First-Year Seminar
University Studies
Montana State University
University Studies Department
P.O. Box 173000
130 Gaines, Bozeman
MT 59717-3000
E-mail: margaret.konkel@montana.edu
Phone: (406) 994-6833

Northern Arizona University
Rebecca Campbell and Kaitlin Hublitz

The Institution

Northern Arizona University (NAU) is a four-year, public, research university located in Flagstaff, Arizona, offering 100 undergraduate majors in seven degree-granting colleges. NAU has an enrollment of more than 25,000 students, of whom 87% are undergraduates and 13% are graduates. Among the first-year cohort (more than 5,000 students), 61% identify as White, 4% as African American, 23% as Hispanic/Latino, 2% as Asian, and 2% as Native American. The average age of this group is 18.1, 60% are female, 90% live in residential housing, and 43% are first in their family to attend college.

Description of the Seminar

NAU offers a letter-graded, three-credit, basic study skills first-year seminar (FYS), NAU:120 Study Skills and College Success, which meets twice weekly for 75 minutes. The FYS is housed within Academic Affairs in an academic department focused on student success. The seminar is required for students admitted with a high school GPA of 2.75 or below (approximately 8%), which institutional assessment has demonstrated is a predictor of poor academic performance and attrition. Other students can petition to enroll in the FYS and make up less than .01% of the enrolled students.

Course development follows the backward design model (see Figure 1), with the learning outcomes identified first. Grounded in self-regulated learning (Schunk, 2015; Zimmerman, 2002), mindset theory (Dweck, 2007), and thriving (Schreiner, 2012), the FYS focuses on the development of academic skills; help-seeking behavior and use of campus resources; personal development resulting from self-reflection; as well as motivational goal setting; metacognition; self-management of time, health, and relationships; and understanding the critical thinking required to meet the expectations of college.

Figure 1. Backward curriculum design model.

The seminar is taught by a three-person Care Team (i.e., one lead faculty and two peer mentors) who follow a course-connected mentoring model (see Figure 2) that embeds individual peer mentoring appointments as a requirement. Most faculty have full-time appointments in an academic department focused exclusively on academic success; part-time instructors may be pulled in from the advising or student success community. The peers serve in an instructional capacity and are formal mentors.

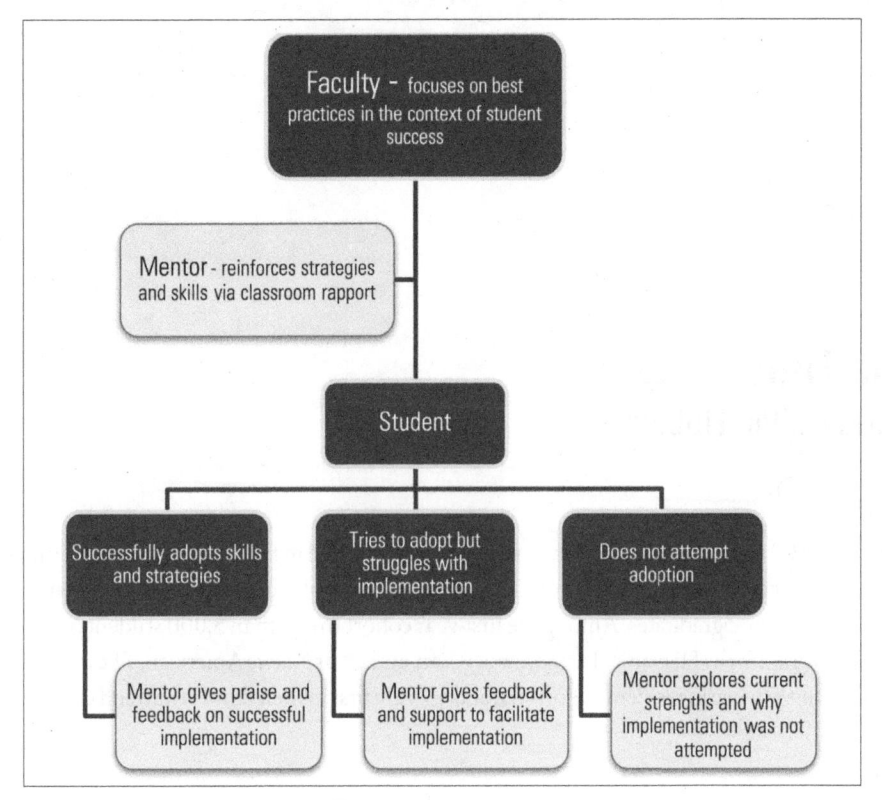

Figure 2. Course-connected mentoring model.

    The pedagogical approach uses active-learning strategies with the faculty and peer mentors fluidly exchanging the instructional role. During weekly Care Team meetings, roles within the lesson plans are assigned to ensure that the peer mentors are optimally positioned (e.g., presenting content or modeling skills). The Team also discusses individual student progress, merging the insights from homework, journals, class interactions, and mentoring appointments.

    Most assignments are constructed as traditional homework with a few additional experiences designed to increase strategy use and help-seeking behavior. For example, the passport assignment requires interaction with campus and community resources along four themes: academic, personal development, campus involvement, and beyond our campus. Students may choose among preselected experiences deemed optimal (e.g., Supplemental Instruction within the academic category) or propose ideas that best fit their needs.

Educationally Effective Practices

    Expectation set at appropriately high level. Students are assigned two writing projects: a transition reflection and a research paper. Expectations for these assignments are set at college level, and faculty are mindful that these writing assignments facilitate the student's transition to more rigorous academic work. Rubrics are provided to articulate standards and expectations, and time is spent in class reviewing steps toward successful completion of the assignment.

    The reflection paper is capstone in nature, supporting all learning outcomes by asking students to think about their goals, expectations of higher education, use of resources, and ability to engage in help-seeking behavior over the course of the semester. In the short research paper, students explore topics they believe are important to first-year students and argue the importance relative to student success. The assignment requires college-level writing and the use of multiple sources, including a peer-reviewed journal article. By asking students to think critically about an article and use those arguments to back up their writing, the paper supports the learning outcome related to the essential role of critical thinking as an expectation in higher education.

    Significant investment of time and effort. The research paper is assigned early in the semester, and students are scaffolded through the writing process in classroom workshop sessions focused on identifying a topic, outlining, close reading of academic articles, thesis writing, breaking down tasks, using resources, and developing a rough draft. These sessions help maintain a productive pace that promotes successful assignment completion.

Interactions with faculty and peers. For a basic study skills seminar, we purport that any topic relating to student academic, personal, or healthy well-being is substantive due to its clear ties to the learning outcomes and its foundational relevance to student success. To foster conversation around these topics, the seminar uses several approaches for formal and informal faculty–student and peer mentor–student interactions both in and out of the classroom.

Faculty–Student. A primary strategy for fostering informal faculty–student interactions is the faculty office hours assignment. The goal of the assignment is to provide students an experience engaging in resource use and demystify the help-seeking behavior related to faculty office hours. This meeting occurs at the beginning of the semester to establish rapport early and uses the student's transition to college and his or her goals as the agenda. Faculty use this information to connect and become more familiar with students' individual needs and experiences, to better match needs to resources, and to identify opportunities for campus engagement.

Additional faculty–student interaction occurs through journaling, creating a two-way dialogue between the student and instructor and a mode for reflection. This dialogue is cued by questions in class tied to course topics (e.g., time management, test taking, feedback) or serves as a vehicle for students to reach out with any concerns. The indirectness of the journal provides a safer space for students to access help. Over the years, the journal has elicited concerns about low-risk issues, such as time management and reading strategies, as well as high-risk disclosure, such as drug abuse, depression, and self-harm. The purpose of the journal is to normalize the self-advocacy that leads to help-seeking behavior and resource use.

Peer Mentor–Student. The course-connected mentoring model allows for peers to have individualized interactions regarding student adoption of strategies and behaviors. These interactions are successful because the peer mentors ask open-ended questions about performance barriers and then tailor approaches. For example, this process might result in identifying Psychology 101 Supplemental Instruction sessions for a student with the goal of an *A* or a developing nuanced time-management strategy around a student's work schedule.

The peer mentors are frequently situated at the intersection of challenging conversations when students self-disclose the underlying reasons behind absences, sleep disturbances, or emotional distress. The peer mentors are provided with a number of strategies to support students through these difficulties, including a campus suicide prevention model, and are adept at making referrals to NAU resources

Frequent and constructive feedback. A unique aspect of the FYS approach is direct instruction on Zimmerman's (2002) model of self-regulated learning, which is simplified as planning, doing, and reflecting. Students are provided a variety of ideas for being metacognitive by reflecting on and monitoring their own learning so they are not solely dependent on instructor feedback or exam results. For example, students are encouraged to place a sticky note at the bottom of a brief section of text. Arriving at the sticky note serves as a cue to reflect on understanding and to implement corrective action if attention has wandered or meaning is not clear. Further, for all assignments, students receive feedback through rubrics, which are available when the assignments are made and verbally overviewed in class. Students are given explicit instruction on how to use rubrics as a feedback mechanism to monitor assignment completion and cued on how to transfer this skill to other courses. After grading, the rubric provides detailed feedback about unmet expectations.

In addition, students receive feedback through the University's Grade Performance Status (GPS) platform, which is tied to course rosters in the student information system and generates individual, small group, or whole class FERPA-compliant e-mails. GPS allows the faculty to provide feedback about attendance, grades, and class participation as well as due date reminders or campus events announcements.

As depicted in Figure 2, a foundational component of the course-connected mentoring model is the peer mentors' ability to provide individualized feedback to students. This feedback occurs intentionally during guided review of a few specific assignments. For example, students develop a planner that includes all assignments for all courses, and one mentoring appointment is focused on reviewing the planner. Feedback is provided on the planner and student's overall approach to time management.

Finally, course feedback is grounded in the growth mindset framework (Dweck, 2007). When faculty or mentors provide feedback, they assume that unmet expectations are the result of a performance barrier that one could grow to overcome, rather than a fixed perspective on which the student is stuck due to lack of motivation, care, or laziness.

Instead of messages stating, "You were absent" or "Where were you?" students receive messages stating, "I didn't see you. Is everything ok?" or "I missed you today. Let me know what I can do help you get caught up." The growth mindset framework provides a gentler access point for returning to class because the message conveys the assumption that the absence could not be avoided. This offsets the shame associated with returning to class or submitting late work and keeps the lines of communication open.

Periodic and structured opportunities for reflection and integration. All sections of the FYS are linked to liberal studies courses (e.g., humanities, biology) that meet degree plan and liberal studies requirements. For example, one section of FYS might be paired with Biology: Unity of Life 1, meaning that all students in that FYS section are co-enrolled in the same section of biology in which 25 seats were reserved for them. This approach applies the self-regulated learning strategies from the FYS to the linked course. Faculty receive the syllabus for the linked course and then create opportunities for applied connections. For example, together they might develop a test preparation schedule for an exam in the linked course that includes the effective study skills and time management strategies learned in the seminar. Faculty are also able to use the notes, tests, and reading passages from the linked course to demonstrate strategies such as note taking, test taking, and text annotation. After major exams in the linked course, instructors model how to reflect on performance feedback to plan for the next exams.

Discussion

In the FYS's backward-design model (see Figure 1), evaluation of the educationally effective practices occurs during the last phase of the model when the faculty and FYS coordinator reflect on the alignment of the learning, instruction, and assessment to the learning outcomes. The extensive use of low-stakes assessments with rubrics allows faculty to informally evaluate whether the learning outcomes are achieved and how the educationally effective practices are supporting that achievement. They can make course corrections by enhancing instruction with additional activities or having the peer mentors address issues with specific students during mentoring.

For the course, the FYS coordinator collects systematic feedback from the faculty to assess the overall effect of the curriculum on the achievement of the learning outcomes. This assessment includes general suggestions about the practices and approaches as well as specific feedback about how each activity facilitates learning outcome achievement as evidenced by student performance. The feedback is part of the course's continuous improvement cycle, during which the coordinator makes adjustments to the learning outcomes, the pedagogical approaches, educationally effective practices, assignments, and rubrics.

Formally, the educationally effective practices are indirectly assessed by examining the efficacy of FYS as a retention strategy. Considerable institutional assessment supports that NAU 120 is effective in retaining students from the first to the second year of college. Before the course was required, NAU 120 demonstrated a positive impact on retention for five semesters after course completion as compared to a matched sample of nonparticipants (Campbell et al., 2016). This is an important analysis, as future assessment will be challenging without a comparison group, now that the course is required for at-risk students. There are further plans to formally assess learning outcome achievement, another indirect measure of the efficacy of the educationally effective practices, by examining the pre- and post-test scores on the Motivated Strategies for Learning Questionnaire (Pintrich & DeGroot, 1990) to determine if the course is effective in enhancing academic abilities.

Implications

NAU's basic study skills FYS incorporates a variety of approaches that contribute to the efficacy of the course. The seminar

- includes several of the educationally effective practices identified by Kuh and O'Donnell (2103);
- addresses many of the criteria attributed to successful seminars (e.g., Keup & Petschauer, 2011), such as being offered for credit and centered in the student's curriculum; including collaboration between student affairs staff and faculty in training, design, and instruction; requiring faculty training and professional development;

using primarily full-time academic faculty; incorporating peer mentors; being housed in an academic department exclusively focused on student success; and regularly communicating effectiveness back to the campus community;

- is linked with a liberal studies requirement to foster applied connections; and
- grounds the curriculum in theories addressing learning and academic success, particularly self-regulated learning.

Due to NAU's intentional inclusion of these practices, the university has seen consistent impacts on student persistence. For example, a longitudinal analysis demonstrated that the course had a positive impact on student retention for as many as five semesters after the conclusion of the course (as compared to a matched sample of students [using propensity score analysis], Campbell et al., 2016). The implications for practice from this basic study skills seminar are to create a structure that is theoretically cohesive, collaboratively designed, and equivalent across all sections. As a highly coordinated course NAU's FYS is able to create a student experience aligned with learning outcomes that foster student success in an at-risk population.

References

Campbell, R. P., Chen, Z., Canning, C., Hublitz, K., Dickson, K. L., & Neff, L. (2016, February). *Longitudinal impact of two different first-year seminars: NAU 100 and NAU 120*. Presentation to the 35th Annual Conference on The First-Year Experience, Orlando, Florida.

Dweck, C. S. (2007). *Mindset: The new psychology of success.* New York, NY: Random House.

Keup, J. R., & Petschauer, J. W. (2011). *The first-year seminar: Designing, implementing, and assessing courses to support student learning and success: Vol. I. Designing and administering the course.* Columbia, SC: University of South Carolina, National Resource Center for The First-Year Experience and Students in Transition.

Kuh, G. D., & O'Donnell, K. (2013). *Ensuring quality and taking high-impact practices to scale.* Washington, DC: Association of American Colleges and Universities.

Pintrich, R. R., & DeGroot, E. V. (1990). Motivational and self-regulated learning components of classroom academic performance. *Journal of Educational Psychology, 82,* 33-40.

Schreiner, L. (2012). From surviving to thriving in transitions. In L. A. Schreiner, M. C. Louis, & D. D. Nelson (Eds.), *Thriving in transitions: A research-based approach to college student success* (pp. 1-18). Columbia, SC: University of South Carolina, National Resource Center for The First-Year Experience and Students in Transition.

Schunk, D. H. (2015). *Learning theories: An educational perspective* (7th ed.). Upper Saddle River, NJ: Pearson.

Zimmerman, B. J. (2002). Becoming a self-regulated learner: An overview. *Theory into Practice, 41*(2), 64-72.

Contact Information

Rebecca Campbell
Department of Educational Psychology
Northern Arizona University
Box 5774
Flagstaff, AZ 86011-5774
Phone: (928) 523-8225
E-mail: Rebecca.Campbell@nau.edu

Southern Methodist University
Caitlin Anderson, Takeshi Fujii, and Donna Gober

The Institution

Southern Methodist University (SMU) is a four-year, private institution located in Dallas, Texas, offering bachelor's degrees in 104 fields, master's degrees in 113 fields, and doctoral degrees in 28 through seven degree-granting schools. Although the main campus is located in Dallas, students have opportunities to complete coursework at SMU-in-Plano, SMU-in-Taos, and more than 150 study abroad programs. SMU enrolls more than 11,000 students, with roughly 6,000 students making up the undergraduate population and an average first-year class size of about 1,400. Approximately half the student body comes from outside the state of Texas; 13% are international students; between 25% and 27% self-identify as minority students; and 70% receive some form of financial aid, which includes both merit and need-based assistance. Undergraduate students are required to live on campus for two years and are assigned to one of 11 residential commons, which integrate the academic, residential, and social experience.

Description of the Seminar

As a graduation requirement, all students must complete Personal Responsibility and Wellness 1101: Concepts of Wellness (PRW-I). This one-credit, pass–fail seminar uses a wellness philosophy to aid students in their transition to college; provide them with the tools to be successful; and encourage them to make positive, relevant, and fulfilling choices ensuring independent growth and a lifetime of wellness. The course focuses on issues of attitude, adaptation to change, personal responsibility, and happiness; awareness of the relationship between thoughts and lifestyle choices; and the connection to an improved sense of meaning, purpose, and well-being. Full-time lecturers in the Department of Applied Physiology and Wellness teach approximately 1,200 students through 36 sections in the fall and 450 students through 20 sections in the spring. Because the seminar is designed to ease the transition to college life, students are encouraged to take it during the first semester of their first year.

Through quality instruction, meaningful content, and student-centered learning environments, the Wellness faculty maintains a curriculum where students are challenged to think critically about their identities and the decisions they are making. Students are introduced to the works of authors, theorists, and researchers as well as current topics in wellness for the college population. Wellness is approached through living a life of quality—a dynamic state where an individual assumes a proactive and holistic approach to life by perpetual assessment of choices, behaviors, and attitudes. The multidimensional aspects of this philosophy are contained in eight domains: spiritual, physical, emotional, occupational, intellectual, environmental, financial, and social. This model provides a foundation for a wide range of interdisciplinary experiences, both in and out of the classroom, in which students are presented with opportunities to progress toward their individual potentials.

Educationally Effective Practices

Interaction with faculty and peers. PRW-I is highly interactive in nature. Sections are capped at 35 students to encourage participation. To create an environment where students feel safe expressing how they think and feel, faculty begin the semester focusing on the social dimension of wellness. Through name games, dyadic encounters, and other get-to-know-you activities, students start to connect with their peers in a more meaningful and authentic way. The goal is that students will report they made new acquaintances because of this class.

The course relies on a variety of small-group discussions and partner work to explore different aspects of the curriculum. At the beginning of the semester, students are given the permission to disagree—with each other and their professor—and are asked to bring their authentic voices to the conversation. By validating student opinions and encouraging respectful discourse, instructors create an environment where students are valued and included. An intended outcome is that students will report their faculty member created an atmosphere where they felt comfortable and relaxed.

Significant investment of time and effort and real-world application. Because PRW-I is an academic, credit-bearing course, students are expected to invest time and effort into understanding the material and applying it to their real-life situations. They are required to attend class for all contact hours (three hours per week), allowing faculty to create a trusting and inclusive environment with the students and to cover the breadth of the multidimensional content.

An integral piece of the course is that students must complete four out-of-class experiences (OCEs) related to one of the eight dimensions of wellness, such as attending a lecture, an artistic performance, a student organization meeting, or a worship service; participating in a volunteer project; or modifying a current behavior. The students write descriptions of these experiences, along with what they learned about well-being and themselves. OCEs provide students with opportunities to apply classroom learning to real-life experiences and to begin to establish new habits. An intended outcome is that through this self-directed, experiential learning, students will be able to find ways to apply lessons learned in the course to everyday experiences for the rest of their lives.

Experiences with diversity. Students come to SMU from all 50 states, the District of Columbia, and nearly 100 foreign countries. It is a diverse group, and they must learn to navigate social relationships with people who are different from themselves. The Elements of Identity assignment is designed to help students learn more about diversity. Students give five-minute presentations designed to reveal more about themselves than what people see on the surface. They have creative freedom with this assignment; some have played instruments, performed monologues, read poetry, and developed games to share with the class an element they feel is integral to their identity. These presentations are deeply personal, which helps foster a trusting, inclusive classroom environment.

In addition, staff from the Office of Multicultural Student Affairs come to the PRW-I classes to discuss diverse perspectives and identity development as it relates to social well-being as well as to make students aware of their services and to create a more inclusive campus environment. Using a Values Line activity, students position themselves along a continuum (*agree* at one end; *disagree* at the other) in response to a series of questions. They are encouraged to bring their own unique narratives to the discussion and openly and authentically share their points of view. Students are immediately confronted with differing perspectives and practice articulating their opinions while allowing for others to bring conflicting, yet equally authentic, perspectives to the conversation. A learning outcome of these activities is that students will be more understanding of others.

Periodic and structured opportunities for reflection and integration. The PRW-I curriculum highlights the interconnection of the intellectual, emotional, and physical dimensions of wellness. Students are introduced to the idea that thoughts impact feelings, which then affect behaviors and choices. Theories related to attitude, cognitive distortions, and habitual mindsets are taught and discussed. An integral piece is challenging students to reflect on their choices and resulting outcomes. In lieu of a final exam, students write reflective essays responding to the prompt, *What I got out of Wellness.* The essays are not graded but are used to measure one of PRW-I's student learning outcomes: Students will demonstrate an understanding of the relationship between lifestyle choices and wellness.

Because the cornerstone of this curriculum is understanding how choices impact wellness, students are introduced to a wide range of topics that encourage self-evaluation as it relates to each of the different dimensions of wellness (e.g., lessons on integrity ask students to examine their core values; financial wellness units have students look at their budgeting and savings habits). In addition, students complete different personality inventories to better understand how they interact with others. These lessons, coupled with the OCEs previously discussed, give students the time to reflect on their own habits. The intended outcome of this is that students report the lessons and time for reflection helped them to better understand themselves.

Discussion

Since 2012, the seminar's educationally effective practices have been assessed through the achievement of course and student learning outcomes using an anonymous, end-of-semester evaluation and a rubric for the final reflective essay. Table 1 presents the average percentage of students giving positive responses across all course offerings since fall 2012 and selected findings related to the reflective essays.

Table 1

Intended Outcomes of PRW-1, Fall 2012 – Fall 2015 (N = 5,882)

Educationally effective practice	Source	Outcome	Percent of positive responses
Time and effort	End-of-semester evaluation	1. Students will demonstrate an attitude change towards wellness.	
		My attitude about wellness before taking PRW-I	51%
		My attitude about wellness after taking PRW-I	91%
Real-world application	End-of-semester evaluation	2. I can use the lessons learned for the rest of my life.	87%
Interaction with faculty and peers	End-of-semester evaluation	3. I have made new acquaintances.	83%
		4. The instructor created an atmosphere in which I felt comfortable and relaxed.	97%
Diversity	End-of-semester evaluation	5. This helped me think with more understanding towards others.	83%
Reflection and integration	End-of-semester evaluation	6. This helped me better understand myself.	78%
		7. This encouraged me to examine the way I think.	85%
	Reflective essay rubric (Spring 2013, n = 1,864)	8. Students will be able to demonstrate an understanding of the relationship between lifestyle choices and wellness.	91%

Note. For Outcomes 2 – 7, percentage of students giving a rating of 3 or better on a 5-point Likert scale where 1 = *Not True* and 5 = *Definitely True*. For Outcome 8, percentage of students demonstrating developing, accomplished, or exemplary understanding of connection between lifestyle choices and wellness.

For the time and effort educationally effective practice (Outcome 1), at the beginning of the semester, an average of 51% of the students surveyed reported feeling positive about the wellness curriculum, with that number increasing to 91% by the end of the term. Students also had overwhelmingly positive responses (ranging from 78% to 97%) for outcomes measured on the semester evaluations (Outcomes 2-7). The final reflection essay, in addition to assessing Outcome 8, provided in-depth and personal testimony, enabling faculty to appreciate student perspectives and obtain feedback to enhance teaching, content, and pedagogy. These essays are rich in qualitative data supporting educationally effective practices, and the Wellness department has submitted a request to secure funding for qualitative data analysis software so that a full study can be conducted.

Implications

The PRW-I seminar at SMU not only assists students in their transition to college but also promotes lifelong learning, constant self-exploration, and a lasting positive outlook. The use of educationally effective practices has enabled the Wellness Department to achieve these goals as well as course and student learning outcomes. PRW-1, and the practices used within it, consistently and positively impact student attitudes and learning.

A crucial piece to the seminar's success is the reputation and credibility of the Wellness department and its faculty. As a well-recognized academic unit for more than 30 years, this department could more easily garner university support for a required course. In addition, because the PRW-1's faculty members do not have research or service requirements, their full attention is on enhancing the course content and pedagogy.

Finally, consistent and thorough evaluation of the seminar and its objectives is essential to this program's success. Measuring student attitudes and learning is important not only for accreditation purposes but also for understanding content and program effectiveness. Assessing vigorously and often has provided our department with the information needed to ensure an ongoing commitment to the wellness curricular philosophy, current pedagogical practices, and analysis of student trends.

Contact Information

Caitlin Anderson
Lecturer of Wellness
Southern Methodist University
Dedman Center for Lifetime Sports
6005 Bush Ave #013
Dallas, TX 75205
E-mail: caitlina@smu.edu
Phone: (214) 768-2327

Southwestern Michigan College
Christi Young, Jeffrey Dennis, and Donald Ludman

The Institution

Southwestern Michigan College (SMC) is a public, two-year community college located in rural Cass County, Michigan, offering 33 concentrations within its Associate of Arts and Associate of Science degree programs. Its Associate of Applied Science program includes 44 degree options. The A.A. and A.S. degrees assist students in completing general education credits in anticipation of eventual transfer to a four-year institution. The A.A.S. is an occupational track degree that prepares students for immediate entry into the skilled labor force.

For fall 2016, SMC enrolled 2,348 students, 638 of whom were degree-seeking first-year students. Among the first-year students, 72% were White, 11% were African American, 5% were Hispanic, 2% were Native American, and 1% were Asian. The remaining 10% were listed as *other* or *unknown*. Females outnumbered males 58% to 42% in this cohort. One in six first-year students lived on campus, and 57.3% represented their family's first generation in college.

Description of the Seminar

Community colleges are characteristically diverse institutions, attracting students of a wide range of ability levels, socioeconomic backgrounds, and future plans. One feature evident, nonetheless, across much of today's community college population is the apparent disconnect between students' present behavior and their ambitions and future expectations. Many entering students appear to lack the self-awareness and plan of execution essential for college success. Consequently, all students now enrolling at SMC in A.A. or A.S. degree programs (as opposed to high school guest students or occupational track students) are advised to register for EDUC 120 (Educational Exploration) with the goal to generate a better informed, more viable academic and post-SMC plan.

EDUC 120 is a two-credit course convening twice each week in one-hour sessions. The course meetings follow a schedule, which integrates reflection journals, in-class activities, full-class discussions, and a broad range of campus engagement opportunities. The seminar helps students prepare for success in college and beyond by focusing on (a) college expectations and practices; (b) self-motivation and study strategies; and (c) personal finance, stress management, and other life skills. Learning outcomes include the ability to

- navigate fluently within essential academic services and policies,
- research relevant college majors and career opportunities,
- understand the transfer process and articulate long-range planning,
- deepen introspection and critical thinking so as to heighten self-awareness and empathy,
- engage in professional college relationships and career networking,
- develop sound financial practices and enhance personal well-being (mind–body–spirit), and
- contribute meaningfully to the success of others in college and future walks of life.

The principal instructors of EDUC 120 are veteran teachers with service on the College Retention Committee and participation at the National Resource Center for The First-Year Experience and Students in Transition's Annual Conference on The First-Year Experience. Thus, the course is entrusted to standouts among the faculty. SMC administrators schedule simultaneous sections to enhance an effective team-teaching approach. Additionally, expert staff members are brought in to assist with instruction for specialized topics (e.g., financial literacy, learning styles, résumé writing, and transfer preparation).

A common syllabus is used by all instructors and includes a helpful overview of course pedagogy. To further ensure consistency among the sections, an instructor's manual was created in 2013, providing major assignments, prompts for reflective journaling and application, and a variety of engaging activities. Beyond offering a general template for teaching the course, the manual is sufficiently flexible and detailed to encourage faculty selection of specific strategies and materials as may best serve the personality of a given class. To wit, the manual seeks to honor academic freedom, even while it maintains a standard of continuity among the instructional sections.

Educationally Effective Practices

Opportunities for reflection, integration, and constructive feedback. The life plan assignment focuses on establishing a set of life goals, including the description, achievement of, and planning for hardships that may interfere with the goals. This assignment consists of a two- to three-page paper that identifies and discusses five leading goals beyond formal education (e.g., career entry and professional service, marriage and family life, personal fitness and stress management, community service and civic engagement, lifelong learning and spiritual development, travel, hobbies and recreation). It requires students to think seriously about what constitutes the highest priorities in their academic and personal lives and guides them in a more informed manner to visualize specifically what a college education can help them to achieve.

Another assignment that fosters reflection and integration is the education plan, which elaborates a formative strategy toward the successful completion of a college program. In a two- to three-page paper, students limn out the particular classes needed using a form prepared by the SMC Academic Advising office. This electronic and highly adaptable document concisely maps the requirements and sequences of courses needed to achieve a chosen degree. Students are required to explain the selection of a major as well as secondary field of study, develop a tentative semester-by-semester (with transfer) agenda, and reflect on likely challenges and rewards to be experienced in higher education. Further, to contemplate beyond their time at SMC, students are urged to begin researching possible choices of four-year major and to identify amenable transfer institutions.

The bulk of student assessment is taken from the major course assignments. Reflection journals, which are submitted and assessed weekly, provide a significant contribution to the course grade. The journals, in fact, have proven a highly meaningful task for the class, as they require students to consider in-depth what it means to be a college student, how to be successful at SMC, and how the college experience can fit naturally within the larger frame of life. Reflections are submitted through an online learning management system, to be read only by the instructor with prompt feedback given to students. In class, journal responses are commonly used as springboards for discussion. EDUC 120 reflection prompts include the following:

- Why am I in college?
- How does SMC fit with me?
- How well am I managing my time?
- How do I prepare for transfer?
- How will I pay for higher education?
- What can I learn from my faculty advisor?
- Which major and career are right for me?
- How can I improve my critical thinking and creativity?
- How can I improve my academic performance?
- How can I improve my fulfillment and contribution in life?

EDUC 120 faculty plan carefully to match activities and to focus a week's discussion on the designated journal topic. For example, professional communication, meeting etiquette, and networking are introduced in class during the week in which students are assigned the task of interviewing their faculty advisors. Similarly, when students reflect on financial literacy, that week's activities include a student-generated budget based on an entry-level post-college job, with consideration given to potential student loan obligations.

Relevance in the curriculum and student interaction with peers and faculty. Students who drop out of college often believe that academic life is largely incongruous with real life. Nothing and no one seems to be there for them. EDUC 120 serves to reduce these beliefs. Students gain experience working proactively and collaboratively through class activities designed to address salient themes such as networking, financial independence, transfer to a four-year institution, lifelong learning, and wellness. These relevant, mutual efforts help reinforce practical resiliency and commitment to college life.

Strength in academic advising, paired with authentic instructor concern for student success, helps build meaningful connections between EDUC 120 students and the SMC faculty and larger college community. Cornerstone to the education plan assignment, for example, are one-on-one consultations with the faculty member teaching the course and with the students' faculty advisors. Such meetings effectively cultivate an understanding and cohesion between students and their mentors that persists long after the course itself ends. It is common to see students seek out their former EDUC 120 faculty for coursework within their discipline and to recognize them at the annual awards banquet or at graduation.

Public demonstration of competence. The EDUC 120 *portfolio* serves to compile and archive all assignments completed in the course. Indexed entries include lecture and discussion notes, class activities and handouts, reading responses and journal reflections, and copies of the life and education plans. Students collate clean copies of each document in preparation for an end-of-semester summative presentation. EDUC 120 content is delivered during the first 11 of the 14 weeks of the course. Beginning in Week 12, students take the lead, revealing in formal presentations what they have learned through the class about themselves, their goals, and their full potential. Students are advised to save their portfolios for future reference and development beyond the course.

From specific portfolio documents, as well as from the general class experience, EDUC 120 students construct their final projects—the *class presentation*. The 8- to 10-minute presentation includes a visual aid (e.g., PowerPoint, Prezi), reflects meaningful introspection, and demonstrates critical thinking about core academic and life goals. The presentation is assessed on its delivery, organization, fluency, engagement, and professionalism.

Discussion

EDUC 120 instructors are expected to engage in timely, accurate review of student progress relevant to course learning outcomes and effective educational practices. Both in-course as well as post-course assessments are consulted in this regard. In-course assessments include the weekly reflection journals, summative assignments (i.e., life plan, education plan, portfolio), formal class presentation, and cumulative final exam. The final has been designed primarily to measure attainment in the specified learning outcomes. An average final exam score of 84% across multiple sections of the course indicates pedagogical effectiveness.

Post-course assessment is undertaken through anonymous student course surveys, which are administered and reviewed with care by EDUC 120 instructors each semester. Almost all students (92%) reported receiving timely and ongoing feedback that allowed them to monitor their academic progress successfully. Student comments highlight the effectiveness of specific educational practice, especially those that support reflection and student–faculty integration. Students point to a variety of course activities that support reflection and integration, as the following comments suggest:

> I really enjoyed the journals and the EDP. It made me sit and think about exactly what I wanted to accomplish in my life, and it helped me map out my college career.

> Even if it might change, I now know how to plan my classes well.

> I really liked the transfer evaluation section. It really helped me get into what I was doing after this college. I now know where to find information and what my outline for the next few courses are! Also it was a bittersweet concept of the cost of college, because it's good to know what I am up for, but it's a pretty depressing fact.

The activity that helped me the most was the EDP activity. That made me able to understand what classes I will need for the upcoming semesters and ... at the college I plan to transfer to.

The journal entries for our portfolio really opened my eyes on how I am as a student and what to look forward to in the future.

The end of the semester project helped me to focus on what I really wanted out of college. It gave me a chance to figure out what course of action I wanted to take during the next years of college and also helped me research which colleges would be best to transfer to.

The presentation ... kept me on track with my goals and made me really think and consider "Is this what I really want to do?" It provided a perfect opportunity for me to see my long term goals as well as my short term goals.

Opportunities for interaction were also highlighted in student comments as being important to their overall engagement in the course and sense of belonging in the larger community.

I really liked the way [my instructor] used classroom discussion. It made us think about a lot of things from a different perspective.

I enjoyed the class discussion. I felt included in the conversation and was encouraged to participate.

She [the instructor] was very understanding, and I knew I could come to her for anything.
[The instructor] created a very comfortable learning environment in which students could speak openly, and I really appreciated how he encouraged everyone to be involved.

With the first full EDUC 120 cohort graduating in spring 2016, SMC students are reaping the benefits of notably improved retention and completion. Institutional analysis reveals that during the program's first three years, 74% of full-time students completing EDUC 120 (285 out of 385) were retained from one fall semester to the next, as compared to 52% of full-time students not enrolling in the course (610 out of 1,183). Among part-time students, the EDUC 120 effect upon annual retention appears yet more pronounced: 68% of EDUC 120 students (15 out of 22) as opposed to 35% of the students who did not complete the course (121 out of 349) were retained to the following semester.

Implications

EDUC 120 undergoes continuous review and revision as helpful student feedback and faculty suggestions are received each semester. The instructor manual serves as a living product that can be adapted and expanded as instructional experience associated with the course grows. EDUC 120 exemplifies how collaboration and innovation could be inculcated across the wider college curriculum. For certainly any subject—indeed, the general college mission—would benefit from the integration of students, faculty, staff, and community and the mix of instructional uniformity and flexibility this course offers.

Given the increased retention and graduation rates, SMC is considering whether EDUC 120 should be required of all on-campus students. In the near future, the course may be required of any A.A. or A.S. candidate. With the data in hand, the institution is giving great attention to the instruction of this class, staffing it with faculty who want to bring fresh energy, expertise, and optimism toward heightened student success.

Contact Information

Christi Young
Chair of Social Sciences
Faculty
Southwestern Michigan College
58900 Cherry Grove Road
Dowagiac, MI 49047
E-mail: cyoung@swmich.edu
Phone: (269) 782-1251

St. Cloud State University
Christine Metzo

The Institution

St. Cloud State University is a midsized, four-year, public, comprehensive university, located in St. Cloud, Minnesota, and offering more than 75 undergraduate majors in its eight degree-granting colleges and schools. In fall 2015, St. Cloud State had an enrollment of 15,461 students, of whom 13,630 were undergraduates and 1,863 were first-year students. Among undergraduate students, 75% are White, 6% are African American, 3% are Hispanic, 5% are Asian, less than 1% are Native American, 6% are international, and 3% identify as two or more races. Additionally, 83% of St. Cloud State's undergraduates are Minnesota residents; 14% are 25 years or older; 47% are male; and 15% live in campus housing, though 69% of first-year students live on campus.

Description of the Seminar

St. Cloud State's Academic Collegiate Excellence (ACE) Program has a long tradition of offering robust support to promising incoming students who do not meet the traditional admission criteria. The ACE population, comprising 18.4% of first-year students in fall 2015, has a higher percentage of students of color than the overall undergraduate cohort (36% vs. 15%, respectively) and is considered academically at-risk, based on low high school rank and/or low ACT scores. Students are referred by Admissions staff to complete a set of short online essays, which address their readiness for college. These are then scored by Admissions and ACE program staff and faculty using a noncognitive variable rubric, and a final Admissions decision is made. The assessed noncognitive variables include long-term goals, the ability to successfully negotiate the system, availability of a strong support person, realistic self-appraisal, community service, leadership experience, knowledge in a field, and positive self-concept. Students admitted into ACE are required to enroll in a pair of two-credit first-year seminars (FYSs): COLL 110: Reading and Study Strategies (focused on basic study strategies) and COLL 150: Discovering the College Experience (an extended orientation).

COLL 110 is taught by a core faculty member in the Department of Academic Support and covers skills such as note taking, learning styles, study habits, and effective reading and test-taking strategies. Diverse instructors, including faculty and staff from University College and other departments campuswide, teach COLL 150 to foster instructor–student mentoring relationships and create a network of campus allies who can support this at-risk population. COLL 150 addresses goal setting, major and career exploration, an examination of identity, and an introduction to campus resources. The FYSs are sometimes linked with an additional general education course, which provides a small learning-community-style model for seminar delivery. FYS class size is capped at 20 to 22 students who take both courses together. If a general education course is added, the COLL 110 instructor attends at least one session in that class and uses that course content to introduce reading and study strategies. Students are further supported by ACE program staff and their academic advisors.

Peer mentors are the final members of the FYS teaching team, and they are often former ACE students, bringing first-hand knowledge of course content, challenges, and successes. They function as role models and cofacilitators both in and out of the classroom. Mentors have their primary assignment in COLL 150; however, because the students are a cohort, mentors may also work with COLL 110, depending on the pedagogical style of the instructors.

Fostering collegiality is an important component of the development of a shared purpose in supporting ACE students in their transition. COLL 110 faculty are invited to the annual spring workshop for new COLL 150 instructors, and everyone (mentors included) comes together for a kick-off reception the week before new students arrive on campus. Instructors are encouraged to communicate periodically about students in their classes who are struggling, and the team approach facilitates collaboration with other team members to devise collective and consistent student support strategies.

Educationally Effective Practices

Interactions with faculty and peers. One of the most important elements of this team approach is the structured, intentional interactions with faculty and peer mentors. Students meet with their peer mentors for three required one-on-one meetings (i.e., beginning, middle, and end of term). In these 20- to 30-minute sessions, mentors provide both formal and informal support. For example, at a typical first meeting, mentors will require students to bring a planner and all their syllabi to help develop a time-management strategy. Although time management is often one of the most articulated student worries, these sessions frequently reveal that students already know a lot of the basics. The individualized sessions simply hone and apply those skills. For the instructional team, this information has made later conversations about time management more meaningful and relevant. The requirement to bring a planner also takes away the inevitable awkwardness of the first mentor meeting. Mentors report greater success and satisfaction with their first meetings when they integrate the formal and practical exercise and report that, in general, students open up more about themselves.

In addition to the mentor meetings, many COLL 150 instructors require one-on-one meetings with their students, often in conjunction with projects or assignments, as well as regular opportunities for reflection on the transition experience. Instructors practice pedagogies that engage the students in frequent and significant small-group activities in class, such as case study analysis or small group scavenger hunts. Further, because the students are in two or three classes together and take both seminars as a cohort, they develop strong bonds over the course of the year.

Periodic and structured opportunities for reflection and integration. Class reflection opportunities include one-minute papers, short responses and assessments, or think–pair–share exercises. Outside class, students complete journal reflections on a regular basis, structured around particular prompts that encourage them to engage with their own development and personal growth as well as reflect on how they are integrating into college life and using campus resources. These assignments allow faculty both to get to know their students more personally and to provide individual guidance and feedback. Sample journal prompts include the following:

- If someone were to ask, "what kind of student are you?" how would you answer? If someone were to ask, "what kind of student would you like to be?" how would you answer? What are three concrete things that you think you can do to become the student you want to be?

- If you had to select only one, which would contribute more to your academic motivation – your values, needs, or expectations? Why? How satisfied are you with your current academic motivation? Explain.

- What experience do you have with research? How has your experience prepared you for college-level expectations? What are your research strengths and weaknesses? How will you improve on your weaknesses?

Every section of COLL 150 has some version of a culminating reflective essay. This essay might be framed as a self-portrait, a college narrative, or simply the last in a series of regular journal entries where the students are asked to consider their personal and academic growth over the course of their first semester in college. Many instructors use the tool of a letter-to-self completed in the first week of classes and returned to students in the final weeks of term. The students are asked to reflect on who they were at the beginning of the semester, how they have grown, and where they see themselves now. This reflection typically integrates a culminating opportunity for an articulation of goals.

Frequent and constructive feedback. In both courses, particularly in COLL 110, there are regular low-stakes assignments on which students receive significant feedback. These assignments range from in-class exercises with immediate instructor verbal feedback to online applications of the reading and study strategies, with immediate correctives and written feedback. Whatever the assignment, students are invited to apply it to their lives. Final culminating essays in COLL 150 are built on the feedback from earlier reflections and assignments, which press students to go deeper into their reflections and apply their first-semester experiences to their future selves. Just as the periodic reflections in COLL 150 focus the student on themselves and their own lives, the COLL 110 assignments are designed to have students work the note-taking, reading, learning, and test-taking strategies through courses in which they are actually enrolled, especially any linked general education courses where they can collectively discuss in the seminar the value and relevance of the strategies and techniques they are learning. The COLL 110 instructor and mentor also facilitate student study sessions for exams and use the principles of the course material in the structure and timing of those sessions.

Discussion

St. Cloud State does not currently have FYSs for the general student population, and institutional data have shown that new students in the bottom half of the regularly admitted first-year cohort do significantly worse than ACE students. In fall 2015, 38% of ACE students had GPAs at or above their high school cumulative GPAs, with 6% earning 3.5 or higher. Non-ACE students with a similar entering profile had cumulative GPAs 0.20 lower than ACE students at the end of their first year.

Data from fall 2015 COLL 150 end-of-course evaluations demonstrate that approximately 80% of students saw the course as significant for building connections to the institution and with their peers. The instructor and mentor were perceived as positive forces in students' educational journeys and genuinely interested in students' success (see Table 1). Further, in responses to a question asking how instructors fostered a connection to St. Cloud State, students recognized instructors' personal engagement as a significant hallmark of the course's success in facilitating their transition. While providing an introduction to campus resources is an explicit FYS learning outcome, in this free-response question nearly a quarter of the students noted the personal engagement they felt from their instructors.

Table 1

Student Evaluation Responses on Selected Questions Relating to Interaction With Faculty and Peers, Fall 2015 (n = 343)

Survey item	Agree/Strongly Agree	Disagree/Strongly Disagree
The course helped me to build relationships with St. Cloud State University faculty, staff, and students.	80.5%	19.4%
The instructor was a positive force in and out of the classroom and challenged student learning in a supportive environment.	83.0%	17.0%
The instructor showed interest in my overall success.	81.8%	18.2%
The peer mentor was a positive force in and out of the classroom and challenged student learning in a supportive environment.	81.8%	18.2%
I talked to and spent time with my peer mentor outside of class.	74.7%	25.3%
The peer mentor showed interest in my overall success.	80.0%	20.0%

The effectiveness of real-world application of the reading and study strategies is demonstrated by The Learning and Study Strategies Inventory (LASSI), given to all COLL 110 students to measure changes in study behaviors over the duration of the semester. The LASSI is a 10-scale, 80-item pre-/post-test assessment of students' awareness and use of learning and study strategies related to skill, will, and self-regulation components of strategic learning. Its focus is on behaviors, attitudes, and beliefs that can be changed through educational interventions, particularly in classes like those offered by the ACE program. Fall 2015 LASSI results, which were similar to previous semesters, revealed that students in COLL 110 improved their performance on every measure on the 10 scales (see Figure 1). Further evidence of the success of this strategy is that ACE students are performing in the top half of the general education courses. St. Cloud State is conducting in-depth data analysis looking at the predictive capacity of the LASSI results for future success.

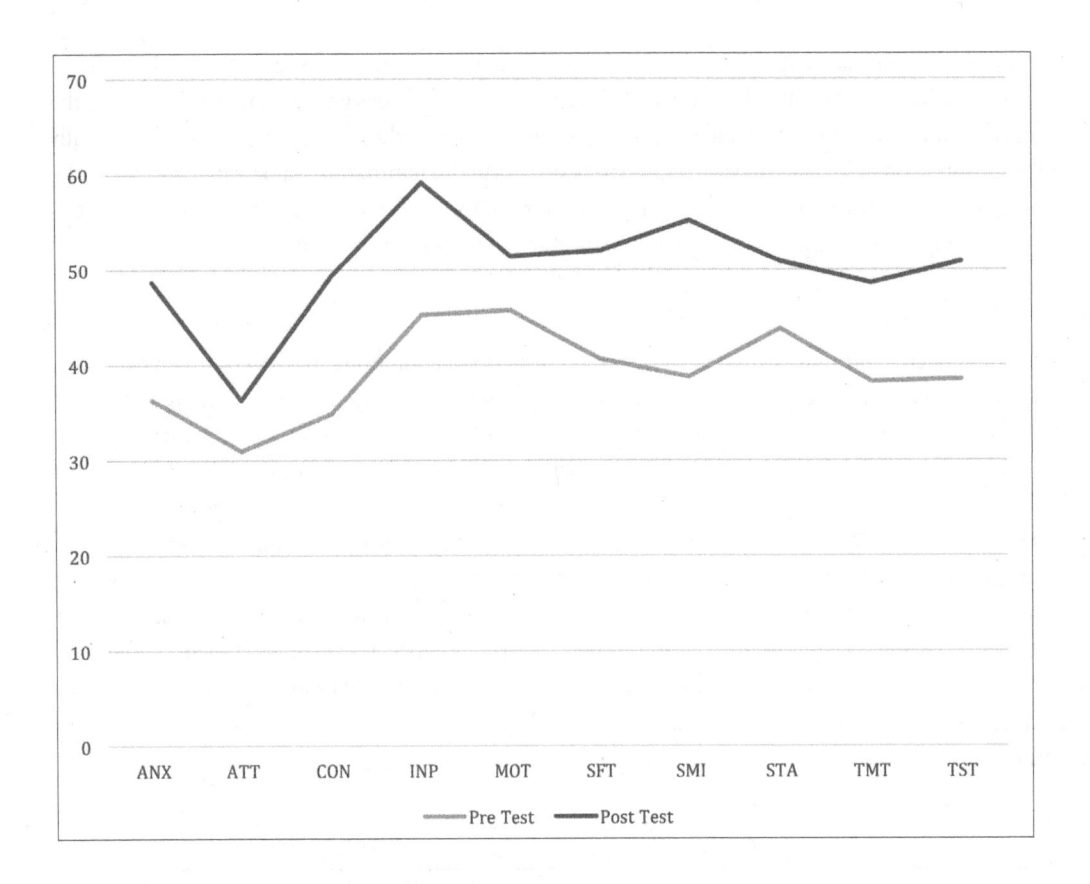

Figure 1. Learning And Study Strategies Inventory (LASSI) pre- and post-test scores, Fall 2015.

Lastly, a noncognitive variables rubric is being developed to assess the effectiveness of the regular and periodic reflection in COLL 150. This rubric will use a more robust 7-point Likert scale to rate each variable, as opposed to the 3-point scale used for admission decisions. It would provide for direct assessment of the growth of noncognitive factors and could use either admission essay data or an early written reflection as the pretest sample for comparison.

Implications

Rather than adopting a single, three-credit course model, St. Cloud State offers two linked courses for a total of four credits. This model also provides at-risk students with instructional teams who work closely with students to foster their success. With a team approach, ACE instructors are also modeling for students what it means to be part of a learning community, something institutions are usually very good at within degree programs with advanced students, but less so at the introductory level. Further, students become part of a community of learning and come to understand the value of college as groundwork for lifelong learning through their personal engagement, individually and in class, with their instructors and mentors, as well as through their observations of the instructor–mentor interactions. Students learn to appreciate the ways people work together to foster success and develop knowledge. Rather than regarding the classes as hoops to pass through in their transition to college, ACE students repeatedly cite these courses as having value for them and contributing to their academic success. As St. Cloud State scales up its FYS program to offer opportunities for other first-year students, the ACE program provides the pedagogical principles to form the basis of that initiative.

Contact Information

Christine Metzo
Director of Academic Initiatives
University College
St. Cloud State University
720 Fourth Avenue South
St. Cloud MN 56301-4498
E-mail: crmetzo@stcloudstate.edu
Phone: (320) 308-5299

Texas A&M University-Corpus Christi
Rita A. Sperry, Andrew M. Garcia, Chelsie Hawkinson, and Michelle Major

The Institution

Texas A&M University-Corpus Christi (TAMUCC) is a comprehensive, Hispanic Serving (HSI), four-year, public university located in Corpus Christi, Texas, and functioning as a primary educational nexus for South Texas. In fall 2015, TAMUCC had a total enrollment of 11,661 students, 9,554 of whom were undergraduates and 2,332 of whom were first-years. Among the undergraduate cohort, 48% were Hispanic, 38% were White, 6% were African American, 6% were international or other, and 2% were Asian.

Description of the Seminar

TAMUCC's First-Year Learning Communities Program (FYLCP) has included all full-time, first-year students since its inception in 1994. Within this program are Developmental Learning Communities (DLCs) designated for alternatively admitted students with high academic risk; these are the focus of this case study. DLCs have a cap of 120 students, with ongoing plans for development and expansion. Potential participants are identified at summer orientation based on their developmental status in math. Because there are more than 600 alternatively admitted students who place into developmental math each year, a number of students are not included in the DLC initiative, allowing for comparisons between those who participate and those who are eligible but choose not to.

All full-time, first-year students enroll in a first-year seminar (FYS), UCCP 1101, during the fall semester at TAMUCC. As part of a two-course sequence, UCCP 1101 is a one-credit, 25-seat, discussion-based course that meets twice a week for 50 minutes and often serves as the central component of a learning community (LC), linking to at least one other core curriculum course. The content of the FYS is variable based on the composition of courses in the LC; however, the 100-plus sections of the seminar all share the same student learning outcomes in an attempt to enhance first-year students' abilities in the following areas: (a) critical thinking, (b) communication, (c) teamwork, (d) quantitative and empirical reasoning, and (e) personal and social responsibility. Activities and assignments are designed in the context of the learning community to help students practice these skills, in addition to connecting them to student resources and introducing them to college-level expectations.

DLC students take one of two specific sections of UCCP 1101: (a) one linked to U.S. history and developmental mathematics (both identified as barrier courses for first-year students) as well as a first-year composition class and (b) the other paired with psychology, developmental mathematics, and first-year composition course. The linked history or psychology lecture is capped at 60 seats and consists only of DLC students. The students are then broken into three blocks of 20 (reduced from the usual 25) for their FYS and composition courses. The developmental mathematics course is intentionally placed in the middle of the schedule to encourage attendance.

DLC-FYSs are taught by full-time, non-tenure-track faculty who are responsible for five to six sections of the seminar each semester and are required to meet with the other instructors in their specific DLCs (i.e., first-year composition, developmental mathematics, and history or psychology). Peer leaders have not been a consistent component of the DLC team, but plans are in place to make that a priority beginning in fall 2016.

Educationally Effective Practices

The impetus for the curricular choices of the DLCs is largely driven and undergirded by established work on high-impact practices. As Kuh (2008) stipulated, emphasis on critical inquiry, opportunities for collaborative work, and the writing process help develop core intellectual competencies and should instruct the formulation process. In addition, related high-impact practices, such as undergraduate research and shared intellectual experiences, coalesce in the final seminar assignment, the First-Year Symposium.

Lessons and assignments in each DLC-FYS are built around learning outcomes from each of the LC courses and strive to differentiate learning to meet a variety of student needs (Tomlinson, 2014). As the semester progresses, courses are adjusted to meet the needs of the students. However, DLCs do not lower expectations for enrolled students. Conversely, the smaller classroom setting provides a better student-to-teacher ratio than other LCs on campus, allowing instructors to devote more time to individualized learning and keep *expectations at appropriately high levels.*

One way that the DLCs engage in individualized learning is by holding conferences with students several times throughout the semester. Repeated conferences have been shown to have significant impacts on engagement and learning for first-year students (Kaufka, 2010). In addition, meeting with students early in the term helps reinforce that they are not invisible and that faculty care they are attending each course in the DLC and completing all assignments. These first meetings are also used to discuss early, low-stakes assignments assigned by LC faculty, such as take-home essays or personal reflections that allow students to apply course content to their own experiences. The early nature of assignments, completed in the first few weeks of the semester, gives faculty a baseline for individual student work and provides students an opportunity to understand college-level expectations without over-penalizing them. FYS faculty return these assignments during conferences and discuss with students how they can improve. Students are encouraged to ask questions about their graded work and to take an active role in their own college learning. In some cases, FYS faculty help students prepare questions to ask another LC faculty member about an assignment and then escort students to the instructor's office to get their questions answered. These intentional and consistent conferences provide opportunities for students to receive *frequent and constructive feedback* as well as deepen their *interactions with faculty.*

Another approach used in the DLC-FYS to individualize learning is a midterm goal-setting assignment. Students set a goal for each of the four courses in the DLC: one personal and one career-focused. They work with FYS faculty during class and in small-group conferences to refine their goals and ensure they are specific and can be achieved within the semester. Students are also encouraged to meet with their other DLC professors for additional input (e.g., the composition instructor might recommend a student focus on improving organization to become a better writer). Next, students work in small groups to complete a photo scavenger hunt of assigned locations, engaging with faculty, staff, and campus resources as well as deepening their *interaction with peers*. Within their groups, students discuss the resources they have discovered together that can help them achieve their goals. For example, they may learn that a Writing Center consultant can assist with organizational skills. Throughout the semester, the FYS instructor provides feedback on adjusting goals or setting new ones. The assignment culminates in the creation of a portfolio, which includes evidence of students' progress and documentation of the scavenger hunt. The portfolio is intended as a *periodic and structured opportunity for reflection and integration* of the entire first semester, including how the student will continue to use the new goal-setting skills and campus resources.

In addition to the attention given to individualized learning, the DLCs provide opportunities for integration of content knowledge and newly acquired skills. For example, the psychology DLC assigns an observational study as a major integrative project. Teams of students are assigned to observe common student behavior in settings around the campus (e.g., the math tutoring center). Students collect data (e.g., the number of students tutored per hour) and keep track of other demographic information. The final product is an oral presentation where the students discuss their original hypotheses, the related literature on the topic, their data, and the implications of their findings. They are required to incorporate content knowledge from psychology about observational studies, research skills from composition, and quantitative literacy skills from their linked math courses to create charts to describe their data, all while observing a situation that is intended make them more aware of campus resources. This project is modeled on best practices for intentional integration to help students make connections between what they are learning in each of the courses (Lardner & Malnarich, 2008). The final event of the semester is First-Year Symposium. Each student is expected to present the observational study to the campus community. The symposium serves as **public demonstration of competence** of students' newly acquired skills and knowledge.

Discussion

TAMUCC has conducted a number of studies on DLCs with findings suggesting a positive impact on students' first-to-second-year retention (Huerta, 2014; Sperry, 2014). Perhaps more significant, however, is the impact of the DLC on academic probation rates. In 2012, 32% of the students who were eligible for a DLC but chose not to enroll or could not because of space limitations were placed on academic probation after their fall semester, compared to 20% of DLC students (Huerta, 2014).

To investigate the impact of the DLC-FYS specifically, a recent pilot study was conducted using the Integrative Learning VALUE Rubric (Rhodes, 2010) to assess reflective work written in a seminar. Student performance met or exceeded that of students in traditional (non-DLC) FYS sections, indicating that students in the DLC-FYS were able to integrate their knowledge at the same level (or higher) than their peers. Plans are in place to continue this form of assessment.

The FYLCP at TAMUCC does not currently deploy qualitative evaluation metrics on an institutional level, and informal measures to assess student satisfaction levels (or otherwise create a constructive feedback loop) are in place. Student comments from conference meetings fell into three major themes: (a) difficulty adjusting to reading and writing processes required for college-level work, (b) confusion understanding course content that required application of basic foundational content from high school coursework, and (c) struggles balancing home and work commitments with the demands of college. As such, the faculty–student conferences serve as anecdotal evidence for participating DLC faculty regarding best practices and provide further impetus for weekly meetings among triad/tetrad leadership. The literature suggests that unstructured, spontaneous student feedback provides an opportunity for students to develop a sense of agency and empowerment (Plank, Dixon, & Ward, 2014). In addition, evidence suggests that students prefer pedagogical shifts as the semester progresses (Plank et al., 2014).

Recognizing the need for a mixed-methods approach to assessment, the FLYCP is engaged in ongoing discussions to institute student focus groups. These moderated sessions would be combined contemporaneously with traditional student evaluations. Fife (2007) indicated that the use of semi-structured questions in a group setting allows students to consider the instructional process in a more thorough and critical way. Moreover, the FYLCP at TAMUCC believes there are some intrinsic limitations to the closed-question standard course evaluation process for DLC students or those otherwise designated as at risk.

Implications

This case study has shown that the deployment of specific, student-oriented interventions can serve as effective pedagogy for an FYS in developmental learning communities. Institutional data indicate that these practices are particularly useful for reducing the percentage of DLC students on academic probation, supporting departmental persistence initiatives. In aggregate, the deployment of these strategies has provided some indication that developmental cohorts have the potential both to integrate knowledge and to perform academically at levels comparable to their peers.

The success of the initial DLC program has been instructive for future programmatic decisions and resource allocation in several ways. First, student performance levels suggest that the DLC cohort should be expanded to include all first-time-in-college students designated through the alternative admissions process. Requests have been made to furnish the requisite staffing and fiscal infrastructure to do so. Second, efforts have been undertaken to ensure that educationally effective practices are cross-applied to non-DLC learning communities. In this way, the DLC program can continue to serve as an effective incubator for innovative pedagogy. Finally, administrative efforts should continue to advocate for reduced classroom size and opportunities for frequent and constructive feedback. This case analysis shows both are ways that faculty can directly encourage students to take active roles in their own learning.

Because developmental learning communities provide administrators an efficient opportunity to showcase impactful strategies as a microcosm for the overall student population, they may provide a particularly useful departure point for new LC programs or those with significant resource constraints. In replicating this design, institutions can avoid the potential for stigmatization of students with developmental need by showing their capacity to succeed when given appropriately high expectation levels.

References

Fife, E. M. (2007). Using focus groups for student evaluation of teaching. *Mountain Rise, 4.* Retrieved from http://mountain-rise.wcu.edu/index.php/MtnRise

Huerta, J. C. (2014). *Star Award Application.* Unpublished manuscript, Texas A&M University-Corpus Christi.

Kaufka, B. (2010). Beyond the classroom: A case study of first-year student perceptions of required student-faculty conferences. *Journal of the Scholarship of Teaching and Learning, 10*(2), 25-33.

Kuh, G. D. (2008). *High-impact educational practices: What they are, who has access to them, and why they matter.* Washington, DC: Association of American Colleges and Universities.

Lardner, E., & Malnarich, G. (2008, July-August). A new era in learning-community work: Why the pedagogy of intentional integration matters. *Change, 40*(4), 30-37. Retrieved from http://www.changemag.org/Archives/Back%20Issues/July-August%202008/full-new-era.html

Plank, C., Dixon, H., & Ward, G. (2014). Student voices about the role feedback plays in the enhancement of their learning. *Australian Journal of Teacher Education, 39*(9). doi:10.14221/ajte.2014v39n9.8

Sperry, R. A. (2014). *Prediction of retention and probation status of first-year college students in learning communities using binary logistic regression models* (Doctoral dissertation). Retrieved from ProQuest Dissertations and Theses database. (UMI No. 3626219)

Rhodes, T. L. (Ed.). (2010). *Assessing outcomes and improving achievement: Tips and tools for using rubrics.* Washington, DC: Association of American Colleges and Universities.

Tomlinson, C. A. (2014). *Differentiated classroom: Responding to the needs of all learners.* Alexandria, VA: ASCD.

Contact Information

Rita A. Sperry
Learning Community Coordinator
Professional Associate Professor
Texas A&M University-Corpus Christi
6300 Ocean Drive
Corpus Christi, TX 78412
E-mail: rita.sperry@tamucc.edu
Phone: (361) 825-3158

The University of Arizona
Marla Franco, Jessica Hill, and Tina Wesanen-Neil

The Institution

The University of Arizona (UA) is a land-grant, public, research university located in Tucson, Arizona, and offering 364 academic programs. Enrollment includes 42,236 undergraduate, graduate, and professional students. In fall 2015, UA welcomed its largest and most diverse class of 8,037 first-year students, of whom 54.5% were Arizona residents, 40.6% were ethnically diverse, and 6.3% were international students. UA was recently identified by *Forbes* as the best college in the state of Arizona (Howard, 2016).

Description of the Seminar

Blue Chip Leadership: The First Year Experience (BCL) is a unique, year-long cocurricular leadership program open to all students and designed to be a gateway experience encouraging students to adopt a sustained interest in engagement throughout their academic careers and beyond. The program encompasses many high-impact practices (e.g., first-year seminar and experience, service-learning, writing-intensive and collaborative assignments) identified by Kuh (2008), making it a valuable experience for students and an effective retention strategy for the institution. The program has supported more than 3,200 students since it began in 1998, averaging 200 new students each year. Recent alignment with the UA's strategic plan has enabled the program to increase its capacity to serve more than 750 students each year.

During fall semester, students participate in a noncredit, extended orientation and leadership development series, comprising experiential team meetings led by third- or fourth-year BCL students who serve as team leaders. During team meetings, students are introduced to leadership topics, including effective communication, team building, problem solving, and resiliency. They also discuss important issues related to transitioning to the University, such as getting involved; navigating risky behaviors; and managing health, wellness, and stress. Students are introduced to the diversity and service core values of BCL by exploring introductory issues of identity and social justice as well as factors to consider when performing community-engaged service. To complement the weekly meetings and give students hands-on experiences, teams participate in three larger events—a teambuilding event (i.e., ropes course or field day competition), a lip-sync contest, and a day of service. These events are intended to highlight the value of team building, working as a team, and engaging with the Tucson community.

During spring semester, students build on the concepts taught in the team meetings through a more formal, one-credit, academic and leadership first-year seminar (FYS), The Leadership Challenge. The class uses Kouzes and Posner's (2014) *The Student Leadership Challenge* as a conceptual foundation to focus on leadership exploration, professional development, community-engaged learning, and diversity and social justice. The course meets for 50 minutes each week, is limited to 15 to 30 students per section, and is taught by staff members from across campus. Peer leaders from years 2-4 of BCL serve as teaching assistants and are responsible for cofacilitating lessons and grading the majority of assignments. All course logistics, including instructor training and curriculum development, are coordinated through the Leadership Programs department to help ensure consistency of experience across the many sections (approximately 15-20).

BCL employs an experiential approach to education. The program is designed with the notion that engaged learning occurs when students process the course material meaningfully by focusing on the activity in the moment, making connections, and drawing conclusions with considerations to future application. In BCL, learning is derived from activities intended to stimulate mental inquiry and reflection. In addition to Kouzes and Posner's (2014) five practices of exemplary leaders (i.e., model the way, enable others to act, inspire a shared vision, challenge the process, and encourage the heart), Kolb's (1984) experiential cycle of learning is used to structure the course: A concrete experience (CE) is processed through reflective observation (RO) and abstract conceptualization (AC) to formulate a new idea or action, which is then used in active experimentation (AE). Almost every lesson plan within FYS incorporates an activity intended to stimulate conversation and reflection. In processing those activities, students are challenged to consider how they can apply the intended lessons in future leadership endeavors.

The experiential learning cycle is also evident in a real-world, community-engaged service experience (i.e., service-learning), which is a central component of the FYS and helps students synthesize lessons introduced in the text and course content. For this project, each course section is assigned a nonprofit partner organization from the Tucson community, such as the Sky Island Alliance, focusing on environmental restoration of native plant species; the Community Food Bank, working to address issues of hunger through a number of different programmatic efforts; and the Living Street Alliance, advocating for sustainable transportation methods. A representative from the community organization comes to speak to the class about the organization and share their vision. This lesson is enlightening to students as they hear the perspectives of the community leaders and are able to see how organizations operationalize the broader leadership concepts of uniting others around a common purpose, mobilizing individuals around that purpose, and addressing barriers to success. Students then apply what they learned from these presentations through a hands-on service experience. In spring 2016, 204 students conducted a total of 1,020 hours of service in and around the Tucson community.

In addition to community-engaged service, major course assignments include

- **Reading reflections:** Students submit one-page reading reflections based on each chapter of the text. Outcome: Students will reflect on their own leadership experiences and apply them to concepts covered in the text.
- **Leadership assessments:** Students take two personality and leadership assessments (i.e., Leadership Practices Inventory and Gallup's Strengths Quest) to develop a deeper understanding of their leadership styles. Outcome: Students will define their leadership style and strengths.
- **Résumé:** Students are taught how to write a résumé, which is reviewed by a professional staff member. Outcome: Students will create a professional résumé.
- **Professional portfolio:** Students are taught the value of showcasing their leadership experiences through the creation of a physical portfolio that includes a personal mission statement, their résumé, leadership assessment results, and one-page summaries of each community service experience in which they have participated and organizations they have joined while attending college.
Outcome: Students create a professional portfolio to showcase their leadership and involvement experiences.
- **Engagement plan:** Students consider how they will continue to be involved during their time at the UA and form college road maps in conjunction with an involvement panel where first-year students hear from BCL peer leaders who share their involvement in research, study abroad, student government, and academic colleges. Outcome: Students will create a goal for future involvement at UA.
- **Personal leadership reflection:** The final project for the course has students reflect on the year, how they grew as leaders, and goals they hope to accomplish in the future. Their reflections are presented in front of their peers in a creative form of self-expression.
Outcome: Students will reflect on their leadership development and practice effective presentation skills.

Educationally Effective Practices

Interactions with faculty and peers. The FYS was designed to accommodate a relatively small class size with the intention of creating a community of learners and to allow students to interact with a staff member in a more intimate environment. The experiential design of the course requires students to work collaboratively during a majority of the class sessions. Additionally, the presence of the teaching assistant and the peer leader involvement panel allow first-year students to develop relationships with potential peer mentors as they plan out their collegiate careers.

Periodic and structured opportunities for reflection and integration. Intentional reflection and application are critical to the outcomes of the FYS. Students engage in meaningful reading reflections where they are asked to apply their own lived experiences to the concepts covered in the text. For example, in the week focusing on the concept of challenging the process, students responded to the prompt: *Think back to a time when you responded to a stressful situation. How did you respond? What did you learn? How has this helped you deal with adverse situations?* Additionally, the professional portfolio serves as a vehicle for students to reflect on their leadership styles and experiences, community service, and goals for the future.

Relevance through real-world application. The service-learning project requires students to apply course material while learning about and analyzing a community organization. Interacting with representatives from the organization and participating in a hands-on experience allow students to consider how organizations apply the five practices of exemplary leadership.

Public demonstration of competence. The capstone presentation for the course requires students to reflect publicly on their leadership growth. In creative presentations delivered before their peers in their sections as well as the staff, students share insights into their leadership styles, personal missions, and future engagement. They also showcase the professional portfolios they created through the class.

Experience with diversity. Diversity and social justice issues are central features of the FYS. Students are asked to consider how they develop stereotypes and how stereotypes are counter to the goals of an inclusive learning environment. They are also introduced to the social justice concepts of privilege and oppression and begin to understand their individual identities as belonging to targeted and privileged groups.

Discussion

Throughout the year, students are asked to demonstrate and reflect on their learning, evaluate their development as leaders, and provide feedback about the program. Formal evaluation of student learning artifacts allows for depiction of student growth over time, self-expression, and the ability of program staff to determine the effects of the experience on student learning.

Rubrics are used to assess multiple assignments. For the written reflections, students are evaluated on the level of depth of the reflection, the extent to which they demonstrate awareness of themselves as leaders, and their ability to make clear and well-articulated connections between their leadership experiences and the readings. The professional portfolio rubric serves as a leadership assessment to examine students' ability to identify and operationalize their leadership styles and strengths using language from the two leadership assessments and to examine the extent to which they demonstrate an understanding and application of their leadership styles and strengths in various contexts and in relation to others. Further, the portfolio is treated as a learning artifact for students to creatively and visually synthesize what they have learned. Additional rubrics assess students' overall ability to produce effective tools for self-branding, including their résumés; the integration of BCL experience in their improved understanding of themselves as leaders; their ability to apply learning to anticipated future experiences to share future action (the engagement plan); and written and verbal communication skills. Finally, the personal leadership rubric evaluates students' ability to convey orally what they learned about themselves, particularly in relation to others. Students are expected to depict new ways of knowing and understanding themselves as leaders as a result of their BCL experiences.

Other assessments of the BCL program and FYS are also made. Informal and open-ended feedback is solicited from community partners regarding individual students' and group's abilities to engage with each other as a team and the group's ability to successfully fulfill commitments of service with the partner. This assessment is in addition to a service-learning section in the portfolio rubrics. A cumulative self-assessment is completed at the end of the course to gauge student learning throughout the entire first year of BCL. In spring 2016, FYS students indicated moderate to significant increases in knowledge in the following areas: applied professionalism (79%), personal leadership style (78%), values and strengths (77%), collaboration (71%), relationship skills (72%), and reflection and application skills (70%). Analysis of students' open-ended responses revealed widespread learning gains in effectively communicating one's personal leadership style, understanding the importance of community engagement, using inclusive language, and effectively presenting oneself professionally through portfolios and résumés. A 2014-2015 retention analysis demonstrated that first-year BCL participants were retained at higher levels than a comparison group (91% vs. 84%, respectively), suggesting the collective impact of this program has not only benefitted student learning but has also demonstrated a strong relationship to positive retention outcomes.

Implications

BCL is a high-impact program for first-year students at UA. The program serves as a model for uniquely integrating pedagogy that is grounded in Kolb's (1984) experiential cycle of learning, while combining elements of leadership development, community service, career readiness, and pathways toward sustained campus and community engagement. Through the use of informal and formal assessment, the program is designed in a way that provides students with opportunities to reflect incrementally on their experiences, apply new ways of knowing, make connections between readings and applied learning, and demonstrate competence publicly in a meaningful way. Demonstrated success of the program, as evidenced by student learning and higher retention rates compared to a comparable student group, has garnered increased attention and resources to support greater program capacity. Blue Chip Leadership: The First Year Experience can provide other campuses with a model that successfully integrates and assesses educationally effective practices, along with experiential learning. This model may provide other institutions with an ideal program design suited to cultivate student learning and retention for their unique student populations.

References

Howard, C. (2016). *The best college in every state*. Retrieved from http://www.forbes.com/sites/carolinehoward/2016/02/22/the-best-college-in-every-state/#2ee28b6323c0

Kolb, D. A. (1984). *Experiential learning: Experience as the source of learning and development*. Englewood Cliffs, NJ: Prentice-Hall.

Kouzes, J. M., & Posner, B. Z. (2014). *The student leadership challenge: Five practices for becoming an exemplary leader*. San Francisco, CA: The Leadership Challenge.

Kuh, G. D. (2008). *High-impact educational practices: What they are, who has access to them, and why they matter*. Washington, DC: Association of American College and Universities.

Contact Information

Marla Franco
Director of Student Affairs Assessment and Research
University of Arizona
1303 E. University Blvd SUMC, Room 319
P.O. Box 210066
Tucson, AZ 85719
E-mail: marlafranco@email.arizona.edu
Phone: (520) 626-2814

University of Kansas
Alison Olcott Marshall and Sarah Crawford-Parker

The Institution

The University of Kansas (KU) is a four-year, public, research university located in Lawrence, Kansas, offering 141 undergraduate majors in 10 degree-granting schools. In fall 2015, KU had an enrollment of 28,091 students, of whom 19,224 were undergraduates and 4,187 were first-year students. Among undergraduate students, 70% are White, 3.8% are African American, 6% are Hispanic, 4.6% are Asian, and less than 1% are Native American. Approximately 9% of KU's undergraduates are over the age of 25, 48.5% are male and 14.4% are first in their families to attend college. Among first-year students, 78% live in campus housing.

Description of the Seminar

Since 2012, the First-Year Seminar (FYS) program at KU has offered all incoming first-year students the opportunity to enroll in a small, discussion-based academic seminar. These seminars are targeted at deciding students and pre-professional students not already admitted to a school and provide an alternative to KU's elective orientation seminar. In 2015, 11% of incoming students took an FYS. Since 2012 the program has expanded from 11 sections to 28 in fall 2015.

The course is designed to inspire intellectual engagement and foster critical thinking by providing students with the opportunity to deeply explore big and exciting questions in an academic content area. Enrollment in these three-credit seminars is limited to 19 students, who spend at least three hours a week in the classroom. FYSs have no prerequisites and share a common set of learning outcomes: that the students will develop their (a) critical thinking skills by being able to analyze and evaluate assumptions and evidence; (b) informational literacy skills, including retrieving useful and relevant information; (c) articulation of critical analysis through writing, media, and/or oral communication; and (d) awareness of experiential learning opportunities and ways to extend learning outside the classroom. Despite this common foundation, the topic of each seminar is defined by the instructor of record for each section. This approach capitalizes on faculty expertise and gives incoming students the opportunity to work closely with researchers who are on the cutting edge in their own disciplines.

Although the majority of these seminars have been in the humanities and the social and behavioral sciences, a growing number of FYSs are being offered in the natural sciences. Geology 177, Exploring Mars, is one example of a successful science-centered seminar available to nonscience majors and is the focus of this case.

Educationally Effective Practices

Geology 177 was divided into two halves, the first of which involved a chronological investigation into the scientific and technological innovations that allowed, and resulted from, the history of Mars exploration from the telescope through the present Rover missions to future plans for human exploration. The second part of the semester focused on science communication, not only the methods by which scientific information is synthesized and presented to the public but also the benefits and dangers inherent in the distillation of knowledge for public consumption. Students were responsible for reading scholarly scientific literature, popular press articles, newspaper reports of scientific events, and the novel *The*

Martian (Weir, 2014), a fictional tale about human exploration on Mars that is, for the most part, scientifically accurate. Students also watched the film (Scott, 2015).

Taught by a professor in the geology department whose professional research is Mars-related, the seminar was structured to emphasize group-based, participatory learning. All activities and assignments were designed around two sets of learning outcomes: the ones common to all FYSs and those specific to the topic of the seminar. Day-to-day classroom activities promoted **interaction with faculty and peers** and provided **periodic and structured opportunities for reflection and integration**. Students whose schedules had common blocks of free out-of-class time were grouped into permanent learning teams representing diverse backgrounds. This grouping was done through CatMe Team-Maker system (CatMe, n.d.), a secure web-based tool allowing teams to be created following collaborative learning best practices (Layton, Loughry, & Ohland, 2010). Students were required to read a set of primary or secondary source articles and complete a reading circle worksheet (Daniels, 2002) prior to each class. These worksheets comprise a series of assigned roles that rotate around the team with each new reading. Each reading circle role guides students through an aspect of dissecting or connecting to the text and places accountability for preparing for class primarily in the hands of the students. The advance preparation meant that each class meeting could begin with an in-depth discussion of the reading, first at the team level and then at the class level.

To promote reflection and integration of learning, each team worked together following the discussion of the reading to produce information maps connecting that day's new material to their prior knowledge on the topic. The form of these maps varied. For example, they could be worksheets that guided students through a process or brainstorming sessions on a whiteboard. These activities culminated in either one-minute papers or think–pair–share activities, where students reflected, wrote on their own, and then discussed their ideas in their teams or as a class.

In addition to these daily tasks, there were three major assignments throughout the semester, each with **high expectations and requiring a significant investment of time and effort.** The first and the third were writing assignments: One required students to write individual entries on a timeline of Mars exploration and to work together in their teams to create a summary of one period of human exploration of Mars. The other had students compose policy memos arguing for or against further funding for Mars exploration. Each assignment offered students time to reflect on and integrate their learning, as successful completion of these projects required them to think critically, seek out and analyze information, and work individually and collaboratively. Further, the timeline provided an opportunity for a **public display of competence**, as it was posted on a front-facing website. Assignments were scaffolded over a month to allow enough time for **frequent and constructive feedback** on the process of researching and writing, including an in-class peer review session of the students' initial drafts. This scaffolding, as well as dedicating in-class time to parts of the assignment, ensured that students spent sufficient time completing the project (approximately 15 hours on the first assignment and 10 hours on the third).

The second assignment involved creating, designing, and holding a public science outreach event at the KU Natural History Museum's Science Saturday—another opportunity for a **public demonstration of competence**. The Science Saturday features hands-on, drop-in, family-oriented events centering on a specific theme and offering activities, demonstrations, and explorations of the intersections of art and science for all members (and ages) of the KU and Lawrence community. A typical Science Saturday involves 5 to 15 staffed tables, each presenting a different educational activity, with visitors guiding themselves through and engaging with the various displays. FYS students, in groups of four to six, prepared Science Saturday displays around the theme of exploring Mars. The learning objectives of this activity were to foster collaboration and teamwork with other students, reflect on and integrate their learning throughout the semester, connect their learning to a real-world application, and communicate their knowledge with members of the public.

Given the scope of the project, this assignment was scaffolded over half the semester, with students spending upwards of 50 hours, both in and out of class, to complete it. They were provided with frequent feedback through this process. Approximately every two weeks, each group was required to meet with the instructor to discuss their progress, share their planning steps, and present any problems they might be having as they moved toward the Science Saturday. Additionally, the student groups and the professor met with the museum educational events coordinator three times: when the assignment was given to the students, halfway through the planning process, and right before the event as a dress rehearsal. Although the process was heavily scaffolded, the students were entirely responsible for content creation, allowing them to discover the relevance of their learning by applying it in a ***real-world context***. The experiential nature of the event required students to be agile and to think on their feet. It also fostered new and authentic connections with the course material, particularly as they responded to audience questions.

Discussion

The educationally effective practices and assignments were assessed both in conjunction with all FYSs and specific to the class. Students in this seminar completed the Student Assessment of Their Learning Gains (SALG) survey, an authenticated, anonymous, online instrument focusing on the extent to which a course supported student learning. The SALG contains both Likert-scale and open-ended questions asking students to assess their skills and attitudes at the beginning of the semester and to reflect on the extent of their learning and the efficacy of the course pedagogy and assignments at the end of the term. This approach allows for an assessment of self-reported gains as well as an understanding of what the students found most effective. Additionally, the anonymous responses can be cross correlated on the website to examine how individual populations of students changed throughout the semester.

The majority of Geology 177 students found all the seminar activities and assignments increased their ability to (a) recognize sound argument and appropriate use of evidence, (b) find relevant articles in professional journals, (c) read articles critically, (d) develop a logical argument, (e) write documents in a discipline-appropriate style, and (e) prepare and give oral presentations (see Figure 1). Running the museum event, the activity with the highest expectations and requiring the most effort, was the most effective activity, with 47% of students reporting it was *a great help* in supporting their learning. Additionally, cross correlation of the self-reported skill levels revealed the majority of students felt that they made *good to great* gains across all dimensions, with some of the greatest gains occurring in the students with the least confidence in their abilities before the semester.

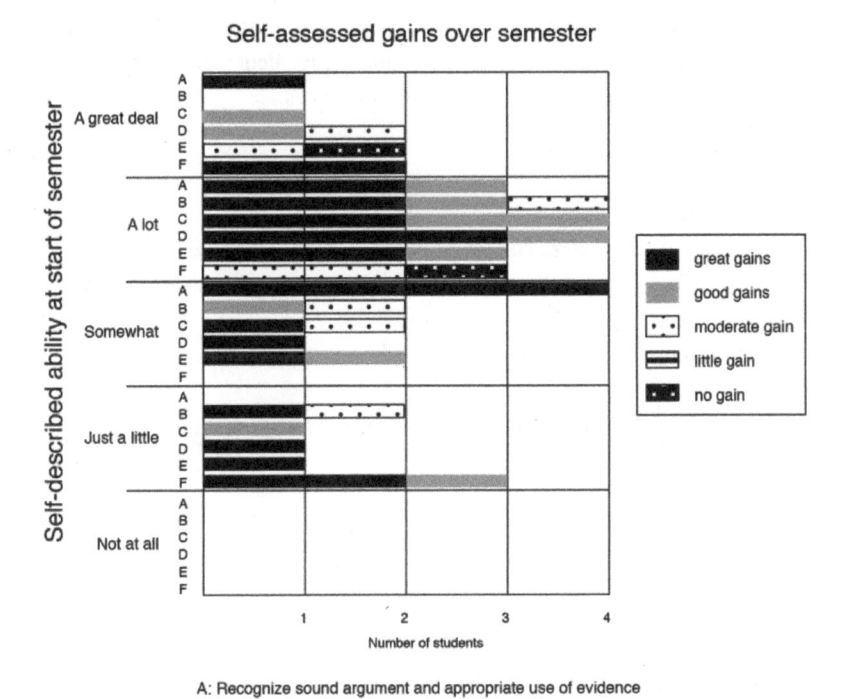

Figure 1. Student self-assessment of gains in critical thinking, informational literacy, and communication skills over the semester. Y-axis indicates students' self-described ability in each of the dimensions at the start of the semester, and X-axis indicates the students' self-assessed gains in each of the dimensions at the end of the semester.

Further, a selection of capstone assignments produced by students in all FYSs are evaluated by a team of assessors against the Association of American Colleges and Universities (AAC&U) critical thinking and writing Valid Assessment of Learning in Undergraduate Education (VALUE) rubrics (Rhodes, 2010). The assessed capstone assignment for Geology 177 was the policy memo. Given how disparate the capstone assignments were, it is difficult to compare data directly across all seminars. That said, more than 95% of the students (including those enrolled in Geology 177) attained benchmark or milestone 2 status in all categories in the VALUE rubric, suggesting developing rather than emerging critical-thinking skills. Thus, it appears, both to outside observers and the students themselves, that this seminar helped the students to improve their ability to think critically.

Implications

This case study has two key implications for practice for seminars inside and outside the natural sciences. First, through careful scaffolding of assignments, which prioritized analysis and reflection on learning, students enhanced their critical-thinking skills in ways that increased their confidence communicating their engagement and facility with the course material. This process began with low-stakes, in-class assignments incorporating peer-to-peer interactions and group learning and culminated in a broader display of knowledge for an external audience. Students were supported in this development through structured writing assignments, peer feedback, interactions with experts, and the production of written and visual materials for the public. Second, requiring work engaging different rhetorical situations enhanced students' critical thinking, particularly their understanding of the influence of contexts and assumptions. The chronological arrangement of the course and the inclusion of scholarly and popular sources from each decade helped students understand how assumptions about science can drive research questions and how the production of new knowledge renders many assumptions obsolete. Interacting with different scientific source types, film, popular fiction, and a natural history museum engaged students in the important processes of understanding and questioning critical decisions that shape how scientific knowledge is communicated, by and to whom, and for what purposes. These questions demonstrate the valuable contribution that the natural sciences make to students' civic knowledge and engagement and the importance of having seminars from the natural sciences in addition to the humanities and social sciences.

References

CatMe. (n.d.). *Home.* Retrieved from http://info.catme.org/.
Daniels, H. (2002). *Literature circles: Voice and choice in book clubs and reading groups.* Portland, ME: Stenhouse.
Layton, R. A., Loughry, M. L., & Ohland, M. W. (2010). Design and validation of a web-based system for assigning members to teams using instructor-specified criteria. *Advances in Engineering Education, 2*(1), 1-28.
Rhodes, T. L. (Ed.). (2010). *Assessing outcomes and improving achievement: Tips and tools for using rubrics.* Washington, DC: Association of American Colleges and Universities.
Scott, R. (producer, director). (2015). *The Martian* [Motion Picture]. United States: Twentieth Century Fox.
Weir, A. (2014). *The Martian: A novel.* New York, NY: Crown.

Contact Information

Alison Olcott Marshall
Department of Geology
University of Kansas
Lawrence KS 66045
E-mail: olcott@ku.edu
Phone: (785) 864-1917

University of Maryland Baltimore County
Lisa Carter Beall

The Institution

The University of Maryland Baltimore County (UMBC) is a four-year, public, research university, offering 55 majors, 35 minors, and 24 certificate programs spanning the arts, engineering and information technology, humanities, sciences, preprofessional studies, and social sciences, in addition to 89 master's degree, doctoral degree, and graduate certificate programs. As of fall 2015, UMBC enrolled 13,839 students, including 11,243 undergraduates, of whom 1,559 were first-year students and 1,228 were entering transfer students. The undergraduate cohort comprises 41% White, 20% Asian, 16% Black, 6% Hispanic, 9% other or unknown ethnicity, and 5% international students.

Description of the Seminar

First-year seminars (FYSs) are three-credit academic courses satisfying general education program (GEP) requirements. Taught by faculty from various disciplines, FYSs are offered on a voluntary basis to first-year and transfer students. Topics range widely and include Social Issues in Business, The Heroic Journey, Beliefs and Behaviors, Mixed Identities, Poverty Amidst Plenty, The Deaf Community and Its Culture, and Images of Madness. Discussion-style classes limited to 20 students promote the active participation of everyone in the seminar.

A recent pilot project linked an IHU or Introduction to an Honors University seminar (a one-credit success course already connected to many discipline-specific core courses) with several FYSs to strengthen students' academic and affective preparation for success. Specific skills instruction (e.g., writing, oral communication, research) in IHU is applied in the FYS, allowing instructors to spend more time delving into the topic of the course. The project is still being evaluated to determine its effectiveness.

Courses meeting GEP requirements promote the development of fundamental skills and intellectual habits of mind, such as written and oral communication, critical analysis and reasoning, information literacy, scientific and quantitative reasoning, and technological competency. FYSs are intentional about their focus on one or more of these competencies and are evaluated accordingly. Instructors use curriculum mapping to design course content, instructional strategies, and assessments that build students' skills in the functional competencies. Sample FYSs, from four different GEP categories, are described herein.

Educationally Effective Practices

Relevance through real-world application, experience with diversity, and public demonstration of competence. The Social Sciences FYS, Diversity, Ethics, and Social Justice in the Context of Schooling, explores the needs of a highly diverse student population in multicultural America. Discussion of Brown v. Board of Education provides students with a foundation for understanding the legal, political, and social forces that affect the education system, including policies aimed at supporting the academic success of all students, regardless of cultural, linguistic, or ethnic backgrounds. Students experience firsthand the challenges faced by educators through a service project in which they work three hours a week in high-need schools or community programs, tutoring and supporting disadvantaged students. They are responsible for proposing enhancements that may increase equity and social justice for their service sites and must present a poster session for a Breaking Ground Grant Proposal—a UMBC initiative engaging the entire campus in civic education and empowered citizenship through implementation grants designed to transform one-time community service projects into forums for the development of civic agency.

Significant investment of time and effort and interactions with faculty and peers. The Mathematics FYS, Mathematics in Literature, takes a unique approach to learning mathematics by examining constructs in literary contexts. Using detective stories, children's literature, science fiction, and other materials, students gain new insights into mathematics and practice their skills by developing their own mathematical narratives. Readings in the course provide a starting point for the discussion of mathematical concepts such that the mystery (and anxiety) surrounding math (e.g., logic, geometry, numbers theory) is reduced. For example, the graphic novel and comic strip *Logicomix* invites conversations on the principles of logic, mathematical logic statements, and symbolic logic problem-solving, while Edwin Abbott's novella *Flatland* allows students to consider one-, two-, and three-dimensional space. Students analyze, interpret, and evaluate readings using their mathematical knowledge and choose methods of reasoning and problem-solving based on the available information. In addition to two required papers (one on logic, the other on cryptology), each student leads a class discussion by incorporating a literary analysis of the text with the mathematical concepts presented. Students demonstrate their understanding by developing puzzles and explaining the problems and solutions to each other, thereby, showing how they are making sense of mathematical ideas.

Periodic and structured opportunities for reflection and integration and experiences with diversity. The Culture FYS, American Orientalism, introduces students to the concept of Orientalism through the lens of the United States' changing relationship with and representations of the Middle East since the late 19th century. Students interact with a variety of cultural sources, including art, literature, film, and the news media, for a critical analysis of how gender, sexuality, race, nation, class, and religion intersect in U.S. cultural productions of the Middle East. They are required to prepare reading responses on a regular basis. Students may connect (e.g., annotations, questions), summarize (using words or images), journal, engage in small-group study, or create (e.g., song, rap) in response to the readings. The purpose is to promote frequency, skill, and comfort in the use of active-reading strategies; to identify understanding and misconceptions about the text; and to prepare students for engaged participation in class discussion.

Expectations set at appropriately high level and frequent and constructive feedback. The Arts and Humanities FYS, Defining and Pursuing Prosperity, introduces widely defined indicators of a successful life, including wealth, career, relationships, intellectual maturity, and social responsibility. Success in college, as a critical step toward later prosperity, is promoted through self-examination of motivation, habits of mind, and typical behavior. Goals, obstacles to goal attainment, and strategies for overcoming obstacles are integrated in all course material. Students consider how they might contribute to the greater good through a success research project, by examining indicators and precursors of success, integrating evidence from research, developing a thesis about planning for prosperity, and articulating practical methods for applying the recommendations. The project is carried out in stages (i.e., using academic resource databases, preparing an annotated bibliography, developing an outline, and writing a summary), with instruction and feedback provided at each stage. The project clarifies the academic expectations of higher education as students develop written and oral communication skills, critical thinking, and reasoning proficiency.

All four of the FYSs described here incorporate significant instructor feedback at various stages of assignments to immediately address issues of skill, motivation, critical thinking, and efficacy. Feedback can take the form of

- rubrics (e.g., the service poster is evaluated for clarity of thought and expression, relevance to BreakingGround values, and practical application to the identified need; Culture FYS reading responses are also evaluated with a rubric to clarify learning objectives);
- required revisions for unsatisfactory work (e.g., success research project);
- classroom discussions (e.g., in the Culture FYS, students can explore their understanding in written form before being asked to discuss the issues among their classmates); and
- evaluations of presentations (e.g., the student-led discussion in the Mathematics FYS allows the instructor to gauge students' critical thinking and their grasp of the quantitative problem or question).

Discussion

The FYS has gained credibility among faculty and students. Course offerings have more than doubled in the past five years (38 sections were offered in the 2014-2015 academic year). Despite being voluntary, most sections are filled to capacity. Student interest in the course can be attributed to the small-group, discussion-style format, specific attention to the needs of first-year students, and the opportunity to earn GEP credit. Faculty members appreciate the active-learning environment in this setting, and several proposals for new courses are submitted each year.

Evaluation of the FYS begins with student input. Students are surveyed at the beginning of the semester to identify their interests, strengths, and concerns. Faculty use the data to tailor instruction and feedback to the specific group of students in their classes, thereby promoting more effective learning in the course. Specific attention is given to students' perception of their skills in the functional competencies. End-of-semester surveys provide feedback that guides curriculum, instruction, and assessment practices. For example, students typically describe the FYS class as "relaxed" and "comfortable"; they receive guidance for contributing to class discussions and are encouraged to participate without fear of criticism. As one student remarked, "the instructor created such a free, expansive, and imaginative thinking place for everyone in the class and this allowed us all to be unafraid of speaking, and it inspired us to think beyond boxes." FYS faculty members regularly share strategies for creating engaging and interactive learning environments that challenge students' critical thinking and communication skills.

Curriculum mapping promotes a systematic link between functional competencies; course content, tasks, and assignments; and assessment at the course and program levels. Online rubrics allow instructors to aggregate data and more easily use formative assessment to promote students' progress. FYS faculty meet monthly with program staff to share instruction and assessment practices. In addition, Faculty Development Center staff provide support and guidance in the improvement of assessment plans. Efforts to strengthen the curriculum and assessment plans for these courses are ongoing and pay particular attention to developing the functional competencies needed for future success.

Retention and graduation data show that students without an established connection (e.g., an academic affiliation such as a scholars program) benefit most from the experience in the FYS. One-, two-, and three-year retention rates are significantly higher for FYS students than for non-FYS students (see Table 1). Further, certain targeted student groups, such as male commuters, especially appear to benefit from the program with respect to one-year retention and four-year graduation rates (see Table 2). Data are used to identify subgroups of students whose progress might be enhanced with a first-year experience and then shared with campus partners who can assist in steering those students toward the FYS.

Table 1

Retention Percentage Rates of Unaffiliated First-Year Students Based on Enrollment in a First-Year Experience, Fall 2006 – Spring 2015

Retention rate	FYE** ($n = 3,004$)	No FYE ($n = 7,671$)
One-year	85%	83%
Two-year	74%	71%
Three-year	69%	65%

Note. Unaffiliated: no connection to a scholars program. First-Year Experience participation: First-Year Seminar and/or IHU (one-credit success seminar).
**$p < .01$

UMBC plans to expand its formal evaluation of effective practices. The student survey will incorporate specific questions about the instructional practices, skill development related to the functional competencies, and suggestions for improving the effectiveness of the practices. Instructors will be asked to provide similar feedback, along with summative assessment data reporting skill improvement related to the functional competencies that can also be linked to the subject practices. Using these data, program staff and instructors will re-evaluate the student learning outcomes that guided development of the instructional and assessment practices used in the course. In collaboration with Faculty Development Center staff, instructors can then consider revisions that may promote improved student performance and growth over time.

Table 2

Retention Percentage Rates of Unaffiliated, First-Year Male Commuter Students Based on Enrollment in a First-Year Experience, Fall 2006 – Spring 2015

Retention/graduation rate	FYE** ($n = 547$)	No FYE ($n = 1,738$)
One-year retention	84%	78%
Three-year retention	66%	59%
Persistence (end of year 4)	65%	58%
Four-year graduation	24%	18%
Five-year graduation	48%	40%
Six-year graduation	55%	44%

Note. Unaffiliated: no connection to a scholars program. First-Year Experience participation: First-Year Seminar and/or IHU (one-credit success seminar).
**$p < .01$

Implications

This case study highlights a sample of the FYSs offered at UMBC. Each seminar has a unique method of achieving programmatic objectives and contributing to student success, but all share the common goals of helping students to develop skills in one or more of the functional competencies and to begin seeing themselves as active members of the institutional community.

Students may enter higher education with naïve attitudes about learning and with immature academic work habits. One of the challenges facing instructors of first-year students is helping them evolve into active learners with greater metacognitive awareness and ownership of the learning process. Students in the FYS are asked, via educationally effective practices, to consider what the take-away messages from the course should be, how assumptions and attitudes shape their understanding of the topic, and what constitutes learning. Actively engaging students in reflection and assessment of their own learning prepares them for success in future courses and other life challenges.

A vision for the FYS program is to build a culminating project into each course that gives students a structured opportunity to consider, reflect on, and express their growth in the course outcomes. The BreakingGround project discussed here is one example; the requirement to present the proposal during a poster session adds to the strength of that project. Other seminars might prompt students to establish goals for applying course material in specific ways that are personally applicable.

Focusing attention on effective educational practices provides the added opportunity for engaging instructors in reflection about what their students learned from the specific methods and how the course might be revised to prompt further improvements. Regular contact with other FYS instructors and collaboration already taking place with the Faculty Development Center allow the program to make the best use of the various forms of data described previously. Instructors are already engaged in conversations about learning outcomes and assessment. We anticipate incorporating the assessment of educationally effective practices into a comprehensive program development and evaluation plan.

Contact Information
Lisa Carter Beall
First-Year Experience Assessment Coordinator
Office of Undergraduate Education
University of Maryland Baltimore County
1000 Hilltop Circle
Sherman Hall 114
Baltimore MD 21250
E-mail: lisabeall@umbc.edu
Phone: (410) 455-1185

University of New Hampshire
Neil Niman, Tamara Rury, and Sean Stewart

The Institution

The University of New Hampshire (UNH) is a land–space–sea grant, public, research institution, enrolling 15,000 students. Approximately 50% of the students are New Hampshire residents, with the remainder coming predominately from the Northeast. UNH offers a traditional residential experience with nearly all of its 3,200 first-year students living on campus. The student body is very homogenous and reflects the broader population trends that exist in the state. The Peter T. Paul College of Business and Economics is one of five colleges on campus offering degrees in business administration, economics, and hospitality management. It has a total enrollment of 2,600 undergraduate and 300 graduate students, of whom 65% are male.

Description of the Seminar

The First-Year Innovation and Research Experience (FIRE), introduced in 2015, provides a comprehensive and immersive first-year experience designed to encourage Paul College students to embrace academics; engage in a meaningful social culture; and recognize the skills, knowledge, and experiences necessary to reach their own goals. FIRE is designed to build a community of engaged learning while tapping into the value of the traditional residential experience. The program is an integrated, team-based, game-like experience promoting the following goals:

- inform students of the resources and opportunities available at UNH for career and academic assistance;
- develop skills needed to succeed at UNH and Paul, as well as in business and professional spaces;
- encourage students to get involved throughout campus;
- give each student an opportunity to stand out;
- teach students how to
    - approach and solve complex problems using a variety of different techniques,
    - effectively present a business concept and the corresponding research, and
    - develop a team culture and be a part of a team;
- guide students to potential majors, internship opportunities, and the corresponding career paths; and
- introduce the importance of mentorship and the value of the broader UNH community network in a low-risk environment.

FIRE relies on three foundational pillars to achieve its learning goals: Mentorship, Grand Academic Challenges, and Gamification. In addition, a required, two-semester, one-credit, first-year seminar (FYS), PAUL 405 and 406: First-Year Academic Experience I and II, provides the academic foundation. To begin the program, students are randomly assigned to teams based on their major: 20 to 25 students per team, approximately 30 teams per academic year. The Director of the Undergraduate Programs with support from the FIRE Program Coordinator are the instructors of record and create the course outline and syllabus, lesson plans, materials, and assignments.

Mentorship is fostered with peer advisors and alumni mentors who assist new students in learning how to transition to college effectively, take advantage of the many opportunities that are available to them, and develop the skills needed to be successful not only in college but also in their professional lives. Each team is assigned a peer advisor who leads the course, facilitates classroom discussion, and serves as the team leader for the academic year. The peer advisors are juniors and seniors selected following an application and interview process; they are enrolled in a supervised student teaching course for the academic year while facilitating the FYSs. Taught by the Director of Undergraduate Programs and FIRE Program Coordinator, the course provides needed training to facilitate the course by reviewing the weekly lesson plans and materials and serves as an opportunity for peer advisors to share experiences and provide feedback that can be used to make adjustments in real time to ensure program success.

To support the efforts of the peer advisors and help the teams achieve success, an alumni mentor is assigned to each team. Many mentors are engaged, younger alumni who want to give back to the College but are not yet in a position to contribute financially. Most live in close proximity to campus; however, with the use of technology, it is possible for mentors to interact with their teams without physically visiting campus. Alumni mentors bring a missing perspective to the first-year experience. They represent a bridge to the real world and have practical experience that reinforces some of the important points introduced during the first year, such as the ability to communicate clearly and work effectively as part of a team, an awareness of the world around them, and professional business etiquette.

To help plan events and ensure the program is meeting participants' needs, each team nominates a student to become a member of the Igniters group. Having shown an extraordinary level of involvement and leadership, the Igniters student group has become the advisory board for the FIRE program.

Grand Academic Challenges are the centerpiece of the experience and give the students a sense of shared purpose as they work in teams to develop business plans tied to current issues or problems. Each team spends the first four weeks of the semester earning points in the game to be the first to select their year-long academic challenge. The challenges for the 2015-2016 academic year were Colonizing Mars, Living Virtually, Prolonging Life, Powering the Northeast, and Surviving Extreme Weather. The goal of the challenge is to help students develop those skills needed to achieve academic success by introducing current topics that have real business applications. To foster a broader perspective, students explore their chosen topic through four different lenses: economic, political, social, and techno-scientific. Each team divides into four groups, and each group is assigned a lens to research. To assist in the research process, staff and campus librarians create research guides for the grand challenge topics (UNH, n.d.) in addition to several activities and mini-games (e.g., watching a video on APA citation, completing a syllabus quiz or library challenge to find the right resource and key word) to help students identify the resources and develop the skills needed to be successful in their endeavors.

In the spring semester with assistance from Business Faculty and Entrepreneurial Studies student mentors, each team focuses on identifying a business opportunity associated with their grand challenge and turns that idea into a business plan. At the University's Undergraduate Research Conference, teams with the same challenge topic compete against each other in front of a panel of judges to determine the best plan.

Gamification provides a methodology, a set of design principles, and the mechanics to create a social architecture intended to increase engagement, motivation, and enthusiasm. The entire FIRE program is centered on a series of friendly competitions that together create a giant game. Students earn points for their grand challenge work and are also given an opportunity to advance in the game by participating in university events and activities. By creating a nexus that facilitates making connections that can serve as either a substitute or a complement for what exists in their residence halls, students in FIRE are provided with an expanded pool of opportunities for building meaningful social relationships.

A majority of a student's point total is earned through engaging in campus events and programs and joining organizations. FIRE students can earn bonus points by bringing a friend or if the entire team attends the same event. Points are also a source of feedback in the form of a reward for engaging in productive behavior or as a tangible sign of success. Subcategories for tracking student achievement allow a larger number of students to be recognized while promoting a set of positive values and establishing expectations for behavior. Small successes become a source of personal pride and, particularly for students who are struggling academically, provide an alternate means for achieving personal success.

To reinforce those positive feelings associated with success, prizes are given at various events and for reaching point levels. FIRE branded merchandise, special access to helpful information, or recognition in the form of a Luminary award at a FIRE event are some of the rewards associated with advancing through the game. In addition, leaderboards are used so that students and their teams can track how they are doing. Enabling students to compare themselves (or their teams) to others serves as a powerful source of motivation.

The FYS meets for an hour a week, and students are expected to spend approximately two hours each week on assignments outside class. The fall course focuses on the academic transition to college and includes three graded assignments. The first is an Academic Autobiography in which students reflect on their past academic experiences and create profiles of their perceived academic strengths and weaknesses. They also write a Lens Summary, presenting their academic challenge topics through their assigned perspectives. Finally, students work in small groups for the Lens Presentation, sharing strategic information with the class from their ascribed viewpoints. These assignments require students to work on key academic and career skills that involve writing, research, and presentation. Course instructors grade writing assignments with the help of teaching assistants. The in-class assignments and presentations are graded by the peer advisors.

The spring semester has an academic and professional career emphasis. Students are given information on the major and minor options at the University and other opportunities such as study abroad, National Student Exchange, research grants, and internships. The alumni mentors actively help students with résumé writing, networking, and identifying skill sets. To further develop these skills, FIRE hosts a networking reception and career boot camp. The semester's four graded assignments include writing a résumé (requiring multiple drafts and peer reviews), pitching a preliminary product or service plan related to the challenge topic, contributing to the team's final business plan either through a written business plan and presentation or a poster presentation, and evaluating their work and that of the team with a group progress report. Throughout the semester, students are challenged to further develop their writing and presentation skills as well as begin to create a professional presence.

Educationally Effective Practices

The very design of FIRE prepares students to be successful not only academically but also socially through ample and structured ***interactions with faculty and peers***, including instructors, campus support staff and faculty, peer advisors, alumni mentors, Igniters, and classmates. ***Relevance through real-world applications*** is supported by the inclusion of alumni mentors in the program to provide career models and real-life assistance and by participation in topical research and the development of a business plan using lenses students will actually encounter in the business realm. ***Periodic and structured opportunities for reflection and integration*** are built into the coursework through the graded written assignments, and students engage in a ***public demonstration of competence*** by presenting their business plans in class and at the University's research conference. Lastly, the gamification concept not only ***sets academic expectations at appropriately high levels*** but also requires collaboration and ***significant investment of time and effort*** to research the challenge topics and achieve points through campus engagement.

Discussion

The FYS has a long history in Paul College. However, in recent years, students seemed disengaged as they questioned the significance of the assignments and attended class meetings with silence and some amount of resentment. The introduction of the FIRE program has led to a major change in student attitudes and engagement. Attending class has become an opportunity to connect with friends, and scaffolding assignments provides a meaningful rationale for the work, with an achievable goal at the end.

The effect that building a first-year experience around a giant game has on student behavior is evidenced by the fact that 50% of the students indicated in an end-of-fall-semester survey that they had participated in at least five events or activities, 84% made friends within their FIRE teams, and 96% of students felt they could contact their peer advisors with problems or issues. Student organizations have also reported increased involvement by Paul students, and the College's internal event tracking data revealed that more than 100 students attended 15 events or activities. Further, the seminar's academic and professional career initiatives led to a doubling of first-year participation at the spring career fair, and the research guides supporting the grand challenges are the most visited webpages at the UNH library.

An examination of academic performance at the end of fall semester comparing students involved in the new 2015 FIRE program with the 2014 cohort (FIRE not available) showed overall increases in cumulative GPA (at or above 3.0, 60.72% vs. 54.03%; at 4.0, 4.2% vs. 1.32%, respectively). In addition, first-semester courses that focused on writing and presentation skills, such as Introduction to Business, First-Year Writing, and Ethics, all showed improvements in course grades (ranging from 6.17% to 14.49% increases) for FIRE students compared to the previous year's class.

Implications

FIRE is intended to strengthen the ties among academics, the student experience, and career preparation by combining a strong foundation with the values instilled by mentorship and the design principles associated with gamification. It supplements the general first-year curriculum populated by large introductory courses with a more personalized, team-based academic challenge related to a current issue. An overarching game framework is used to create a shared purpose, making it easier for students to form meaningful social relationships that emerge from academics rather than residential experiences. In doing so, it harnesses the power of healthy competition to motivate students and build self-esteem.

The FIRE program can easily be adapted for use outside a business school environment. For example, FIRE's business plan final product could be changed to a public policy recommendation, opportunity for scientific discovery, or something relevant to a subset of the student population at a particular university. Expanding student involvement and building basic research and career skills are desired outcomes regardless of academic discipline or structure. The interdisciplinary approach that underlies FIRE's grand challenges is consistent with the goals and aspirations of any general education program.

References

University of New Hampshire (UNH). (n.d.). *Research guides*. Retrieved from http://libraryguides.unh.edu/fire/weather

Contact Information

Neil Niman
Associate Dean of Academic Programs
University of New Hampshire
10 Garrison Ave.
Durham, NH 03824
E-mail: neil.niman@unh.edu

University of North Carolina - Wilmington
Zackary W. Underwood

The Institution
The University of North Carolina Wilmington (UNCW) is a four-year, public, research university located in Wilmington, North Carolina, offering 49 undergraduate majors in four degree-granting colleges. In fall 2015, UNCW had an enrollment of 14,969 students, of whom 13,261 were undergraduates and 2,024 were first-year students. Among undergraduate students, 78% are White, 5% are African American, 6.7% are Hispanic, 2% are Asian, 3% are members of two or more races, and 3.5% are of unknown ethnicity.

Description of the Seminar
UNI 101: First-Year Seminar (FYS) is a three-credit, required course in the University Studies general education curriculum and a graduation requirement. The seminar is based on uniform content and encourages students to "develop [and apply] effective academic and personal strategies; hone critical thinking, writing, and oral presentation skills; engage in academic major and career exploration; and become familiar with the expectations of the university as well as campus resources" (University College, n.d., para. 2).

The FYS is taught by UNCW faculty, staff, and administrators who are dedicated to first-year student learning and success. The seminar emphasizes student interaction. Instructors and peer mentors (Seahawk Links) are encouraged to create a community within the 25-student classes through readings, discussions, assignments, and out-of-class activities. A final group project is a requirement of all FYS sections. One example, the Film Festival Group assignment, highlights the use of educationally effective practices in FYS.

For this project, students, in groups of four to five, create a three- to five-minute film highlighting their first-semester experiences at UNCW. Films are built around a theme common to all FYS sections (e.g., Chasing Dreams: Your First Year Experience at UNCW), which provides a consistent element upon which films can be judged in a friendly competition. Past film topics touch on common transition issues, such as fitting in, time management, and getting involved in the community. Topics have also included academic issues, such as the rigor of a difficult major or how to speak with a faculty member. The project is intended to encourage group collaboration, offer a public venue for the display of work, incorporate opportunities for timely and consistent reflection, and support improvement of students' reflective writing and ability to make connections to learning through instructor and peer feedback.

Once the initial assignment is presented, student groups are responsible for setting up times outside class to meet and create their films within a two-month time span. The project is structured in three stages: preproduction (i.e., role assignment, scripts, and storyboards); production (i.e., filming, directing, and acting); and postproduction (i.e., turning in raw footage and editing). Films are first submitted to the FYS instructor for a grade and are then entered into a campuswide film festival. To further increase motivation, films are judged by a panel of faculty, staff, and students.

The judges choose the top 10 films from all entries, and these are shown at The Premiere, which takes place in the campus movie theatre. A winner is announced at the end of this event. All students, faculty, and staff are encouraged to attend The Premiere, and for many FYS students it is a class requirement accompanied by a reflection activity. Further, in 2013, the winning film was e-mailed to more than 2,000 incoming students as an example of campus life and belonging at the University.

Educationally Effective Practices

Periodic and structured opportunities for reflection and integration. As part of the Film Festival assignment, three written critical reflections are required. The first happens prior to filming to guide students in examining their expectations of the project and working with their groups. The second occurs midway through the assignment to explore current progress as well as the group dynamics. The final paper is written after The Premiere to allow students to reflect on their first-semester transitions, their filmmaking experiences, the films of their peers, and their initial expectations articulated in the first critical reflection.

What distinguishes these assignments as critical reflection, as opposed to simply a personal one, is that students are asked to examine their group dynamics and how learning is affected by expectations, group interactions, and the process of capturing their experiences on film (Brookfield, 1995). Students are given a series of prompts based on the DEAL model (describe, examine, and articulate learning; Ash & Clayton, 2009) to guide them toward making learning connections:

- Describe situation
  - How are you effectively organizing your group to work on this project?
  - Based on previous group work, what are some challenges that you may face? What strategies could you use to make this group more effective or productive than previous group experiences?
- Examine situation
  - Describe any life experiences, values, or beliefs that you will bring to the group that could impact this project.
  - What academic or personal skills will you or did you use to create the short film?
- Articulate learning
  - In your opinion, how does the process of creating a short film relate to this course?
  - How will the process of creating a short film influence future Seahawks (high school students) or the general community?
  - (Only for the last two reflections) By creating a film, did you learn something about others? Describe this finding.

At The Premiere event itself students are able to make connections to their own and their peer' experiences, as well as with each other, through the medium of film. Further, they can engage in self-reflexivity, which Dancyger (2011) described as "viewers watch[ing] or reflect[ing] upon themselves dreaming ... simultaneously very involved and not involved at all...it is a film being watched (as opposed to reality), this creates a tolerance for ranging more widely" (pp. 170-171).

In the same capacity, the films are reflective tools for instructors. Products from the film festival can help them adapt their teaching to incorporate a particular subject differently for the future. The films also offer discussion catalysts in the classroom for students to interact with their peers through common transitional issues. Viewing the final films gives instructors the opportunity to look introspectively at their teaching over time and offers additional awareness of the student perspective.

Interactions with faculty and peers. Faculty members are able to supervise the work among groups and provide written and oral feedback, which helps students focus their efforts and use their creativity to explore new ways to examine common transitions. For example, instead of showing a typical day-in-the-life scenario, one student, in collaboration with the instructor, came up with the idea of a film trailer about the first college year. Sometimes this feedback leads to faculty members becoming actors in the films. It is also a reminder that faculty members are integral pieces of the first-year experience, and interactions with faculty are a common theme among all films.

Peer mentors (undergraduate teaching assistants) are also available in every class to give a seasoned student's perspective for the films. The peer mentors are usually mediators for faculty members, providing quick answers or suggestions to students. They often form relationships with students outside class and are a readily available resource as an extra actor, camera person, or source of feedback. Similar to the real film industry, peer mentors are consultants who are readily available to help students with their films.

Public demonstration of competence. The Premiere highlights a variety of filmmaking styles, student experiences, and transitional issues. Awards for the top two films as rated by students, faculty, and staff are given, along with an award for crowd favorite as determined by applause level. The crowd favorite award serves as an incentive for students to bring their film crews, friends, actors, and instructors to the event and cheer their films to victory.

Frequent and constructive feedback. Instructors provide feedback on all three reflection papers, evaluating them for the application of critical-thinking skills as well as the integration of previous group experiences and assumptions with new learning. They also provide feedback at key points of film development, helping shape each group's film. In preproduction, faculty provide written feedback on scripts and storyboards, encouraging the groups to expand or focus certain ideas. Students commonly misjudge the amount of detail and complexity of a short film. Feedback encourages them to examine each decision thoroughly before filming.

As part of production, faculty members have students turn in raw footage and receive oral or written feedback about production decisions, such as camera angles, audio quality, or the general direction of the film. In postproduction, faculty use a rubric available on the film festival website to judge the final films. Based on this feedback, groups may have the opportunity to reshoot certain scenes or clarify certain points to improve their films prior to the Premiere. Some instructors preview the films in their classrooms, allowing for student feedback prior to the public screening.

Discussion

Though the goal of the assignment is to create a film, learning is reflected as much in the process of filmmaking as it is in the final product. Social constructivism suggests human experiences shape initial knowledge, but meaning-making occurs through social interactions with others (Crotty 1998). This project and reflection engage students in content creation, which McHaney (2011) believed is part of taking responsibility for learning. Comments from student reflection papers highlight positive experiences with the assignment despite initial negative assumptions about the film project. For example, students commented:

> I honestly learned a lot more about this project than I expected to. I learned more of how to be successful in a group assignment ... it gave me the opportunity to see this semester from a new perspective, a wiser and informed perspective, as well as be prepared for the journey to come.

> Through this project, I learned that each person has a particular skill set that they bring to the group and the team functions best when everyone applies their specific skills to create the project.

The best moment of critical reflection is reading about a student's *a-ha moment* regarding learning about their own transition or making a connection that was not there before. Even though the film festival assignment is powerful, without the critical reflections, students would miss out on what is really taking place. The reflections and films give the student an opportunity to see transitional issues in college from multiple viewpoints: through their own critical reflections, feedback from faculty and peer mentors, and the films of other first-year students at the Premiere event.

Implications

The film festival assignment and critical reflections are educationally effective practices that allow students to collaborate with peers, gain constructive feedback, and experience reflective moments within the process. Students are able to create products that are reflective of the transition to college life at UNCW and display their work to their peers. Instructors are able to interact with students and encourage them in their group work through preproduction, production, and postproduction activities.

Critical reflections can be applied to nearly any group project or even the entire first-year experience. Through implementing critical reflection, instructors can make decisions, see pedagogy in action, gain feedback about teaching, and keep students actively engaged in the classroom (Brookfield, 1995). The most challenging aspect of teaching students to reflect critically is assisting them in differentiating personal and critical reflections. This includes helping students find the connections between group dynamics and previous and current experiences.

References

Ash, S. L., & Clayton, P. H. (2009). Generating, deepening, and documenting learning: The power of critical reflection in applied learning. *Journal of Applied Learning in Higher Education, 1*(1), 25-48.

Brookfield, S. (1995). *Becoming a critically reflective teacher.* San Francisco, CA: Jossey-Bass.

Crotty, M. (1998). *The foundations of social research: Meaning and perspective in the research process.* Thousand Oaks, CA: Sage.

Dancyger, K. (2011). *The technique of film and video editing: History, theory, and practice.* Burlington, MA: Elsevier/Focal Press.

McHaney, R. (2011). *The new digital shoreline: How Web 2.0 and Millennials are revolutionizing higher education.* Sterling, VA: Stylus.

University College. (n.d.). *First-year seminar.* Retrieved from http://www.uncw.edu/uc/fys/index.html

Contact Information

Zackary W. Underwood
Academic Advisor
University of North Carolina Wilmington
University College
601 S. College Rd.
Wilmington, NC 28403
E-Mail: underwoodz@uncw.edu
Phone: (910) 962-7908

University of Northern Iowa
Deirdre Heistad, April Chatham-Carpenter, Kristin Moser, and Kristin Woods

The Institution

The University of Northern Iowa (UNI), located in Cedar Falls, Iowa, is a four-year, comprehensive university offering a distinctive educational experience to 10,169 undergraduate and 1,812 graduate students. Among undergraduate students, 83% are White, 3% are African American, 3% are Hispanic, and less than 1% are Native Americans or Asians. The majority of first-year students are from Iowa, and 70% are from hometowns within 100 miles of the Cedar Falls campus. Whereas 37% of the total student population lives on-campus, 93% of first-year students live in one of 10 on-campus residence halls. Data from the fall 2015 MAP-Works transition survey indicate that the top five issues and concerns of UNI's first-year cohort ($n = 1,916$) are homesickness, test anxiety, low numbers of study hours per week (five hours or fewer), a sense of struggling in two or more courses, and low confidence in the ability to pay for college.

Description of the Seminar

Growing out of the results of a 2011 Foundations of Excellence self-study of first-year practices, UNI piloted First-Year Cornerstone, a year-long, six-credit, integrated communication course, meeting three hours per week. Cornerstone has grown from 10 sections, serving 243 students in fall 2011, to 30 sections in fall 2015, serving 682 students, nearly 40% of the incoming first-year class. Students who enroll in Cornerstone must do so their first semester and must successfully complete both sections to satisfy general education writing and oral communication requirements.

The vast majority of Cornerstone instructors come from the writing and communication departments, although participation in the program is open to faculty from all disciplines. To create the course, nine faculty participated in a month-long professional development workshop devoted to the pedagogies of oral and written communication, assessment, student development, and engaged learning. All Cornerstone instructors continue to participate in an annual four-day summer workshop to review assessment data, revise the course learning outcomes, and create the common major assignments.

Cornerstone focuses on three integrated areas: communication, student success, and civility. Learning outcomes include (a) improved communication through the composition, presentation, and demonstration of effective written and oral messages in a variety of contexts, both individually and in groups; (b) success in college as demonstrated by the identification and use of campus resources and support programs as well as engagement in campus and community activities; and (c) enhanced civility exhibited by the recognition of multiple perspectives and worldviews and an examination of the impact of personal beliefs and views on others. As students work to achieve these goals, they engage in numerous low-stakes writing and speaking tasks in preparation for the multistep, major assignments.

Educationally Effective Practices

Expectations set at appropriately high level. During the first semester, students are expected to complete three major assignments: (a) a narrative essay and speech, (b) a rhetorical analysis, and (c) an annotated bibliography and informative speech. The second semester is devoted to developing group decision making and persuasive writing and speaking competencies. Students also put together portfolios of their work from both semesters, including reflections on their improved communication skills, student success strategies, and considerations of diverse points of view. Faculty- and peer-supported scaffolding is present in all major common assignments. For example, within the narrative essay and speech assignment, students create outlines, write multiple drafts, engage in guided peer reviews, and reflect on all aspects of the writing and speaking processes. As the assignments become more research-oriented, additional expectations, such as topic justifications, library consultations, and external reviews, are added.

Experiences with diversity. The major assignments are carefully designed to emphasize the nature and importance of integrated communication within the context of diversity, civility, and student success. This is achieved via the use of a common read book connected to a university-wide project related to social justice issues, Reaching for Higher Ground. Because the writing and speaking assignments in the first semester are developed around the topic of the common read, students quickly encounter diverse ideas while studying and practicing communication in an academically rigorous environment. For example, in a narrative assignment linked to Isabel Wilkerson's *Warmth of Other Suns*, focusing on the migration of African Americans from the South, students were asked to consider the book within the context of their own lives, experiences, and personal storytelling.

Significant investment of time and effort and frequent and constructive feedback. Students encounter increasingly complex assignments and engage in research and discussions of the great migration of African Americans to the northern United States over the course of the seminar. They use their annotated bibliographies as the foundation of research upon which they prepare informative speeches to educate their classmates on issues surrounding the great migration, with the goal of helping each other understand all aspects of that complex topic. Students also create rhetorical analyses of some aspect related to the great migration (e.g., songs, poems, speeches, passage from common read) in a writing assignment that goes through multiple drafts.

Periodic and structured opportunities for reflection and integration. Along with communication activities integrated with the common book and linked to the course's civility theme, Cornerstone students are required to participate in a variety of university activities, many tied to the common read. On average, students engage in at least 5 to 10 activities per semester, including a theatrical adaptation of the common read or theme and a discussion designed specifically for Cornerstone students. They write a reflective essay for their course portfolios upon completion of each activity, relating what they learned to course goals.

Interaction with faculty and peers. Cross-divisional collaboration between faculty and staff who share a common goal—to help students engage in activities and learn about communication and civility—is key to Cornerstone. Along with the diverse faculty who teach the course, almost the entire Student Affairs division, from Wellness to Financial Aid, play an integral role in Cornerstone's success. Further, to build on the course's student success theme, peer mentors are part of the classroom, offering engagement in a personalized academic community and connection to University and personal resources. Peer mentors attend every class session, hold office hours as well as individual and group meetings, make referrals through MAP-Works, provide written feedback on assignments, facilitate classroom and cocurricular activities, plan lessons, and give presentations. This integration of academic and social support within the classroom creates a rich environment for promoting student engagement and persistence (Tinto, 1997).

Discussion

To measure educational effectiveness, the faculty who teach First-Year Cornerstone have maintained a rigorous assessment plan that includes a variety of direct and indirect measures. The ongoing cycle of assessment has instructors measure one to two outcomes per year, including communication skills, both written and oral, as well as student engagement and civility. For example, to evaluate students' proficiency in composing and presenting effective written and oral messages in a variety of contexts, writing and speech samples are collected and evaluated by a team of faculty, using modified versions of American Association for Colleges and Universities' (AAC&U) VALUES rubrics (Rhodes, 2010). After identifying the strengths and weaknesses of the work samples, faculty use the summer curriculum development workshop to identify ways to improve student learning.

Value-added indirect assessment, in the form of students' perceptions of their own learning, helps to contextualize and corroborate the direct assessment. In a pre- and post-survey of self-reported gains in the 2015-2016 academic year, students perceived a significant increase in how well they *understand what is meant by the writing process* (61% to 84%); *use the writing process* (57% to 85%); and *adjust the writing process to account for audience, context, and purpose* (50% to 82%). On similar survey questions related to speaking and integrated communication, students reported significant gains in their ability to *prepare and give oral presentations* (54% to 85%) and their level of comfort *giving an oral presentation* (37% to 63%).

The direct and indirect assessment data illustrate the academic rigor and learning that is taking place in this class. However, student learning gains are not just limited to communication. The following comments from Cornerstone portfolios are representative of the ways in which students also expand their understanding and appreciation of diversity through the use of the common read and required participation in related campus-life activities and the Reaching for Higher Ground project:

> Over the past year, I have participated in many civility activities. I have become more accepting of other people's ideas. I am able to have a discussion with other students and professors without being offended or upset by something they said. I have learned a lot about cultures and ideas that are different from my own and can understand their point of view.

> Before coming to college, I lived in a small Iowa town full of stereotypes of those who are 'different.' College has taught me that those stereotypes are false, and that diversity is a great thing. Diversity is one of my favorite aspects of college. Cornerstone specifically has also made me more appreciative of diversity. ... I have always been respectful of others, but I feel that now that the negative stereotypes are out of my mind, I am even more respectful.

National Survey of Student Engagement (NSSE) data have also been used to compare Cornerstone to non-Cornerstone students and corroborate other assessment findings. For instance, when asked about learning to use a *multiple-step writing process*, 73.3% of Cornerstone students responded favorably, whereas only 49.2% of the non-Cornerstone students did so. Likewise, when asked about the use of drafts, 58.8% of Cornerstone students reported having *prepared more than one draft* as compared to 37.8% of their non-Cornerstone classmates.

While much of the assessment has focused on learning outcomes, efforts are also made to evaluate the program's overall effectiveness. For example, the fall-to-fall retention rate of Cornerstone students is 85.8% as compared to 77.4% of a similar group of non-Cornerstone students. The impact of Cornerstone on academic success and progress continues to be observed through graduation. The first cohort of Cornerstone students had a four-year graduation rate of 34.0%, compared to a 31.5% graduation rate for a similar group of non-Cornerstone students.

Implications

UNI's First-Year Cornerstone course reflects many of the effective educational practices identified by Kuh and O'Donnell (2013). Building rigorous writing and speaking assignments, which include multiple feedback loops around a common read focusing on diversity and social justice, allows students to explore themselves and others in ways that increase their writing, research, speaking, civility, and student success skills. Furthermore, because students have opportunities to connect their learning to their own lives and current social contexts, they are finding the course to be relevant to them.

Students indicate in end-of-course surveys that they feel challenged and have grown in their information literacy, writing, and speaking skills, as evidenced by this comment:

> When coming to UNI, I never thought that one class would have so much impact on my learning. I'll admit that I was skeptical about Cornerstone when I first signed up for the class. With that said, I don't regret one minute of it. I learned more in Cornerstone than I did in any of my other classes.

The frequent and persistent opportunities a two-semester sequence offers to engage writing and speaking skills about different viewpoints and life experiences is an educationally effective practice, which is paying off for the Cornerstone program and its students.

References

Kuh, G. D., & O'Donnell, K. (2013). *Ensuring quality & taking high-impact practices to scale.* Washington, DC: American Association of Colleges and Universities.

Rhodes, T. L. (Ed.). (2010). *Assessing outcomes and improving achievement: Tips and tools for using rubrics.* Washington, DC: Association of American Colleges and Universities.

Tinto, V. (1997). Classrooms as communities. *Journal of Higher Education, 68*(6), 599-623.

Contact Information

Deirdre Heistad
Director of Undergraduate Studies
University of Northern Iowa
381 Rod Library
Cedar Falls, IA 50614
E-mail: d.heistad@uni.edu
Phone: (319) 830-6375

University of Texas at Austin
Ashley N. Stone and Tracie Lowe

The Institution

The University of Texas at Austin (UT Austin) is a four-year, flagship, public, research university located in the south central portion of the United States, offering 119 undergraduate degree programs and 223 graduate programs in 18 colleges and schools. The institutional enrollment in fall 2015 was more than 39,000 undergraduates and over 11,000 graduate students. The first-year cohort was approximately 8,000 students. Among the total enrollment, 45.1% of students were White, 19.5% were Hispanic, 17.2% were Asian, 9.7% were foreign, and 3.9% were Black. Approximately 11% of students are from out of state (representing all states).

Description of the Initiative

The UGS 303 Signature Courses at UT Austin are unique learning experiences designed to engage first-year students in the academic and cocurricular life of the university and expose them to elite faculty on campus. The course is one of several that are implemented to support students in their first year at the university. These three-credit, first-year seminars (FYS) meet twice a week in a lecture setting and once a week with discussion leaders (i.e., other faculty members and graduate research assistants) and peer leaders. Faculty members are recommended by their deans to teach signature courses, which are developed based on innovative or current topic areas of interest. The large lecture sections for each course can range from 50 to 250 students; however, the accompanying discussion sections accommodate approximately 17 students each. This case study focuses on a signature course titled Race in the Age of Obama, designed to connect students to the campus and help them gain an awareness of the social issues pertaining to the larger Austin community.

The objectives for this FYS are to develop students' (a) consciousness of how various identity constructs pertaining to race affect individuals and societies, (b) ability to apply competencies and skills they have learned in the classroom and cocurricular setting to other areas of their collegiate life, and (c) understanding of how to engage in society in a critically conscious way. To achieve these goals, students read assigned literature, such as *Dreams from My Father: A Story of Race and Inheritance* by Barack Obama, *The Short and Tragic Life of Robert Peace* by Jeff Hobbs, *Enrique's Journey* by Sonia Nazario, and *The Glass Castle: A Memoir* by Jeannette Walls. Lectures involve discussion and reflection on topics such as the complexity of race in America, hip-hop culture, music, politics, the prison industrial complex, immigration, and other related areas. Students also engage in a service-learning component, offering them firsthand experience with the inequities in their own community. They are required to complete one service activity outside the classroom with the guidance of peer leaders.

Educationally Effective Practices

Interactions with faculty and peers. This FYS is taught by a history faculty member, who also serves as the senior associate vice president for the Division of Diversity and Community Engagement. Although the lecture component in the seminar is a large group (i.e., more than 250 students per section), the instructor moves through the auditorium drawing students into conversations about the week's readings, the ways issues that arise in the text relate to current events, and their own real-life experiences with the issues being discussed. During their small group sections, students interact with each other and their instructors through engaging in semi-structured debates, connecting their readings to current events by watching video clips and critiquing the content, or participating in other activities.

Experiences with diversity. Students encounter diversity in a variety of ways throughout the course. First, they encounter it in the other students of the seminar, of whom approximately 45% identify as Latino; 32% identify as White; 18% identify as Asian; 14% identify as Black; and 1% identify as American Indian or Alaskan Native, or Native Hawaiian or Other Pacific Islander. Students also come with a variety of educational interests, with all 12 schools or colleges on campus represented in the class. Students in the course are also involved in the different programs connected to the Longhorn Center for Academic Excellence, which intentionally serves a diverse cross-section of the UT student population and accounts for the increased diversity of this particular class. Additionally, students encounter diversity through the course content, which draws on biographical texts and memoirs to help students understand the lived experiences of people from different racial and socioeconomic backgrounds. These texts frame discussions of how racial issues shape and are shaped by societal structures and policies.

Relevance through real-world application. Students are able to see how these policies and structures play out in their new community through the service component of the course, which was implemented to help students become active and engaged citizens within their new community from the start of their time on campus. Students are required to participate in only one service event during the semester; however, many of the students go beyond the minimum requirement. Students have the opportunity to reflect on the service experience when they report completing the requirement through the online service management system, GivePulse. The service component helps students see the real-life implications of the social issues discussed inside the classroom. One student who volunteered at a community garden stated, "the various types of green thumbs I encountered reinforced Dr. Moore's lessons on the importance of diversity and how preconceived ideologies, while unavoidable, are unrealistic." Another student reported, "I have also learned that ignorance toward immigration and issues related to race are still problems until this day and that is something that needs to change." These responses show how students connected the course content to the issues addressed through service in Austin.

Periodic and structured opportunities for reflection and integration. Finally, students are given the opportunity to reflect on how the course content, community service component, and their own personal experiences are connected in a number of different ways, such as classroom discussions, the post-service survey, and a required reflection essay connected to the final exam. Each activity allows students to critically consider society in new ways and to examine their own assumptions and biases about the world and those who live in it. Creating space for students to reflect within the classroom setting in small and large group discussions, virtually through the online service management system, and through written assignments provides them with important opportunities to not simply check off each reading or required activity but to examine how their own lives and lives of those around them are impacted and shaped by the issues they are studying.

Discussion

To assess the service-learning component of the FYS, students participated in pre- and post-assessments (81% and 47% response rates, respectively) to measure the impact of their experience on their academic career. Preliminary data analysis yielded four major themes demonstrating the way students articulated their understanding of service-learning in their FYS: (a) impacting the local community, (b) gaining personal awareness, (c) connecting to diversity, and (d) engaging in teamwork.

The impacting the local community theme indicated students' desire to gain knowledge of the issues within their community and to make positive changes. The pre-service survey revealed that 90% of students began the course with the belief that they could make a difference in their community. As a result of participating in service-learning, 89% of students agreed or strongly agreed that the component showed them how to become more involved in the Austin community. Nearly 80% asserted that their service experience helped them gain a better understanding of their role as a citizen in the community, a key objective of the course.

Students further expressed that their service-learning was a catalyst for them to be self-reflexive and self-aware. More than 60% of students reported that the service experience contributed to them becoming more aware of their own values. One student claimed, "I was able to be a part of the Austin community while understanding my biases and trying to fix them." The reflection process led students to think about issues of diversity with an intentional and critical lens. Students also articulated their ability to work with others from different backgrounds and their interest in connecting with diverse populations through service, as demonstrated in these comments from the post-service survey:

> I learned not to judge a person based on their differences. Everyone is fighting their own battles, and negativity from others only makes it harder.

> I gained leadership skills as I learned to work with people who I usually do not socialize with. I learned how to work in teams and speak up on my opinions.

Another student noted in the qualitative reflection question on the post-service survey,

> My eyes were open to a world I [k]new existed, but never paid much attention to. Growing up I recognize[d] my privilege and have always wanted to serve others, but until this service-learning experience I failed to recognize the strong disparities between local children in low-income areas versus privileged children I am used to interacting with.

Once again, the quantitative and qualitative data gathered to evaluate the course emphasized how the effective educational practices, such as real-life applications through the service component, experiences with diversity, and opportunities for reflection, worked together to achieve the course objectives.

In fall 2015, in addition to the traditional course evaluations and the pre- and post-service surveys, ethnographic research methods were used to study the seminar. Researchers looked at artifacts, such as the syllabus and texts for the course, conducted field observations in both the large lecture and discussion sections, and conducted formal and informal interviews with students. These additional measures offered an opportunity to examine how the many components of the FYS work together. The student interviews highlighted the power of reading memoirs and biographies to frame the conversations in the classroom. Students were excited about the readings, which provided examples of how the societal structures discussed in class played out in the lives of real people. Furthermore, observing the lectures and discussion sections revealed that faculty members, discussion leaders, and students shared stories from their own lives or the lives of people they knew to highlight these issues in real-world scenarios; the observations demonstrated the high level of interaction between all those involved in the course. Students' reflections showed how they witnessed firsthand in Austin those things they had read about and discussed in class. This holistic evaluation approach provided an understanding of the impact of the course beyond the students' final grades.

Implications

As previously mentioned, UGS 303 Signature courses are designed to engage students in the campus academic life by giving them opportunities to engage with elite faculty across the campus in their first semester. Race in the Age of Obama is an exemplary model of how a variety of educationally effective practices can be implemented in first-year seminars. Students are introduced to critical social issues and the importance of active citizenship through their readings, lectures, and class discussions and then have the opportunity to participate in a service-learning experience, exposing them to how these issues manifest in the communities around campus. This reinforces an understanding that justice, respect, and trust must not remain within the walls of academia but should reach beyond the scope of the institution to encompass the communities where students work and live.

The use of varied educationally effective practices in the learning environment is important to the growth and development of first-year students. Practices such as application of knowledge in real-world settings, exposure to diversity, and extensive interactions with faculty and peers provide opportunities for critical engagement between academia and the community. By encountering diverse ideas through the course readings, discussion, and in their new community, students are able to think more critically about the ideas they brought with them to college and their understanding of the world around them. They can also use these critical-thinking skills as they investigate the new ideas they are exposed to in other courses and as they become more civically engaged. Reflection, along with high levels of interaction with their instructors and peers, enables students to synthesize their understanding of the diversity they are exposed to through their peers and course content and the service they complete in the community and amplify the effect of such exposure.

Combining multiple high-impact practices together (e.g., service-learning and the first-year seminar) allows each one to reinforce the others, creating a synergistic effect. Universities should consider additional ways to embed these practices in the curriculum as a means of connecting students to their peers, their campus, and the surrounding community. These connections play an important role not only in the retention of students but also for instilling an ethic of active citizenship among them. Students become engaged with the community beyond the campus from the very start of their collegiate careers, allowing for a greater amount of time to develop their understanding of their roles as citizens and their relationships to the campus and community.

Contact Information:

Ashley Stone
100 West Dean Keeton St., SSB 4.426
1 University Station A6300
Austin, TX 78712
E-mail: Ashley_Stone@utexas.edu

Tracie Lowe
E-mail: tracie.aj.lowe@gmail.com

University of Texas at San Antonio
Kathleen Fugate Laborde and Tammy Jordan Wyatt

The Institution

The University of Texas at San Antonio (UTSA), a public, four-year, Hispanic-serving (HSI), research institution, serves the San Antonio area as well as South Texas and offers 158 degree programs. The institution's vision is "to be a premier public research university, providing access to educational excellence and preparing citizen leaders for the global environment" (UTSA, 2016). During fall 2015, UTSA enrolled approximately 28,800 students with a 4,976 first-year cohort. Of the new entering students, 54% were Hispanic/Latino, 23.1% were White, 9.8% were Black or African American, 7.5% were Asian, 53.7% were female, and 43% identified as first-generation. UTSA is ranked sixth in the nation in awarding degrees (both undergraduate and graduate) to Hispanic students, and the Carnegie Foundation for the Advancement of Teaching awarded UTSA a Community Engagement Classification in recognition of the University's commitment to serving the local community.

Description of the Seminar

UTSA's First-Year Experience program (FYE) was implemented in fall 2014. The FYE is designed to help first-year students transition into the university by addressing both academic and social needs. As part of FYE, students complete Academic Inquiry and Scholarship (AIS 1203), which is a three-credit, core curriculum first-year course. They also participate in University Peer Mentorship (UPM 1000), a zero-credit, year-long experience. In UPM, new students are paired with trained, upper-division peer mentors to help them explore UTSA's academic and social resources, build university connections, and learn college success strategies. The peer mentors are part of the AIS class during the semester, and they meet with students throughout their first year.

First-year students take AIS before they declare majors and move into the college of their directed study. AIS is designed to introduce students to undergraduate research and critical-thinking skills, epistemologies, and inquiry practices within the academic cultures of the humanities and arts, social sciences, and natural sciences. Students self-select the AIS class that matches their interests. Each section has an enrollment cap of 50 students and is taught by a team consisting of a faculty member and graduate teaching assistant (TA), for a student–teacher ratio of 25:1. Faculty who teach these sections represent a variety of academic cultures and disciplines and are encouraged to share their own research agendas with the students. TAs receive training in best practices for teaching in higher education and attend all classes. The instructors and the TAs each hold regular office hours. Much of the curriculum uses collaborative teaching techniques to foster relationships among first-year students and to allow for some self-teaching. The class meets for 150 minutes per week, and the classroom environment is designed to encourage critical thinking and analysis, with minimal lecture.

Educationally Effective Practices

Expectations set at appropriately high levels. All sections are guided by state-required core curriculum assessment outcomes of critical thinking, communication skills, and personal and social responsibility. Because AIS has more than 60 sections in a typical fall, and 40 in the spring, instructors are encouraged to use their own lenses to discuss and demonstrate research. The Pathways Project, one option for AIS class curriculum, fits into the social and academic objectives for the comprehensive first-year program and is adapted by several AIS instructors.

The Pathways Project is grounded in Rendón's (1994) validation theory, which proposed that the unique experiences of each student (particularly students of minority or first-generation status) are significant, should be intentionally and proactively affirmed, and can be used to create knowledge. The research assignment was based on a program developed to build bridges between communities and educational institutions (Gonzalez & Moll, 2002; Rendón, 2002). This UTSA initiative introduces students to the idea that their transition from their community of origin to the higher education community is important. They are encouraged to explore their own thoughts and feelings to develop self-knowledge of their life transition.

Thus, Pathways is used as a way for students to have direct experiences with research while developing self-knowledge of their important transition. In these select classes of AIS, students participate in hands-on research projects that exposes them to qualitative and quantitative methodologies and real-world applications. They conduct case studies of their class's experience as first-year students, creating an interview protocol and conducting interviews. In exploratory sequential mixed-methods research, students use the results of class interviews to create surveys to distribute to other UTSA first-year students.

Periodic and structured opportunities for reflection and integration. At the beginning of the semester, course content focuses on epistemologies, different ways of creating and understanding knowledge, and academic cultures (i.e., humanities and arts, social sciences, and natural sciences). As students explore these new approaches to learning, they are given two 500-word journaling assignments in the first and second months of the semester. The prompt is to record their feelings as they transition from their home community to the University. Because many are first-generation and/or minority students, the journal entries often reflect conflicts and emotions related to their backgrounds. The students explore their individual experiences within the context of what they are learning about the creation of knowledge.

The students use what they consider to be the key aspects of their journals to create visuals to present to class that synthesize and demonstrate their thoughts on their transition experiences. They are asked to include 10 images from the Internet, personal photographs, or original artwork that represent their transitions from their communities of origin to the higher education community. They also prepare brief narratives (300 to 500 words) describing the images and their significance.

Significant investment of time, effort, and interactions with faculty and peers. In addition to examining their individual and personal experience through the journaling assignments, students explore the experience of the first-year cohort as a whole in a mixed-methods research project. They begin the study by exploring the first research question in the classroom setting: *For first-year students, what are the themes that describe the transition from the community of origin to the higher education community?*

After receiving instruction in how to write and conduct interview questions, students work in groups creating five or six good questions to probe for answers to the research question. They practice interviewing within their groups, gradually refining their work until they have four or five solid questions to be used in interviews, as well as follow-up questions. Groups are paired so that members of each group have the opportunity to interview members of the paired group.

Each student is interviewed, conducts an interview, and observes and takes notes on at least three other interviews. The interview begins with a student presenting his or her visual project, followed by a classmate presenting the questions their group has developed. The other group members observe and take notes. The interviews are conducted in the classroom, a procedure that allows the instructor and teaching assistant to observe and assist as needed. All interviews are completed over the course of one or two class periods. Students are instructed in using thick description by making note of everything they observe in the interview process. They use a standard worksheet to document the interviews and reflect on whether they have captured the nuances, adding anything they remember as being significant (e.g., from the visual project, the interview answers, observations of gestures or language). Returning to their own groups, the students collaborate to find four or five key themes that define their observations.

Students list on the board the quotations and observations that best represent what they have experienced and examine these for common themes. The class discusses the similarities and differences in the postings. The themes then serve as the foundation for the creation of a survey to broadcast to other first-year students at UTSA, based on the second research question: *What are the experiences of FYE students at UTSA, and are these experiences aligned with those of the 50 students in our class?*

Using a format similar to the interview protocol, each group writes six or seven closed-ended survey questions (i.e., multiple choice, Likert scale, yes–no). Groups post their questions on the online survey tool (SurveyMonkey), and students take these draft surveys, recording the questions they think are most effective. The class uses peer review procedures to examine the questions and, as a class, choose the best questions for a final 8- to 10-question survey. The final survey is posted on SurveyMonkey for the cohort, and AIS students invite other FYE friends and colleagues to take the survey. The findings from the survey are compiled and discussed in class. Students are then able to draw from these rich data sources to answer their research questions using their journaling essays, individual student interview information, and campus-wide survey responses.

Public demonstration of competence. Finally, students write the entire case study and create an academic poster to illustrate the most significant findings. Each group is assigned a section of the research report to write, including an introduction explaining the theoretical grounding and research questions; descriptions of the interview and survey methodologies; results from the interviews, such as themes and key examples or quotes; a discussion of the survey findings; and a conclusion. These individual sections are then assembled as a class research paper, which is organized on a poster template and presented at UTSA's undergraduate research event.

Frequent and constructive feedback. Students receive feedback from the teaching team and fellow classmates at various points during the project. Journal entries and the visual assignment are graded using a rubric evaluating the students' abilities to examine their experiences thoughtfully and select representations that present their unique stories in a meaningful way. Interview notes are graded for quality of observations and useful data, as are the individual survey questions and survey analysis. In addition, classmates provide feedback to each other during the individual and cohort survey question process. Contributions to the final poster also receive a grade. In total, the research project reflects 15% of the semester grade.

Discussion

The desired outcomes for the project reflect those of the AIS course. Students are expected to demonstrate and are assessed on state-mandated core curriculum requirements, including critical-thinking skills, both oral and written communication, and personal and social responsibility. Roughly three fourths of the Pathways students measured either strong or excellent in gauging their mastery of these core assessment areas. In terms of student satisfaction, sections implementing the Pathways project were higher in both the overall rating of the course and in the overall rating in the teaching of the course by more than 10% than the average of AIS course sections.

Via the Pathways Project, students develop self-knowledge and examine their own first-year experiences. They synthesize personal recollections and demonstrate the results in their visual projects. As one student wrote: "It was nice to look back at the first few months of the semester compared to … the end. I was able to see where I was able to grow mentally and grade-wise." In addition, students learn to design research protocols for interviews meant to collect data and to analyze the results to find important themes illuminating the research question. Students also create a quantitative survey, based on their qualitative findings, that measures the extent to which identified themes are present throughout the first-year cohort. Another typical student response: "I like that we conducted a unique kind of research relating to our transition from high school to college. I enjoyed making questions for the surveys and seeing the results after the study was conducted."

Finally, students have the opportunity to discuss findings and prepare a scholarly poster presentation with introduction, methods, results, and conclusion sections. Students build skills in working collaboratively at both the group and classroom levels. Although first-year students may be accustomed to class assignments that link lecture to theories and methods, having their work arranged and described in a scholarly poster is a new experience for many. When students are able to present their work at a campus-wide event, the results are inspiring: "I got to see what it was like to feel professional and be part of a (research) community."

Implications

Many entering UTSA students arrive from high school having focused on empirical learning and writing in order to pass standardized tests, rather than engaging in critical thinking. In the Pathways AIS course, as in all the AIS sections, students are encouraged to ask questions that have not yet been answered and to consider methods for finding those answers. The Pathways Project helps them to understand that they can accomplish their own research.

Further, students who have not been raised in a college-going environment (e.g., first-generation and/or minority students) may lack the cultural capital to maneuver successfully through the higher education landscape. The Pathways Project assists these students in two important ways. First, they become more aware of the questions they have concerning their unique experiences; and, second, they realize that other students are experiencing many of the same things, regardless of the diversity of their backgrounds. By treating these experiences as important, the Pathways Project validates the students and invites them to share their strengths as well as their insecurities.

UTSA's first-year students have benefited from the AIS course as well as the Pathways Project. Academic first-year seminars that develop basic research skills help students transition from high school to higher education (Brent, 2006) and build skills that can be used throughout the college journey. The Pathways Project model has been shown to be a valuable first-year experience and can be inserted in many first-year curricula.

References

Brent, D. (2006). Using an academic-content seminar to engage students with the culture of research. *Journal of The First-Year Experience & Students in Transition, 18*(1), 29-60.

Gonzalez, N., & Moll, L. C. (2002). Cruzando el puente: Building bridges to funds of knowledge. *Educational Policy, 16*(4), 623-641.

Rendón, L. I. (1994). Validating culturally diverse students: Toward a new model of learning and student development. *Innovative Higher Education, 19*(1), 33-51.

Rendón, L. I. (2002). Community college puente: A validating model of education. *Educational Policy, 16*(4), 642-667.

University of Texas at San Antonio (UTSA). (2016, March). *About UTSA*. Retrieved from http://www.utsa.edu/about/mission.html

Contact Information

Kathleen Fugate Laborde
Lecturer II
University of Texas at San Antonio
University College
1 UTSA Circle
San Antonio, TX 78249
E-mail: Kathleen.laborde@utsa.edu
Phone: (210) 458 5930

University of Wisconsin-Madison
Susan Brantly and Sorabh Singhal

The Institution

The University of Wisconsin – Madison (UW) is a four-year, public, research university located in Madison, Wisconsin, offering 232 undergraduate majors and minors spread between its eight undergraduate schools and colleges. In fall 2015, UW had an enrollment of 43,389 students, of whom 29,580 were undergraduates and 4,685 were first-year students. Among undergraduate students, 76% are White, 3% are African American, 5% are Hispanic, 7% are Asian, 8% of students are international, and 1% are Native American. Approximately 3% of the undergraduate cohort is over the age of 25, 49% are male, and about 25% live in campus housing.

Description of the Seminar

Founded in 1996, the Bradley Learning Community is an exclusively first-year residence hall at the UW, providing a living–learning environment that promotes a successful transition from high school to college life; encourages collaborative learning among students, faculty, and staff; and prepares students to become integrative scholars and active participants in the university community and beyond. In addition to professional staff members associated with the community, Bradley houses 246 residents who are served by 17 faculty members, 17 peer mentors, seven live-in student house fellows, and two part-time students dedicated to promoting leadership development and intentional programming. Over the past few years, Bradley has seen a steady increase in the number of international students it attracts, and for the fall 2015 semester, 24% of the residents were international students.

One of the flagship opportunities offered through Bradley is the Integrated Liberal Studies (ILS) 157 Roundtable first-year seminar (FYS). This is one of a variety of first-year seminars offered on campus, some through University Housing and others through various academic programs, such as the College of Agricultural and Life Sciences or the Center for the First-Year Experience. Although the seminar is not required of residents, 80% to 85% choose to participate. Classes are limited to 14 students, guaranteeing strong interactions with faculty and peers as well as frequent feedback. The one-credit, ungraded seminar meets for one hour per week, mostly within the residence hall. Five times during the semester, all sections convene to listen to a featured speaker and share a meal. With 20 years of refinement, this service-learning course has played a pivotal role in many students' transition to university life.

Educationally Effective Practices

Interactions with faculty and peers. Many sections begin with a Highs-and-Lows check-in, where students are able to share the highest and lowest parts of the previous week. By offering a structured setting for every student to speak to the small group, the activity gives them an opportunity to have a glimpse into each other's lives. Moreover, faculty can hear about students' transitional issues, which can be addressed in future classes. The small size of the sections means that the faculty fellows and peer mentors can pay individual attention to the needs of the residents, providing opportunity for frequent and constructive feedback.

Outside the classroom, faculty and peer mentors work to develop meaningful and structured assignments to ensure students have multiple opportunities to interact with campus professors. For example, to address students' fear of speaking with their instructors in large classes, Bradley residents must attend a faculty member's office hours and report back to the seminar group on their experience. Another common assignment is the Roundtable Presentation where students are challenged to teach their peers topics about which they are passionate, with talks ranging from Chinese New Year celebrations to how to engineer an alarm clock. By reflecting on their own experiences, developing short presentations, and sharing their passions with the group, students have opportunities to mentor others, and the activity allows faculty to connect with their Roundtable participants on a more personal level. It further promotes the value of intellectual curiosity as an important tool for taking charge of their own educations and succeeding in university life.

Expectations set at a high level. FYS activities are also designed to support first-year students in their transition to UW. For instance, to help students adapt their study habits to accommodate the rigor of college academics, FYS faculty integrate a Perceptual Thinking Patterns activity into their lesson plan. Within a workshop format, students discover their own comfort with visual, auditory, and kinesthetic learning styles, which in turn suggests different techniques for studying and notetaking. Students become better aware of their own learning styles and also develop an appreciation for those with different learning styles. The result of this activity is that in conversation with faculty and peers, residents are able to develop effective study practices for succeeding in the university academic environment. Faculty have also used other instruments to assist students in learning more about themselves and how they can best succeed, such as True Colors and Myers-Briggs.

The weekly meetings are also opportunities to address common misperceptions students may have about college and academic expectations (e.g., the importance of attending class). As students share their experiences from the first semester, it becomes clear that different strategies are required for success than those familiar from high school. Peer mentors are able to provide especially valuable advice because they have just experienced the first-year transition themselves. The personal connections formed with faculty members help residents realize that faculty do care about the effort put into their classes. The point is to raise students' own expectations for themselves and their understanding of the contributions they can make to their own success.

Relevance through real-world applications and experiences with diversity. One of the hallmarks across all FYS sections is the final project. Throughout the semester, students learn the importance of community involvement through service-oriented projects, where they work directly with their classmates, peer mentors, and instructors to make changes in the larger community. Increased community engagement is part of the mission of the Bradley Learning Community. The students themselves research the possibilities for service projects, inspired by Roundtable themes such as Just Connect, Pay it Forward, or Explore, thereby learning more about campus, city, state, and global communities. These projects, which have included a one-day fast to raise awareness of and money for the homeless through the Porchlight Foundation, making hats and scarves for homeless elementary students, and a fundraising event for Heifer International to send a girl to school and purchase livestock for families in developing countries, among many others, allow FYS students to learn from the perspectives of the people they serve while making a difference locally and globally. Students prepare presentations on their projects, which involve the reflection component essential to service-learning.

To maximize opportunities to connect the classroom learning to real-world applications and the community experience, FYS students attend monthly Roundtable Dinners that feature a campus or community member who shares insights on the semester's theme. The Dinners are opportunities for all 200 students to come together and draw parallels between their small-section activities and real-world challenges. For example, for the fall 2015 Make a Change theme, a campus faculty member was invited to speak on a canoe-building project connecting UW and the Ojibwe Nation, a Native American community within the state of Wisconsin. FYS students learned how this collaborative effort increased esteem for native traditions among young people and resulted in improvements in educational success among the Ojibwe. The Roundtable Dinners serve both to unite the Bradley group and to expand their community learning.

In an attempt to learn from the diversity that exists within Roundtable sections, some faculty ask students to write poems about their hometowns, using a template (First, 2005). The poems provide an opportunity for learning about each other's differences with curiosity and respect.

Public demonstration of competence and periodic and structured opportunities for reflection and integration. To promote reflection on the service projects and support a sense of achievement, FYS students present what they have learned through their service projects to the entire Bradley community. Encouraged by their faculty members and peer mentors, the students take this unique opportunity to personalize their presentations with creative ideas, such as writing short songs, performing skits, or bringing small prizes for their audience. These presentations are delivered to the entire seminar group during the final, capstone Roundtable dinner. In a supportive and relaxed environment, students are introduced to large-audience public speaking early in their college journey, a valuable skill for many future careers.

The individual Roundtable sections provide weekly opportunities for reflection, promoting integrated learning. Students are called upon to write letters to themselves at the beginning of the course, describing their expectations for the semester. These letters are returned at the end of the semester, providing an opportunity for students to consider how their transitions have gone.

Discussion

At the end of each semester, FYS participants complete an online course evaluation. Every three years, the Bradley Learning Community participates in the National Survey of Student Engagement (NSSE) and in the intervening years supplies its own Bradley Survey of Student Engagement (BSSE). University Housing also conducted surveys of learning communities during the fall 2014 and fall 2015 semesters.

One of Bradley's operating assumptions is that if students are able to interact with instructors in small-class and informal environments during the first semester, then they will be more likely to approach faculty for help, advice, and information in the future, resulting in a successful academic career. The 2014 NSSE indicated that Bradley residents spoke with faculty about career plans at a somewhat higher rate than the general population (82% vs. 75%). Similarly, Bradley students discussed course topics, ideas, or concepts with instructors outside of class at a somewhat higher rate than other first-year students (75% vs. 67%). Residents also worked with faculty members on activities other than coursework at a significantly higher rate (62% vs. 48%) compared to other students. On the 2015 Roundtable course evaluation, 82% of residents said they got to know their faculty fellows differently than other faculty, a rate that is typical of previous years as well.

In the 2014 NSSE, 60% of Bradley residents reported that they found their entire educational experience excellent, as compared to 51% of the general UW population. According to the University Housing Assignments Office, 48.4% of 2015 Bradley residents indicated they would be returning to live in University Housing in 2016, which is a much higher return rate than any other dormitory on campus: further evidence of residents' satisfaction with their Bradley experience.

Students' qualitative comments on the FYS course evaluation suggest a range of important outcomes for students, including the value of civic engagement, openness to diverse others, and academic skills, among others:

Professors are normal people and are a resource to help with all types of problems.

[I learned about] the importance of making a difference in the community.

I learned how to be more open to other people because I interacted with people from other countries and regions.

Roundtable helped make my transition into college much easier. I also learned how to get involved in the Madison community and how to make a change.

There was a huge culture shock for me. It helped tremendously to just sit and talk about life with people.

I picked up study habits from talking to those around me.

Implications

An important feature of Bradley's Roundtable seminar is its small size. Learning environments that foster informal interactions are key to reducing student stress and facilitating the transition to college. Another key component is the access residents have to faculty and peer mentors. The connections that are forged through the Roundtable seminar will serve these residents throughout their educational careers and will encourage students to continue creating connections with other faculty and useful resources. Roundtable sections seek to urge students to set high expectations for themselves and to be mindful of their study habits and the effort required for academic success. The emphasis on community fosters a collaborative spirit, so that residents can help each other succeed and feel comfortable seeking help when necessary. The service-learning component of the course teaches students that they can make a difference, gaining valuable insights from the experiences of diverse others. Although living–learning communities are not an option at many institutions, simple practices such as the Highs-and-Lows check-in, poetry about hometowns, and student presentations help to promote intellectual curiosity and can easily be integrated into a wide range of first-year seminars to support the transition of first-year students, increase their engagement with the campus community, and promote student success.

References

First, F. (2005, March 5). *Where are you from?* Retrieved from http://www.swva.net/fred1st/wif.htm

Contact Information

Susan Brantly
Birgit Baldwin Professor of Scandinavian Studies
Faculty Director of the Bradley Learning Community
University of Wisconsin, Madison
1306 Van Hise Hall
1220 Linden Dr
Madison, WI 53706
E-mail: sbrantly@wisc.edu

Virginia Commonwealth University
Melissa C. Johnson and Beth Kreydatus

The Institution

Virginia Commonwealth University (VCU) is an urban, public research university with 13 schools and two colleges, located in Richmond, Virginia. In fall 2015, VCU had an enrollment of 31,163 students, of whom 23,962 were undergraduates and 4,090 were first-year students. Among first-year students, 45% identified as White, 19% as African American, 15% as Asian, 8% as Hispanic, 3% as international, 6% as two or more races, and less than 1% as Native American or Hawaiian/Pacific Islander. In this cohort, 87% of first-year students are in-state residents, and 63% are female. Many students are the first in their families to attend college. In fall 2013, VCU's first-year student retention rate was 87%. VCU has been recognized by the Education Trust for boosting graduation rates and closing the graduation gap among underrepresented minority students (Eberle-Sudré, Welch, & Nichols, 2015; Nguyen, Bibo, & Engle, 2012).

Description of the Initiative

To improve student engagement in the first year, in fall 2007, VCU replaced one semester of the first-year composition requirement (English 101) with a two-semester, three-credit (each), first-year seminar requirement known as Focused Inquiry (FI; UNIV 111 and UNIV 112). The course sequence serves as the first tier of the core curriculum. Initially, 42 full-time, term (non-tenure track with renewable contracts and promotion) faculty members were hired to teach these classes in the University College. Presently, the Department of Focused Inquiry is made up of 63 full-time, term faculty members from a variety of disciplinary backgrounds who collaborate to design and teach three required, sequential intensive seminars to first- and second-year students (UNIV 111, 112, and 200).

The FI seminars engage students in the process of sustained, rigorous academic inquiry in a small, cohesive, learning community. Classes of 22 students remain with the same faculty members and peers for both UNIV 111 and 112. Using a common theme, a faculty-developed reader based on that theme, and two common books, students explore big questions through an interdisciplinary lens. The faculty-developed shared curriculum outlines learning outcomes and core assignments in the two courses. The learning outcomes prioritize critical thinking, oral and written communication, information fluency, ethical reasoning, quantitative reasoning, and collaboration. The core assignments are designed as a spiral, enabling students to build on previous learning, while being broadly defined to give faculty some autonomy. All faculty design their courses to promote and encourage student engagement through active learning. With the exception of students enrolled in the Honors College or with advanced placement (AP), international baccalaureate (IB), or dual-enrollment credits, all first-year students take both courses. During fall 2015, 3,381 students from the first-year class of 4,090 students were enrolled in UNIV 111 and UNIV 112.

The faculty of the Department of Focused Inquiry come from a range of disciplines, including English, creative writing, comparative literature, education, American studies, sociology, history, philosophy, and ethnomusicology. In addition to their own disciplinary research, FI faculty share a common interest and expertise in pedagogy, and many faculty members present and publish on the scholarship of teaching and learning. Faculty typically teach four sections per semester and engage in substantial service through departmental and university-wide committees. The faculty are highly collaborative, regularly sharing assignment ideas and lesson plans, participating in mutual observation, and engaging in pedagogical research together in Faculty Learning Communities. Faculty members regularly incorporate experiential learning, gaming, thoughtful use of technology, collaborative or layered assignments, and other innovations into their pedagogy. In addition, many faculty members work with the Division of Community Engagement to offer service-learning experiences for their students.

The Department also has a robust Undergraduate Teaching Assistant (UTA) program. The UTAs offer support and encouragement to their first-year peers, model successful student behaviors, and confer with their faculty mentors to offer student insights into the curriculum. In addition to the UTA program, the Department has a Graduate Teaching Assistant program through which graduate students are mentored and trained to teach FI courses.

Educationally Effective Practices

Significant investment of time and effort. The FI program intentionally and successfully incorporates educationally effective practices into the curriculum. For example, the course requires significant investment of time and effort from students. Students are required to complete three semesters enrolled in intensive seminars that demand substantial thinking, writing, revision, and collaboration. In the first-year seminars (UNIV 111 and 112), students are expected to produce three formal written assignments and complete two oral presentations in each course, along with substantial process and group work, including informal writing on the University's Rampages WordPress blogging platform each semester.

Interactions with faculty and peers. FI also prioritizes frequent, high-quality interactions with faculty and peers. In addition to the peer mentoring many students receive through the UTA program, all students in FI are expected to collaborate both within and outside the classroom. The shared curriculum and common UNIV 112 syllabus ask students to "effectively collaborate on activities and projects" and "provide peer response and participate in group feedback." Faculty understand student support to be a key professional responsibility. The Department works closely with other units on campus—including the Writing Center, the Learning Center, Academic Advising, and Student Affairs—to connect students to resources that support their intellectual and personal development. Relatively small class sizes accommodate close faculty–student collaboration; typically, FI faculty are responsible for 88 students each semester. Almost all faculty have a practice of conferencing with students, either individually or in small groups, as they work on major assignments, and faculty also tend to have well-attended office hours. Finally, many FI faculty build community collaboration into the classroom by offering service-learning sections of UNIV 111 and 112 to their students.

Collaborative assignments and projects and experiences with diversity. Collaboration among VCU's exceptionally diverse first-year student population creates regular opportunities for students to learn about differing viewpoints, ways of knowing, and life experiences. "Acknowledging alternate viewpoints and values" is a chief intended outcome for the FI's shared curriculum, and readings, assignments, and themes are chosen with this priority in mind. Additionally, faculty have worked hard to make the FI classroom an inclusive environment for all students by pursuing training to better serve LGBTQ+ students, students affiliated with the military, and international students. VCU has recently revived a week-long Institute for Inclusive Teaching, and in just the first two years of this program, more than a quarter of FI faculty have participated. These experiences help FI faculty take advantage of VCU's diversity and create inclusive spaces for exchange of diverse perspectives.

Periodic and structured opportunities for reflection and integration. The shared curriculum identifies "reflect[ing] on experiences, texts, the writing process, and class activities" as an intended outcome of the course. To this purpose, most instructors require students to submit a writer's memo with major products, asking students to assess their process, their strengths and weaknesses, and their goals for future assignments. The FI spiral curriculum provides an overall shape to the semester that explicitly encourages and rewards student reflection. Further, it allows students to repeat activities and revisit concepts through increasingly complex and involved assignments intended to deepen their understanding, internalize the steps of the analytical process, and build critical-thinking skills.

Public demonstration of competence. Finally, students have multiple opportunities to demonstrate their competence before peers and before the University community at large. In addition to required class presentations, first-year students benefit from participating in the end-of-year FI Expo—a celebration and exhibition of the academic work accomplished in the FI classrooms. Hundreds of students are invited to give oral presentations, display academic posters, or demonstrate digital compositions for the University community at large. At the Expo, winners of a departmental student essay contest are publically recognized, and their work is published in the subsequent year's FI Reader. Lastly, the department has spearheaded a university-wide drive to incorporate online writing into the curriculum by asking every student to create and maintain a blog throughout the class. Increasingly, other departments at VCU are asking students to build on that first-year portfolio and add to it as they do upper-level course work. The public nature of these blogs creates opportunities for students to engage with audiences beyond their immediate first-year FI classrooms and to engage in connected learning.

Discussion

Since 2007, assessment of the FI seminars has been a high priority for the program. For example, the faculty assess learning outcomes, especially critical thinking, written communication, and ethical reasoning, in FI courses by employing a pre- and post-assessment of student writing. This assessment suggests that students improve significantly in these areas over the course of their first year.

Along with annual reports by faculty members and peer observation, the course evaluations used in UNIV 111 and UNIV 112 have allowed VCU to assess the prevalence of high-impact practices. The course evaluation instrument is derived from the CLASSE, a course-level instrument based on questions from the National Survey of Student Engagement (NSSE). The NSSE is used for assessment of student engagement on an institutional level and calls for student reporting on activities, experiences, and behaviors that correlate with student engagement and learning and include Level of Academic Challenge, Active and Collaborative Learning, Student–Faculty Interaction, and Enriching Educational Experiences (NSSE, n.d.).

Department averages from course evaluations (see Table 1) show that educationally effective practices are common in FI. Student responses on these course evaluations suggest the educationally effective practices employed in the FI courses have had a meaningful impact on their experiences in the seminar.

This high level of engagement in FI courses translates into increased persistence and academic performance. As the graph in Figure 1 illustrates, the rate at which first-year students at VCU are retained into their second year and complete their first-year coursework in academic good standing has improved significantly with the creation of the FI program. Enrollment in UNIV 111/112 and the second-year course UNIV 200 has had a similarly positive impact on five-year graduation rates. For first-year students beginning fall 2010 who took all three courses (UNIV 111, 112, and 200), the five-year graduation rate is 66.45%, compared to an overall rate of 56.63% and a rate of 60.71% for students who took none of these courses. Of those students who took none of the courses and who are not in the Honors College, the five-year graduation rate was 53.69%, a 12.75% difference. The five-year graduation rate for those who took UNIV 112 and UNIV 200 only (based on AP and IB credit) is 76.53%.

Implications

Since 2007, first-year students at VCU have participated in an interdisciplinary seminar sequence that has made rigorous inquiry and skill acquisition central to its shared curriculum. The FI seminars have successfully incorporated a range of educationally effective practices in their design. Given that the FI courses are taken over two semesters and that most students report spending more than three hours a week preparing for these classes, it is clear they require significant investment of time and effort from students. Frequent interactions with peers and faculty are the norm in the FI classroom: Students overwhelmingly indicated on their evaluations that FI instructors were readily available outside the classroom, and students noted they frequently worked with peers to prepare for class. FI classes make consideration of diverse perspectives central to their curriculum, and students stated they regularly considered multiple perspectives in completing course assignments or in class discussions. By employing a spiral curriculum, FI has made periodic and structured opportunities for reflection and integration inherent in the course design. The Expo, Rampages blogging requirements, class presentations, and student essay contests have created opportunities for students' public demonstrations of competence. It is evident these measures have led to increased student retention, improved learning, and enhanced engagement.

Table 1

Department Averages From Course Evaluations

Educationally effective practice	Question from course evaluation completed by students	Department average, Fall 2015
Expectations set at appropriately high levels	Had to engage in critical thinking to meet the expectations of the course	4.46
	Made connections between your learning in this course and other courses	3.72
	Used skills and techniques learned in this course for work in other courses	3.92
	Made judgments about the value and reliability of information, arguments, or research sources	4.25
Significant investment of time and effort	Used writing to explore and develop ideas	4.53
	Engaged in a process of writing that involved drafting and revision	4.52
	Spent more than three hours per week preparing for class (e.g., writing, reading, doing homework, analyzing data, using support services, rehearsing, other academic matters)	4.06
Interactions with faculty and peers	Shared written work with peers for feedback	4.23
	Asked questions or contributed to a class discussion in other ways	4.23
	Worked with classmates on class activities and or projects	4.29
	Discussed ideas from this class with others outside of class (e.g., students, family members, roommates, coworkers)	3.85
Experiences with diversity	Learned something that changed my own views or enhanced the way I understand an issue or concept	4.05
	Considered multiple perspectives in completing course assignments or in class discussions	4.32
Frequent and constructive feedback	The feedback I received from my instructor on my work enhanced my learning	4.32
	The instructor was available as a resource for students outside of class (e.g., office hours, appointments, e-mail or other electronic communication)	4.64
Periodic and structured opportunities for reflection and integration	Reflected on my own learning or performance and acted to improve it	4.18
Public demonstration of competence	Gave a presentation, whether group or individual, spontaneous or prepared	3.96
	Used an online medium (e.g., blogs, Blackboard, wiki, Google Docs) for writing, discussion, and/or to otherwise enhance learning in the course	4.41

Note. All questions are on a frequency scale that is then translated into a numerical scale of 1-5: *Very Often* = 5, *Often* = 4, *Sometimes* = 3, *Infrequently* = 2, *Never* = 1.

First-Year Cohort: Retention and Good Standing

— Percentage of First-Year Cohort Retained into Second Year
— Percentage of First-Year Cohort in Good Standing at the End of Its First Year

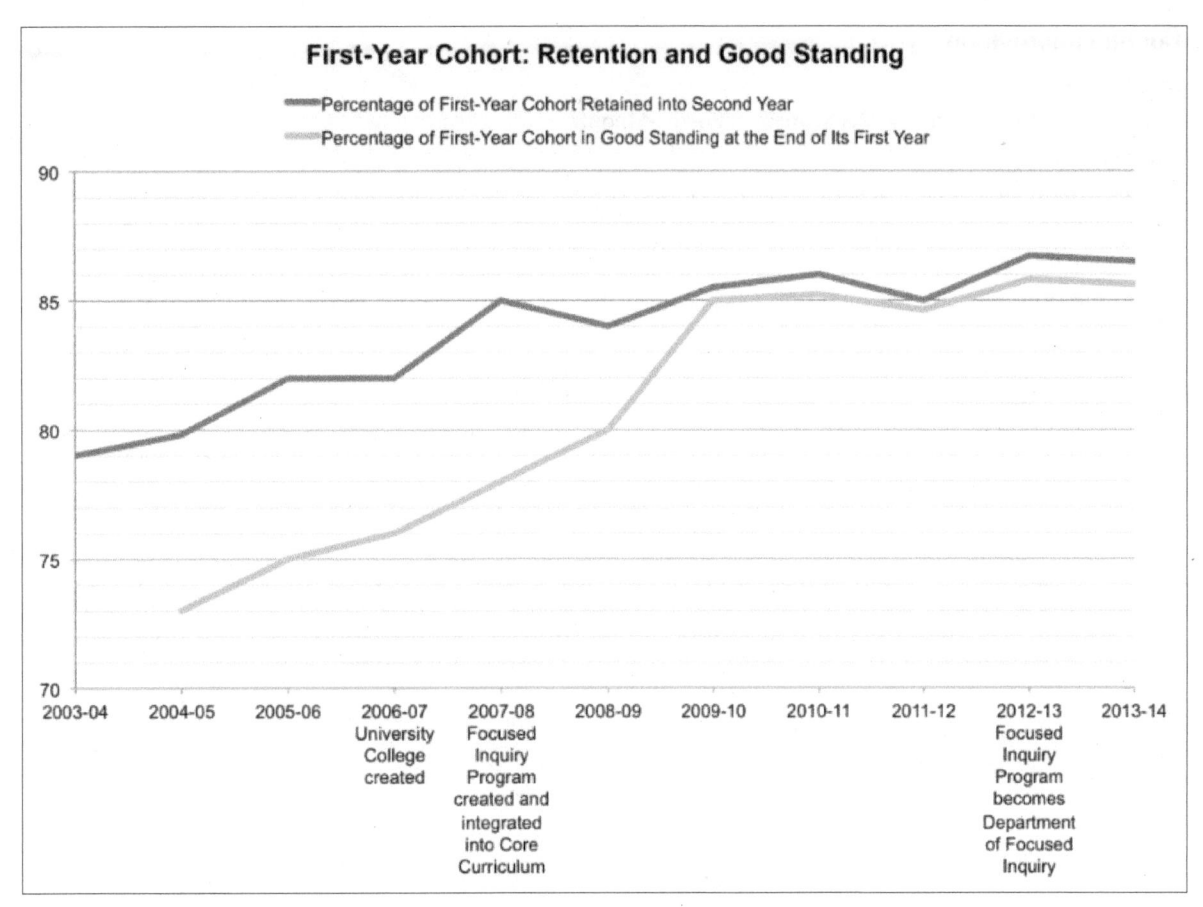

[2006-07: University College created]
[2007-08: Focused Inquiry Program created and integrated into Core Curriculum]
[2012-13: Focused Inquiry Program becomes Department of Focused Inquiry]

Figure 1. First-year retention and first-year cohort in good academic standing.

As VCU approaches the 10th anniversary of teaching these courses, the University endeavors to maintain and expand educationally effective practices in these courses by providing additional opportunities for community-engaged experiential learning and exploring the possibility of incorporating a study-abroad option for first-year students into the curriculum.

The primary reason for VCU's success with its first-year seminars is that they are taught by a full-time, dedicated interdisciplinary faculty fully invested in curricular design and revision, pedagogical and scholarly collaboration, and student success. The level of faculty investment that this structure both results in and demands allows VCU to continuously build on its achievements, to largely avoid the pitfalls of high turnover and faculty burnout, and to strive for excellence in teaching and learning.

References

Eberle-Sudré, K., Welch, M., & Nichols, A. H. (2015, December). *Rising tide: Do college grad rate gains benefit all students?* Washington, DC: The Education Trust. Retrieved from https://edtrust.org/wp-content/uploads/2014/09/TheRisingTide-Do-College-Grad-Rate-Gains-Benefit-All-Students-3.7-16.pdf

National Survey of Student Engagement (NSSE). (n.d.). *About*. Retrieved from http://nsse.indiana.edu/html/about.cfm

Nguyen, M., Bibo, E. W., & Engle, J. (2012, September). *Advancing to completion: Increasing degree attainment by improving graduation rates and closing gaps for African-American students*. Washington, DC: The Education Trust. Retrieved from http://edtrust.org/wp-content/uploads/2013/10/Advancing_AfAm.pdf

Contact Information

Melissa C. Johnson
Chair and Associate Professor, Department of Focused Inquiry
University College
Virginia Commonwealth University
PO Box 842015
Richmond, VA 23284
E-mail: mcjohnson@vcu.edu
Phone: (803) 827-3614

Conclusion: What Does It Mean to Be High Impact?
Tracy L. Skipper

The purpose of this collection was to gather evidence about the characteristics of first-year seminars that make them high-impact practices (HIPs). If all first-year seminars were small, faculty-led courses exploring a scholarly topic related to the instructor's area of research and focused on critical inquiry, writing, collaborative learning, and other essential practical and intellectual skills, such an exploration might not be necessary. However, national survey data suggest that many first-year seminars do not meet this definition. The academic seminar as described here may be offered on less than one third of U.S. college campuses (Young & Hopp, 2014). Even on those campuses where it is offered, other seminar types are also likely to be part of the course catalog. How do we know whether students are receiving a high-impact educational experience when the first-year seminar in which they are enrolled does not meet the definition most often cited in the HIPs literature? How do we judge the quality or effectiveness of different types of seminars—or even different sections of the same seminar—on the same campus?

Here, we have attempted to discern answers to these questions by asking authors to describe the first-year seminars on their campuses and to demonstrate the presence of conditions that support high levels of student engagement and learning. Minimally, authors had to provide evidence that the seminar included at least two of the eight effective educational practices associated with HIPs (see Kuh & O'Donnell, 2013) to be considered for inclusion. Moreover, we sought to include robust descriptions of what those practices looked like in action. We also attempted to include cases where the effective educational practices informed or were the focus of first-year seminar assessment, although we placed less emphasis on that. This concluding essay summarizes what the authors suggest about the presence and qualities of effective educational practices in various first-year seminars while highlighting potential gaps or possibilities for strengthening the seminar as a HIP.

Evidence of Effective Educational Practices

Five different seminar types—extended orientation, academic – uniform content, academic – variable content, basic study skills, and hybrid—were represented among the cases selected for inclusion in this collection. On average, authors described the presence of 5.3 effective educational practices per case study. Academic variable content seminars included the most effective educational practices, with an average of 6.3 per case; this finding may offer some indication of why this type of first-year seminar persists as the ideal in the HIPs literature. That said, the average number of effective educational practices cited by authors describing other seminar types ranged from 4.5 (basic study skills seminars) to 5.8 (hybrid seminars), suggesting that students enrolled in other types of seminars are also exposed to a range of high-quality educational experiences. With the exception of experiences with diversity, the effective educational practices were present in each of the different seminar types represented in this collection. That is, no effective educational practice appears to be the exclusive domain on any one seminar type. Put another way, all types of first-year seminars have the potential to be high-impact educational practices.

In the remainder of this section, I summarize the prevalence and ways in which these practices were enacted in the first-year seminars described in this collection (see also Table 1).

- ***Periodic, structured opportunities to reflect on and integrate learning.*** All of the authors described opportunities for reflection that were embedded in the seminar. The most common strategy was journaling. Alternately, students were asked to write reflective papers or assignments, some of which were letters to themselves, essays written at the beginning and end of the course to demonstrate growth or change, or culminating essays reflecting on the course or the first semester. A range of other reflective activities were also described, including personal narratives, self-assessment inventories, portfolio development, practicing the principles of self-regulated learning, concept maps, reading responses, and writer's memos. An electronic portfolio is the cornerstone of the University College's first-year seminar at Indiana University – Purdue University Indianapolis. Sections within the portfolio encourage students to explore their identities, make connections between their experiences and possible careers, and document their involvement and its impact on them. The emphasis on reflection may stem from the fact that many first-year seminars are process-oriented in nature, rather than focused on mastery of a specific content area.

- ***Interactions with faculty and peers about substantive matters.*** Peer and faculty interaction also figured prominently among the effective educational practices incorporated in the seminars. One third of the authors described peer mentor involvement in the delivery of the seminar. Strategies for engaging students with their more immediate peers include group projects (i.e., papers, presentations), structured classroom discussions designed to involve all students, collaborative learning activities, learning teams, and peer teaching. For example, in a mathematics-focused seminar at the University of Maryland Baltimore County, students developed puzzles and explained the solutions to their classmates; each student was also responsible for leading one class discussion. Strategies supporting faculty interactions were less robust, though some described using the reflective journal as a site for dialogue between students and faculty. In some cases, faculty held conferences with individual or small groups of students. Because the importance of faculty engagement extends beyond the first-year seminar, some courses included a requirement that students meet with a faculty member teaching one of their other courses at some point during the academic term.

- ***Frequent, timely, and constructive feedback.*** The third most frequently incorporated effective educational practice focused on feedback. Seminars included rubrics to provide feedback on specific assignments, incorporated writing conferences with instructors and/or peer review workshops, scaffolded assignments and required revisions, and encouraged students to visit the campus writing center. Students at the American University of Rome use feedback from peers and their instructors to hone their oral communication skills following review of videotapes of their first presentations.

- ***Opportunities to discover relevance of learning through real-world applications.*** A variety of strategies help students connect what they are learning in the seminar to the real world. Service-learning experiences were most commonly mentioned, followed by a requirement that students participate in a prescribed number or type of out-of-class learning experiences. Other practices included field trips or field experiences, activities that emphasized the connection between college experiences and future careers, alumni mentors, and research on real-world problems. Seminars at LaGuardia Community College and Montana State University, for example, engage students in primary research on real-world issues.

- ***Public demonstration of competence.*** Most commonly, seminars included symposia or showcases—for first-year students or for all undergraduates—where students could make presentations of significant work completed in the course. Students frequently were expected to give oral presentations in class and occasionally were encouraged to submit class work for publication in print or online (e.g., creation of a website or blog) formats. Several seminars involved students in primary research, with students presenting their findings to their seminar sections or larger audiences. The University of Kansas offered one of the most unique practices connected to demonstration of competence: Students in a science-oriented first-year seminar designed and taught an interactive lesson as part of a family-focused discovery day at a local museum.

- ***Experiences with diversity.*** Of the 15 seminars that highlighted diversity as an effective educational practice, five had diversity as a primary course theme (e.g., a focus on social justice issues or culture and diversity). In other seminars, the course texts were intentionally chosen to represent a variety of perspectives, genres, and

Table 1

Evidence of Effective Educational Practices in First-Year Seminars

Effective educational practice	Implementation strategy
Opportunities to reflect on and integrate learning ($n = 27$)	Reflective journal/weekly reflective exercises Reflective papers/assignments Personal narrative Self-assessment inventories (e.g., LASSI, personality inventories) Reflective essay (final) or pre/post reflective essays/letters to self Portfolio development Teaching and practicing principles of self-regulated learning (i.e., planning, doing, reflecting) Personal goal setting/life planning/values clarification Education plan Classroom assessment techniques (i.e., one-minute paper, think-pair, share) Creation of concept maps Reading responses Writer's memos
Interactions with faculty and peers ($n = 24$)	Group/partner paper/presentation/project Group discussions/structured classroom discussions Collaborative learning activities/small-group activities Learning community configuration Learning teams/peer teaching Replies to journal entries; dialogue in journals Assigned visits to faculty One-on-one conferences
Frequent, timely, and constructive feedback ($n = 18$)	Encouraging use of campus writing center Videotaping presentations Writing conferences Peer review workshops (writing/presentations) Use of rubrics Scaffolded assignments Required revisions
Relevance of learning through real-world applications ($n = 17$)	Field trips/field experiences Participation in on-campus/off-campus experiences/out-of-class learning experiences Activities emphasizing connection between college and future careers Service-learning Research on real-world problems Alumni mentors
Public demonstration of competence ($n = 15$)	Participation in undergraduate symposium/research showcase; oral presentations in a public forum Oral presentations (in-class) Submission of class work for publication (print or online, such as a blog) Conducting primary research/presenting findings Public teaching demonstrations/outreach
Experiences with diversity ($n = 15$)	Establishing diversity as a primary focus of the seminar Community service experiences Social barometer activities Course texts representing a variety of perspectives, genre, etc. Elements of identity presentation/structured opportunities for sharing Connection to common read, emphasizing diversity issues Faculty development on inclusive teaching

Table continues on page 152

Table continued from page 151

Effective educational practice	Implementation strategy
Significant investment of time and effort ($n = 14$)	Research papers (on academic topic, major) Academic papers (i.e., thesis-driven, argumentative) Attendance requirement Required reading Direct research experience Three-course sequence demanding substantial thinking, writing, revision, and collaboration
Performance expectations set at appropriately high levels ($n = 13$)	Discussions about purpose of the course/introduction to college-level academic expectations Scaffolded/staged writing assignments/expectations for college-level writing Student-led discussions/peer teaching Significant reading (quantity, difficulty) Gamification Direct research experiences

so forth. When the common reading emphasized diversity issues, connecting to that text was a strategy for incorporating this effective educational practice. Community service experiences were also used to expose students to diversity, as were social barometer activities and structured opportunities for sharing personal aspects of the self with other class members. Virginia Commonwealth University encouraged a focus on diversity and inclusivity by having faculty participate in a week-long workshop on inclusive teaching.

- ***Significant investment of time and effort by students.*** To show investment of time and effort, case study authors frequently pointed to the kinds of assignments students completed in the seminars—research papers on an academic topic or major/career field or other academic writing (e.g., thesis-driven essays, argumentative pieces). Other strategies included attendance requirements or required readings. Students participating in Pathways seminars at the University of Texas at San Antonio designed a mixed-method study to explore their own transition experiences and those of other first-year students at the university. At Virginia Commonwealth, students participate in a three-course sequence that emphasizes substantial thinking, writing, revision, and collaboration.

- ***Performance expectations set at appropriately high levels.*** Closely related to investment of time and effort, evidence related to performance expectations included engaging students in scaffolded or staged writing assignments, having students conduct primary research, and assigning a significant quantity of college-level reading. The base level of this practice included discussions about the purpose of the course or introduction to college-level expectations. At Ithaca College, students assume management of the class during the second half, selecting the readings, creating instructional materials, and developing activities and discussion prompts.

Reviewing the descriptions of effective educational practices across different seminar types for consistent themes revealed two primary issues. First, the authors sometimes provided descriptions of a seminar at a high level (i.e., institutional or program level); at other times, they focused on a single section of a seminar. Still other authors explored the seminar as it was embedded in various programs or majors across the campus, emphasizing different principles across seminars or describing different strategies for enacting them. Depending on the vantage point, the practices that were highlighted might be a function of a larger departmental mandate or intentional course design, the style and goals on an individual instructor, or a reflection of course goals/purpose as related to its position within the institution (i.e., a discipline-specific seminar). Such variability points to the challenge of assessing the quality and effectiveness of the first-year seminar as a HIP on a broad scale. Where institutions provide different types of seminars and/or offer opportunities for customization at the program or section level, instructors will need clear guidance on how their institutions define these effective educational practices and suggested strategies for implementing them. Table 1 provides a good starting point, as it summarizes the range of strategies brought to bear in a variety of different seminars. Individual instructors could still have broad latitude in how they embed the practices in their sections, but providing operational definitions and options may help ensure a more consistent experience for students.

Second, there seems to be a good bit of fluidity in how case authors categorized learning experiences with respect to effective educational practices. For example, service experiences were cited as exposing students to diversity and as providing a vehicle to connect learning to real-world applications. Similarly, scaffolded writing assignments were variously presented as evidence of expectations set at appropriately high levels and significant investment of time and effort. Primary research experiences were connected to appropriately high expectations, significant investment of time and effort, real-world applications, and public demonstration of competence. The convergence of several practices under a particular type of assignment or learning experience suggests the potential of those experiences to engage students at high levels. Seminars that include one or more such high-value experiences may represent a better quality HIP than those without such experiences.

Assessing the Quality of High-Impact Practices

All case authors were asked to describe formal or informal evaluation of the effective educational practices embedded in the seminar. Specifically, we wanted to see the evidence to suggest that these practices contributed to seminar outcomes. The descriptions of assessment vary widely, as some authors explored a single section of the seminar, whereas others described assessment conducted at a program level. The range of assessment methods reflects the scope and purposes of the assessments (i.e., Was it designed to improve course delivery within the current academic term? Was it designed to demonstrate program effectiveness and drive program improvement?). Authors also described the measured outcomes and/or highlighted specific findings from institutional assessment studies. A summary of methods used and outcomes described follows.

Assessment measures. The most frequently mentioned assessment measures were end-of-course evaluations, followed by rubrics and portfolios or capstone assignments. Rubrics were used to examine specific assignments or to measure a particular capacity, such as critical thinking or writing ability. Several institutions described using or adapting the VALUE rubrics developed by the Association of American Colleges and Universities (Rhodes, 2010). Other campuses used student presentations or papers as direct evidence of student learning. Student artifacts were assessed with a rubric or were subjected to textual analysis to demonstrate the presence of particular outcomes.

Although most of the assessment measures focused on summative assessment, several cases included formative approaches, such as the use of one-minute papers or other CATs (i.e., classroom assessment techniques) and mid-semester evaluations. Rubrics were sometimes used to explore performance at the program level, but in other cases rubric use was described as a strategy for offering feedback to students about their own learning and development or for providing insight to instructors about where course adjustments may be needed. In this way, rubrics functioned as a valuable formative assessment technique.

Student performance was a focus of many assessments, yet some authors described strategies that were designed to examine the effectiveness of course delivery. Florida SouthWestern State College used a 360-degree evaluation technique to assess peer mentor involvement. Coastal Carolina and Virginia Commonwealth Universities used classroom observations to gauge instructor performance. The University of Texas at Austin conducted an ethnographic research project that included the analysis of course artifacts (e.g., the syllabus, assignment prompts), observations, and interviews with students.

Outcomes. Given the focus on end-of-course evaluations, it is perhaps not surprising that the most commonly assessed outcomes were self-reported gains in learning and development. Other frequently noted outcomes that can also be drawn from course evaluations are related to satisfaction or perceptions of effectiveness—of the seminar, of peer mentors, and of faculty. High-impact practices, and first-year seminars in particular, have been linked to improved retention. Thus, it is not surprising that the third most commonly reported outcome—following learning and satisfaction—was retention or persistence. Closely related are academic progress (i.e., course completion) and graduation rates. Academic performance outcomes (i.e., GPA, academic probation rates) were also cited by a number of authors.

A range of specific student learning outcomes—those with a direct connection to the educational effective practices explored here—appeared throughout. Writing and critical thinking skills were well represented, but many of these outcomes were only described in one case, or two at the most. These outcomes included appreciation of cultural differences, oral communication skills, integrative learning, leadership development, engagement with faculty, and ethical reasoning.

Few of the cases offered compelling evidence of how the intentional incorporation of effective educational practices supported seminar outcomes, though several cases pointed to places in their current assessment plans where that evidence might be found. These authors highlighted the end-of-course evaluations, event critiques, journals, capstone projects, and rubrics tied to specific assignments or course products. A more thorough understanding of the potential impact of these practices might not necessitate introducing new assessment measures; rather, it may simply involve a more nuanced understanding of the kinds of evidence already being collected and discussion of how that evidence provides insight into the presence and impact of effective educational practices.

Final Thoughts

Without a doubt, first-year seminars other than an academic seminar in a content area have the potential to offer students a high-impact educational experience early in their college careers. That said, first-year seminar administrators can undoubtedly be more intentional about the prevalence of effective educational practices in these courses and the care with which they are administered. A first step might simply be to audit the first-year seminar(s) on campus. Which practices are readily apparent in the seminar as currently delivered? Should some less visible practices be prominent because of their alignment with larger program or institutional goals? How can those practices be more frequently and effectively incorporated into the seminars?

The implementation of effective educational practices depends on front-line instructional faculty. As such, discussion of what is meant by those practices, and possibilities for bringing them into the classroom, should be a cornerstone of faculty development initiatives related to the first-year seminar.

In addition to being more intentional about making sure effective educational practices are threaded throughout seminars, program administrators may need to be more thoughtful about how to assess these practices. Where cases highlighted connections between effective educational practices and first-year seminar assessment, they seemed focused primarily on documenting the existence of the practices. For example, students might be asked whether they received feedback from instructors, were asked to consider multiple perspectives in completing course assignments, or participated in a service experience. Their collective responses would indicate whether opportunities for feedback, exposure to diversity, and application to real-world experiences were present in the seminar, but not much more. Having these conditions present increases the likelihood that an educational experience will be high impact, but it is no guarantee.

As such, documenting the presence of these educational practices seems like a necessary but insufficient step in demonstrating the effectiveness of a seminar. If feedback is designed to help students improve their performance on a particular task, such as writing, are we measuring task performance (e.g., improved writing) as part of the larger assessment plan for the seminar? Similarly, exposure to diverse perspectives might help students develop greater intercultural competence or engage in higher levels of critical thinking. How are those outcomes being measured? Finally, one of the purposes of applying classroom content to real-world settings is to promote integrative learning. Is that one of the goals of the first-year seminar, and if so, how is it assessed?

In other words, it is not enough to say that we have incorporated three, four, or eight of these effective educational practices into a seminar. We have to know why we have embedded particular practices in the first place (i.e., they help us meet specific course, program, or institutional goals), and we have to assess outcomes aligned with the reason for selecting that practice. Not all practices will make sense within the context of every first-year seminar. Moreover, adding assessment keyed to effective educational practices where it is not already being done may strain an already overloaded assessment agenda. Several of the cases featured here described assessment cycles, where certain outcomes might be measured only once every three years. Even then, evidence does not have to be collected from every student or every seminar section. Thoughtful sampling procedures can ensure an accurate picture of seminar performance without examining every case.

An Alternate Definition

This project began from a desire to expand the definition of first-year seminars most often presented in the high-impact practices literature—a definition that emphasized "critical inquiry, frequent writing, information literacy, collaborative learning, and other skills that develop students' intellectual and practical competencies ... [and] involve[ment] with cutting-edge scholarship and with faculty members' own research (Kuh & O'Donnell, 2013, p. 49)—and that really only spoke to one type of seminar. Other definitions of the first-year seminar tend to focus more broadly on the academic and/or social development of new college students, making room for a wider variety of seminar types. For example, Hunter and Linder (2005) define the seminar as a course designed to

> assist students in their academic and social development and in their transition to college. A seminar, by definition, is a small discussion-based course in which students and their instructors exchange ideas and information. In most cases, there is a strong emphasis on creating community in the classroom. (pp. 275-276)

Yet, this definition only points to one of a number of conditions (i.e., faculty–student interaction) that makes the first-year seminar high impact.

In closing, I would like to offer an alternate definition of the first-year seminar as a high-impact practice.

The first-year seminar is a course that intentionally includes a range of effective educational practices in its design and delivery to support the development of skills and dispositions leading to academic and personal success in college and in 21st century global society. The practices are selected to support course, program, and/or institutional goals and woven into a seamless curricular and pedagogical fabric rather layered onto an existing course structure. Such practices emphasive opportunities for substantive conversations with peers and faculty members; significant investment of time and effort; frequent and constructive feedback; reflection, integration, and synthesis; exposure to diverse others and way of knowing; application of knowledge to real-world situations; and public demonstrations of competence, among others. The content of such a course could be an introduction to a discipline or field of study; an interdisciplinary exploration of a vexing social problem; or a student-led investigation of their own transition experiences, learning styles, and/or vocational aspirations.

The variability of first-year seminars suggests that no single combination of practices will ensure that these courses are engaging learning experiences for new undergraduates. The definition I offer here may be aspirational for many, but I believe it more accurately captures the promise and flexibility of one of the most ubiquitous courses in American higher education. I hope the cases collected in this volume provide readers with insights into how the thoughtful incorporation of effective educational practices can make any first-year seminar a high-impact practice.

References

Kuh, G. D., & O'Donnell, K. (2013). *Ensuring quality and taking high-impact practices to scale.* Washington, DC: Association of American Colleges and Universities.

Rhodes, T. L. (Ed.). (2010). *Assessing outcomes and improving achievement: Tips and tools for using rubrics.* Washington, DC: Association of American Colleges and Universities.

Young, D. G., & Hopp, J. M. (2014). *2012-2013 National Survey of First-Year Seminars: Exploring high-impact practices in the first college year* (Research Reports on College Transitions, No. 4). Columbia, SC: University of South Carolina, National Resource Center for The First-Year Experience & Students in Transition.

Index

Institutional Type

Four-year
The American University of Rome, 23
Cabrini University, 27
Clark University, 31
Coastal Carolina University, 35
Florida SouthWestern State College, 45
Indiana University – Purdue University Indianapolis, 51
Ithaca College, 55
Loyola University Maryland, 65
Malone University, 71
Montana State University, 77
Northern Arizona University, 81
Southern Methodist University, 87
St. Cloud State University, 95
Texas A&M University-Corpus Christi, 101
The University of Arizona, 105
University of Kansas, 109
University of Maryland Baltimore County, 113
University of New Hampshire, 119
University of North Carolina Wilmington, 123
University of Northern Iowa, 127
University of Texas at Austin, 131
University of Texas at San Antonio, 135
University of Wisconsin – Madison, 139
Virginia Commonwealth University, 143

Two-year
Durham Technical Community College, 41
LaGuardia Community College, CUNY, 59
Southwestern Michigan College, 91

Institutional Control

Public
Coastal Carolina University, 35
Durham Technical Community College, 41
Florida SouthWestern State College, 45
Indiana University – Purdue University Indianapolis, 51
LaGuardia Community College, CUNY, 59
Montana State University, 71
Northern Arizona University, 84
Southwestern Michigan College, 91
St. Cloud State University, 95
Texas A&M University-Corpus Christi, 101
The University of Arizona, 105
University of Kansas, 109
University of Maryland Baltimore County, 113
University of New Hampshire, 119
University of North Carolina Wilmington, 123
University of Northern Iowa, 127
University of Texas at Austin, 131
University of Texas at San Antonio, 135
University of Wisconsin – Madison, 139
Virginia Commonwealth University, 143

Private, not-for-profit
The American University of Rome, 23
Clark University, 31
Ithaca College, 55
Loyola University Maryland, 65
Malone University, 71
Southern Methodist University, 87

Private, for-profit
Cabrini University, 27

Institutional Mission
Hispanic-serving institution
LaGuardia Community College, CUNY, 59
Texas A&M University-Corpus Christi, 101
University of Texas at San Antonio, 135

Religiously affiliated
Loyola University Maryland, 65
Malone University, 71

Seminar Type
Extended orientation
Coastal Carolina University, 35
Durham Technical Community College, 41
Indiana University – Purdue University Indianapolis, 51
St. Cloud State University, 95
The University of Arizona, 105
University of Wisconsin – Madison, 139

Academic seminar with generally uniform content
The American University of Rome, 23
Malone University, 71
Montana State University, 77
Southern Methodist University, 87
Southwestern Michigan College, 91
University of North Carolina Wilmington, 123
University of Northern Iowa, 127
University of Texas at San Antonio, 135
Virginia Commonwealth University, 143

Academic seminar on various topics
Cabrini University, 27
Clark University, 31
Texas A&M University-Corpus Christi,
University of Kansas, 109
University of Maryland Baltimore County, 113
University of Texas at Austin, 131

Basic study skills seminar
Northern Arizona University, 81
St. Cloud State University, 95

Hybrid
Florida SouthWestern State College, 45
Ithaca College, 55
LaGuardia Community College, CUNY, 59
Loyola University Maryland, 65
University of New Hampshire, 119

Educationally Effective Practices
Expectations set at appropriately high levels
Coastal Carolina University, 35
Durham Technical Community College, 41
Ithaca College, 55
Loyola University Maryland, 65
Montana State University, 77
Northern Arizona University, 81
Texas A&M University – Corpus Christi, 101
University of Kansas, 109
University of Maryland Baltimore County, 113
University of New Hampshire, 119
University of Northern Iowa, 127
University of Texas at San Antonio, 135
University of Wisconsin – Madison, 139
Virginia Commonwealth University, 143

Significant investment of time and effort
Cabrini University, 27
Clark University, 31
Coastal Carolina University, 35
Ithaca College, 55
LaGuardia Community College, CUNY, 59
Loyola University Maryland, 65
Northern Arizona University, 81
Southern Methodist University, 87
Southwestern Michigan College, 91
University of Kansas, 109
University of Maryland Baltimore County, 113
University of New Hampshire, 119
University of Northern Iowa, 127
Virginia Commonwealth University, 143

Interactions with faculty and peers
The American University of Rome, 23
Cabrini University, 27
Clark University, 31
Coastal Carolina University, 35
Florida SouthWestern State College, 45
Ithaca College, 55
LaGuardia Community College, CUNY, 59
Loyola University Maryland, 65
Malone University, 71
Northern Arizona University, 81
Southern Methodist University, 87
Southwestern Michigan College, 91
St. Cloud State University, 95
Texas A&M University – Corpus Christi, 101

The University of Arizona, 105
University of Kansas, 109
University of Maryland Baltimore County, 113
University of New Hampshire, 119
University of North Carolina Wilmington, 123
University of Northern Iowa, 127
University of Texas at Austin, 131
University of Texas at San Antonio, 135
University of Wisconsin – Madison, 139
Virginia Commonwealth University, 143

Involvement of peer mentors

The American University of Rome, 23
Coastal Carolina University, 35
Florida SouthWestern State College, 45
Ithaca College, 55
Loyola University Maryland, 65
Malone University, 71
Northern Arizona University, 81
St. Cloud State University, 95
The University of Arizona, 105
University of New Hampshire, 119
University of North Carolina Wilmington, 123
University of Texas at San Antonio, 135
University of Wisconsin – Madison, 139
Virginia Commonwealth University, 143

Experiences with diversity

The American University of Rome, 23
Cabrini University, 27
Clark University, 31
Ithaca College, 55
LaGuardia Community College, CUNY, 59
Loyola University Maryland, 65
Malone University, 71
Montana State University, 77
Southern Methodist University, 87
The University of Arizona, 105
University of Maryland Baltimore County, 113
University of Northern Iowa, 127
University of Texas at Austin, 131
University of Wisconsin – Madison, 139
Virginia Commonwealth University, 143

Frequent and constructive feedback

The American University of Rome, 23
Cabrini University, 27
Clark University, 31

Indiana University – Purdue University Indianapolis, 51
Ithaca College, 55
LaGuardia Community College, CUNY, 59
Loyola University Maryland, 65
Northern Arizona University, 81
Southwestern Michigan College, 91
St. Cloud State University, 95
Texas A&M University – Corpus Christi, 101
University of Kansas, 109
University of Maryland Baltimore County, 113
University of North Carolina Wilmington, 123
University of Northern Iowa, 127
University of Texas at San Antonio, 135
Virginia Commonwealth University, 143

Periodic and structured opportunities for reflection and integration

The American University of Rome, 23
Cabrini University, 27
Clark University, 31
Coastal Carolina University, 35
Durham Technical Community College, 41
Florida SouthWestern State College, 45
Indiana University – Purdue University Indianapolis, 51
Ithaca College, 55
LaGuardia Community College, CUNY, 59
Loyola University Maryland, 65
Malone University, 71
Montana State University, 77
Northern Arizona University, 81
Southern Methodist University, 87
Southwestern Michigan College, 91
St. Cloud State University, 95
Texas A&M University – Corpus Christi, 101
The University of Arizona, 105
University of Kansas, 109
University of Maryland Baltimore County, 113
University of New Hampshire, 119
University of North Carolina Wilmington, 123
University of Northern Iowa, 127
University of Texas at Austin, 131
University of Texas at San Antonio, 135
University of Wisconsin – Madison, 139
Virginia Commonwealth University, 143

Relevance through real-world applications

Cabrini University, 27
Clark University, 31

Coastal Carolina University, 35
Indiana University – Purdue University Indianapolis, 51
Ithaca College, 55
LaGuardia Community College, CUNY, 59
Loyola University Maryland, 65
Montana State University, 77
Southern Methodist University, 87
The University of Arizona, 105
University of Kansas, 109
University of Maryland Baltimore County, 113
University of New Hampshire, 119
University of Texas at Austin, 131
University of Texas at San Antonio, 135
University of Wisconsin – Madison, 139

Public demonstration of competence
Cabrini University, 27
Clark University, 31
Coastal Carolina University, 35
Indiana University – Purdue University Indianapolis, 51
Ithaca College, 55
Southwestern Michigan College, 91
Texas A&M University – Corpus Christi, 101
The University of Arizona, 105
University of Kansas, 109
University of Maryland Baltimore County, 113
University of New Hampshire, 119
University of North Carolina Wilmington, 123
University of Texas at San Antonio, 135
University of Wisconsin – Madison, 139
Virginia Commonwealth University, 143

Connections to Other High-Impact Practices
Learning community
Cabrini University, 27
Loyola University Maryland, 65
Northern Arizona University, 81
St. Cloud State University, 95
Texas A&M University – Corpus Christi, 101
University of Maryland Baltimore County, 113

Service-learning
Loyola University Maryland, 65
The University of Arizona, 105
University of Maryland Baltimore County, 113
University of Texas at Austin, 131
University of Wisconsin – Madison, 139

Undergraduate research
Texas A&M University – Corpus Christi, 101
University of Texas at San Antonio, 135

Assessment Methods
360-degree evaluation of peer mentors
Florida SouthWestern State College, 45

Classroom assessment techniques
Coastal Carolina University, 35
Durham Technical Community College, 41

Classroom observations
Coastal Carolina University, 35
Virginia Commonwealth University, 143

End-of-course evaluation
The American University of Rome, 23
Clark University, 31
Coastal Carolina University, 35
Durham Technical Community College, 41
Ithaca College, 55
LaGuardia Community College, 59
Southern Methodist University, 87
Southwestern Michigan College, 91
St. Cloud State University, 95
University of Maryland Baltimore County, 113
University of New Hampshire, 119
University of Texas at Austin, 131
University of Wisconsin – Madison, 139
Virginia Commonwealth University, 143

Ethnographic study
University of Texas at Austin, 131

Externally developed assessment tools
California Critical Thinking Inventory (CCTDI)
Florida SouthWestern State College, 45

Learning and Study Strategies Inventory
St. Cloud State University, 95

Motivated Strategies for Learning Questionnaire
Northern Arizona University, 81

National Survey of Student Engagement (NSSE)
Malone University, 71
University of Northern Iowa, 127

University of Wisconsin – Madison, 139
Virginia Commonwealth University, 143

Student Assessment of Their Learning Gains (SALG)
University of Kansas, 109

Survey of Entering Student Engagement (SENSE)
Florida SouthWestern State College, 45

Faculty evaluation of student performance
LaGuardia Community College, CUNY, 59

Mid-semester evaluation
Montana State University, 77

Portfolio/capstone assignment
Coastal Carolina University, 35
Durham Technical Community College, 41
Indiana University – Purdue University Indianapolis, 51
Southwestern Michigan College, 91
The University of Arizona, 105

Pre/Post surveys of course objectives/experiences
Malone University, 71
University of Texas at Austin, 131

Pre/Post writing assessment
Virginia Commonwealth University, 143

Rubric
The American University of Rome, 23
Cabrini University, 27
Durham Technical Community College, 41
Florida SouthWestern State College, 45
Texas A&M University – Corpus Christi, 101
The University of Arizona, 105
University of Kansas, 109
University of Maryland Baltimore County, 113
University of Northern Iowa, 127

Student interviews/focus groups
Clark University, 31
Florida SouthWestern State College, 45

Assessed Outcomes
Academic performance (e.g., GPA, academic probation)
Indiana University – Purdue University Indianapolis, 51
LaGuardia Community College, CUNY, 59
St. Cloud State University, 95
Texas A&M University – Corpus Christi, 101
University of New Hampshire, 119

Academic progress
LaGuardia Community College, CUNY, 59

Adjustment to college
Indiana University – Purdue University Indianapolis, 51

Appreciation of cultural differences
The American University of Rome, 23
University of Northern Iowa, 127
University of Texas at Austin, 131

Career decision-making
Indiana University – Purdue University Indianapolis, 51

Connection to a faculty member
University of Wisconsin–Madison, 139

Critical thinking
Florida SouthWestern State College, 45
Loyola University Maryland, 65
University of Kansas, 109
University of Texas at San Antonio, 135
Virginia Commonwealth University, 143

Graduation rates
Virginia Commonwealth University, 143

Engagement
Florida SouthWestern State College, 45
University of Northern Iowa, 127

Ethical reasoning
Virginia Commonwealth University, 143

Information literacy
University of Kansas, 109

Integrative learning
Texas A&M University – Corpus Christi, 101

Involvement on campus
University of New Hampshire, 119

Leadership development
The University of Arizona, 105

Learning and development (self-reported gains)
Florida SouthWestern State College, 45
Indiana University – Purdue University Indianapolis, 51
Montana State University, 77
Southern Methodist University, 87
St. Cloud State University, 95
The University of Arizona, 105
University of Kansas, 109
University of Northern Iowa, 127
University of Texas at Austin, 131
University of Texas at San Antonio, 135
University of Wisconsin - Madison, 139

Oral communication skills
Montana State University, 77
University of Kansas, 109
University of Texas at San Antonio, 135

Persistence
Cabrini University, 27
Durham Technical Community College, 41
Florida SouthWestern State College, 45
Indiana University – Purdue University Indianapolis, 51
LaGuardia Community College, CUNY, 59
Northern Arizona University, 81
Texas A&M University – Corpus Christi, 101
The University of Arizona, 105
University of Maryland Baltimore County, 113
University of Northern Iowa, 127
Virginia Commonwealth University, 143

Satisfaction/Effectiveness
Course
The American University of Rome, 23
Clark University, 31
Ithaca College, 55
LaGuardia Community College, CUNY, 59
Malone University, 71
Southwestern Michigan College, 91
St. Cloud State University, 95
University of Texas at San Antonio, 135

Faculty
Clark University, 31
St. Cloud State University, 95

Peer Mentors
The American University of Rome, 23
Florida SouthWestern State College, 45
St. Cloud State University, 95

Writing skills
Cabrini University, 27
Durham Technical Community College, 41
Loyola University Maryland, 65
University of Kansas, 109
University of Northern Iowa, 127
University of Texas at San Antonio, 135
Virginia Commonwealth University, 143

About the Editor

Tracy Lynn Skipper is assistant director for publications for the National Resource Center for The First-Year Experience and Students in Transition at the University of South Carolina. An accomplished editor and writer, Skipper edited (with Roxanne Argo) *Involvement in Campus Activities and the Retention of First-Year College Students* (2003), wrote *Student Development in the First College Year: A Primer for College Educators* (2005), and served as managing editor of the five-volume series, *The First-Year Seminar: Designing, Implementing, and Assessing Courses to Support Student Learning and Success* (2011-2012). Most recently, she co-authored the volume *Writing in the Senior Capstone: Theory and Practice* with Lea Masiello. She holds degrees in psychology, higher education, American literature, and rhetoric and composition. In addition to her writing and editorial work, she has served as a student affairs administrator, taught writing at the college level, and presented writing workshops for higher education professionals. She has presented on the application of student development theory to curricular and cocurricular contexts and what national datasets suggest about the organization and administration of high-impact educational practices. Her research interests include the application of cognitive-structural development to composition pedagogy and the use of writing in first-year seminars and senior capstone courses.